Huskerville

Huskerville

A Story of Nebraska Football,
Fans, and the Power of Place

Roger C. Aden

McFarland & Company, Inc., Publishers
Jefferson, North Carolina, and London

LIBRARY OF CONGRESS CATALOGUING-IN-PUBLICATION DATA

Aden, Roger C. (Roger Craig), 1962–
    Huskerville : a story of Nebraska football, fans, and the power
of place / Roger C. Aden.
        p.   cm.
    Includes bibliographical references and index.

    ISBN-13: 978-0-7864-3206-6
    softcover : 50# alkaline paper ∞

    1. University of Nebraska—Lincoln—Football.   2. Nebraska
Cornhuskers (Football team)—History.   I. Title.
GV958.U53A34   2008
796.332'6409782—dc22   2007033732

British Library cataloguing data are available

Front cover: Memorial Stadium, Lincoln, Nebraska (Scott Bruhn/NU
Media Relations). Back cover: Memorial Stadium crowd (Gloria Strope)

Manufactured in the United States of America

McFarland & Company, Inc., Publishers
  Box 611, Jefferson, North Carolina 28640
  www.mcfarlandpub.com

Table of Contents

For the important women in my life:
my grandmother Varla Aden;
my mother, Harriett Aden;
my wife, Christina Beck;
and my daughters,
Brittany Pangburn, Chelsea Pangburn, and Emmy Beck-Aden

Preface: The Long Road to Huskerville

In the fall of 1999, I was granted a faculty fellowship leave from Ohio University for the fall quarter. During that quarter I worked in several different directions, each of which I hoped would culminate in some insight to some basic questions: "What does it mean to be a Nebraskan?" "How do the performances of the Nebraska football team reflect the state's identity?" and "How do the performances of Husker football fans reflect the state's identity?"

To investigate them, I collected information about the history of Nebraska football, read some of the work of Nebraska literary giants Mari Sandoz and Willa Cather, visited Web sites related to Husker football, developed questionnaires to be distributed among Nebraska fans across the country, and solicited stories from Husker fans through Internet contacts, newspaper stories, and University of Nebraska Alumni Association chapter leaders.

I began to write this book in the fall of 2000, thanks to a generous reassignment of duties granted by my immediate supervisor, Professor David Descutner. After completing drafts of four chapters, though, I realized that the manuscript lacked focus. So, rather than force the issue, I retreated. I paused, I read, I thought, and I took some time to enjoy my new role as husband and parent.

Not to sound too noble, I also stalled, fought writer's block, and gave a higher priority to work around the house than I might ordinarily have. I also, unfortunately, gave what turned out to be overly optimistic assessments of my impending progress to those Husker fans who inquired about the book. I am extraordinarily grateful for their patience, participation, and assistance.

In gathering ideas, and in organizing them in some manageable form, I relied on the generosity of these fellow Husker fans. I spoke with, and heard from, friends, relatives, and strangers. I benefited from the cooperation of University of Nebraska Alumni Association groups, small-town Nebraska newspaper publishers, and small-business owners—all of whom helped to spread the word about my project. I searched through Internet discussion group archives, which served as a kind of public records depository of the hopes, concerns, and beliefs of some of the most dedicated Husker fans on the planet. And, through the generosity of folks at my academic home of Ohio University, I was able to hear from over 100 Nebraska residents who answered questions over the phone.

All of this took some time and required the assistance of some extraordinary people. Let me explain.

I developed four versions of a questionnaire that was distributed through alumni groups, Internet discussion groups, and newspapers and small businesses in Nebraska communities. A total of 211 people graciously completed those questionnaires. I thank Ed Vinton in Atlanta and Monty and Darren Seidler in Washington, DC, in particular, for encouraging the members in their alumni groups to complete the questionnaires (Sean McLaughlin was also instrumental in organizing the DC questionnaire collection). Ohio University student Stacie Baske did a marvelous job of reading my chicken scratches to compile documents that included the highlights of the questionnaires.

In addition, I had the good fortune to have friends and friends-of-friends visit watch parties (groups of Husker fans who gathered in public venues to watch the Husker football team play on TV) in Austin, Denver, Phoenix, Louisville, Minneapolis, and Portland where they collected audio-taped interviews and shared their observations with me. Thanks to Innes Mitchell (Austin), Amy Grim and Shannon Davis (Denver), Fred Corey and his students Jeff Sands, Kristy Strong, and Tonja Woody (Phoenix), Alena Amato Ruggerio (Louisville), Kirstin Cronn-Mills (Minneapolis), and Natalie Dollar (Portland) for graciously talking to Husker fans in places that I could not visit.

I talked to Husker fans in Lincoln prior to the 1999 Homecoming game against Iowa State (thanks to the University of Nebraska Sports Information Office and the University of Nebraska Alumni Association for their assistance during this visit), in Chicago at a watch party for the 1999 Texas A & M game, and in the Seattle suburb of Kirkland at a watch party for the 2000 Kansas State game (thanks to Tony Joyce of the Lucky 7 Saloon and Bob

Paine for their kindness in helping me arrange a visit to the Kirkland watch party). I also talked to a few folks over the telephone. All told, 126 Husker fans agreed to have their thoughts audiotaped and transcribed for this book. I want to thank to Sook Young Lee and Usha Matta for their transcription of these interviews.

One hundred thirty-six Nebraska residents—not all of them Husker fans—agreed to be interviewed over the phone through Ohio University's Scripps Survey Research Center. This survey would not have been possible without the generous support of Dean Kathy Krendl in Ohio University's College of Communication and Professor Greg Shepherd, director of the School of Communication Studies at Ohio University. Professor Guido Stempel and the staff in the Scripps Survey Research Center worked magic over the course of four nights to complete these 136 long surveys. The survey instrument itself could not have been developed, and its results analyzed, without the expertise of my Ohio University colleague (and fellow University of Nebraska alum) Scott Titsworth.

My colleagues at the School of Communication Studies at Ohio University have been especially supportive. Scott Titsworth and Lynn Harter read drafts of my work and offered suggestions for reading. My supervisors during the course of the project—David Descutner, Gregory Shepherd, Nagesh Rao, Claudia Hale, and Kathy Krendl—have provided logistical support and assistance.

Along the way I received research assistance at Ohio University from graduate students Paiwen Lee, Devendra Sharma, Sirintorn Bhibulbhanu-vat, and Chintana Monthienvichienchai. In addition, I benefited greatly from tips, information, and conversations I had with these folks in Nebraska: Sue Sitzmann of the Nebraska Department of Economic Development, Cheryl Wiese of the University of Nebraska–Lincoln's Bureau of Sociological Research, and the late Sue Rosowski of the University of Nebraska–Lincoln's Department of English.

My research was also made possible through funding provided by the School of Communication Studies and the College of Communication at Ohio University as well as the Ohio University Research Council.

In the course of my collecting these questionnaires, interviews, surveys, and other tidbits of information, Husker fans also shared some remarkable stories with me. Between the questionnaires and interviews, I heard from 473 Husker fans in 33 states (plus the District of Columbia) and six countries other than the United States (Ireland, Germany, Japan, Italy, Taiwan, and Armenia). Their ideas were supplemented by the ideas of Husker fans who posted their thoughts on Internet discussion boards such as Mike Nolan's Husker List, HuskerPedia.com, and Huskerscentral.com. I also found a number of valuable insights in newspaper articles and books written about Cornhusker football players and coaches.

I have organized the book into three types of experiences: Rooting, Homesteading, and Cornhusking. These experiences are by no means entirely distinct from one another. I'll point to shared interests among them, and you will undoubtedly notice a few on your own.

In Rooting, we'll learn how one kind of rooting (cheering) produces another type of rooting (anchoring) in Huskerville. In other words, while illustrating the devotion of Cornhusker fans, I also explain how our devotion is about more than football; it's about anchoring ourselves to the cultural identity of being a Nebraskan. Our rooting is terribly important to us because, as the final chapter in this section indicates, changes are also working to uproot us.

In Homesteading, we'll explore three types of doings that we Huskervillers seek to re-affirm as part of our collective memory: working hard, being neighborly, and remaining down-to-earth. These types of performances endow our experiences with traces of the legacy of Nebraska's early homesteaders, for they had to enact these characteristics in order to survive and succeed.

In Cornhusking, I'll illustrate how the experience of coming together or congregating is a critical part of being a Huskerviller. Just like cornhuskings of years past brought distant neighbors together for a productive party that blended work and play, Nebraska football games bring us Huskervillers together to enjoy ourselves in a way that does important cultural work. Specifically, the cornhusking experience reminds us that (1) our cultural identity is unique, (2) we can collectively generate a presence that puts Nebraska on the cultural map, and (3) we live in a small world.

Finally, I'll conclude by illustrating how the experiences of Rooting, Homesteading, and Cornhusking coalesce to reflect what I believe is a universal human impulse: to find a meaningful place to dwell together.

I am especially grateful to a number of fellow Husker fans who read drafts of portions of the book.[1] John Strope was so encouraging and helpful that my wife and I half-jokingly began referring to him as my agent. For example, the very day that I asked him if he knew of anyone who could take photos in Lincoln for me, John served as assistant to his wife, Gloria, as she took the photos that you'll find in the following pages. Cindy Koziol, Tim Hindman, and Matthew Grosz were extraordinarily helpful in their careful review of chapter drafts. Not only did they read every chapter, they sent me detailed line-by-line suggestions for editing, proofreading, and fact-checking. I am indebted to them for their diligence. I also received valuable feedback, tips, and encouragement from a number of other Husker fans around the country: Candy Hodge, Gary McGirr, Jack Kovacs, Beth Townsend, Stew Price, Antone Oseka, Jon Johnston, Todd Wolverton, Matthew Waite, Loren Wagner, Bob and Andy Sklenar, C. Thomas Preston, Jr., and Harriett Aden. In addition, I want to thank David Max of HuskerPedia.com and Ed Paquette and Andrea Cranford of the University of Nebraska Alumni Association for their willingness to help spread the word about *Huskerville*. I am especially grateful for the help of my wife, Christina Beck, who helped me sort through several important issues and made sure that I had time to write.

The ideas, stories, and experiences of all the Husker fans who shared their thoughts with me ultimately helped me make sense of my own questions. I hope that, in the following pages, I have done their ideas justice.

Introduction: Welcome to Huskerville

"Is this some sort of nostalgia thing?"

The question hurt. My soon-to-be fiancée (now wife), Christie, had just responded to my brief and unfocused explanation of why I wanted to take a short leave from my teaching and service duties at Ohio University to work on a project about Nebraska Cornhusker (Husker) football fans.

The question hurt for a number of reasons. One, Christie is one of the smartest people I know—a distinguished author and editor whose opinion I value professionally and personally—and she did not sound at all confident that I had a worthwhile project. Two, Christie's confusion and doubt stemmed from my inability at that point to explain how I thought the project would have scholarly merit (a necessity if you want to take a leave from teaching). Three, "nostalgia" was a nasty word; we're not supposed to "live in the past"[1] and here I was talking about Nebraska football during an Ohio University basketball game timeout. To make matters worse, our conversation was occurring in December 1998, almost ten years after I moved from Nebraska.

I stumbled through an incoherent, defensive answer. My gut said this was not exactly a "nostalgia thing," but darned if my brain and mouth could work together to articulate exactly what it was. Not that I should have been surprised. I had never been successful in explaining to Christie exactly how Nebraska football, and its fans, were—from my perspective at least—different from other dedicated fans of sports teams. "It's more intense" seemed a pathetically insufficient answer, especially when I'm supposed to—from my perspective at least—be able to put my Ph.D. degree to better use in explaining cultural phenomena. That Christie grew up within an hour's drive of South Bend, Indiana (home of Notre Dame University), and earned her

Ph.D. degree from the University of Oklahoma didn't help. She knows sports fans, and she is a sports fan. "It's more intense" wasn't especially persuasive to her, and rightfully so.

It's not that compelling an explanation for other sports fans, either. Even with the 2006 expansion of Nebraska's Memorial Stadium, another 11 universities host their home football games in stadiums that hold more people.[2] Even with Nebraska's dedicated alumni watching games around the country (see chapter 2 for more on this), no university can compare to Notre Dame's international fan base.[3] Dedicated sports fans are everywhere, not just in Nebraska. Heck, some *defunct* professional sports teams still have passionate fans who gather to celebrate and honor their teams. The California Golden Seals booster club meets monthly, even though the professional hockey team has not existed since 1976.[4]

So, yes, Nebraska football fans are, in all kinds of ways, just like sports fans around the globe. We know that, of course, but our knowledge of that fact doesn't keep us from believing that we are somehow different from everybody else, too. To answer Christie's question, I had to figure out what exactly makes us think we are different.

As I searched for an answer to Christie's question, I eventually realized that I was also searching for something else: orientation. If, as author Patricia Price notes, "we are, in a profoundly important sense, who we are because of where we are, and vice versa,"[5] then any sudden change in location will send our internal compasses whirling. My compass was thrown out of whack back in 1989, when I took a job as a professor at the University of Wisconsin–Eau Claire. As I visited with Christie nearly 10 years later in Athens, Ohio, I felt as if I were still trying to re-set my own internal compass. Let me explain.

I called Nebraska home from the day of my birth in 1962, until the completion of my Ph.D. degree at the University of Nebraska at Lincoln in the summer of 1989. Scottsbluff was my hometown. Nebraska was where I lived and earned an education. But in the summer of 1989, I moved to Eau Claire, Wisconsin. In addition to its "funny" spelling, Eau Claire was not much like Scottsbluff or Nebraska. Still, like many people who move away from home, I rather naively assumed that my new place of residence was now my home.

It didn't work that way.

My heart was still in Nebraska. And, in some ways, the rest of me lingered there, too.

Scottsbluff is a small town, really, holding just under 15,000 people. But in terms of proportional scale, Scottsbluff is a good-sized burg, for you have to travel nearly three hours to reach a larger town in Nebraska. To reach a larger town of any size still requires a lengthy drive of almost two hours to Cheyenne, Wyoming. Eau Claire was as big as Cheyenne. However, in less time than a Scottsbluff-to-Cheyenne drive would take, I was in the Twin Cities of Minnesota. This shift in scale was a bit hard to take.

So, too, was the shift in topography. Scottsbluff is situated in the middle of farm and ranch country on relatively flat land. Some of my junior high friends who lived too far out of town for efficient school bus service were driving themselves to school thanks to school permits that allowed them to drive solo to school at age 14. They didn't have too much trouble getting around town because the city streets were laid out in grids just like the county roads that intersected and bordered their farms and ranches. These grids ran much like these kids were supposed to run: on the straight and narrow.

I still vividly remember the ease with which my mother and father taught me the cardinal directions of north, south, east, and west one day in our living room; the wall facing the street was west, the wall facing my grandmother's house down the street was south, etc. Of course, living in a town with streets labeled primarily with numbers and letters helped; I lived at 2023 Avenue E, which was easily described as being located between West 20th and West 21st. As a child, then, I knew that Scottsbluff was the center of the region and that you could give (and receive) directions by using phrases like "two miles north of town" and "between 17th and 18th on Avenue H." (The only orientational difficulty I recall concerned the Oregon Trail landmark called Scotts Bluff. I remember asking why this large rock formation, from whose summit you could see over 100 miles on a clear day, was known by two words while the town was known by one word, and why the bluff was closer to the neighboring town of Gering than Scottsbluff.)

In Eau Claire, I lived on a street called *South* Hastings Way, but darned if I could ever get a handle on the cardinal directions. As the Eau Claire and Chippewa rivers meandered through town, city planners worked around them, creating a web of twisting streets that seemed to change names at bends instead of turns. On the drive to work, for example, I navigated a single street whose name changed from Brackett Avenue to Harding Avenue to Washington Street. Western Wisconsin's slightly hilly terrain didn't help matters much either, for in both Scottsbluff and Lincoln I had grown accustomed to having a horizon. In Eau Claire, both geography and topography reminded me that I didn't live in Nebraska anymore.

The nagging feelings of disorientation that I suffered in Wisconsin were compounded upon my move to the beautiful foothills of the Appalachians in Athens, Ohio, in 1991. Although southeastern Ohio is gorgeous and tremendously green six months a year, the green is—to me—monotonous and sometimes suffocating; I live for October's eruption of autumn colors. The foothills also make me a bit claustrophobic; I sometimes feel trapped inside their walls and long to see a horizon. The lack of grid-like streets and highways disorients me; ask me which direction is north and I'll feel like I'm playing pin the tail on the compass point. The university at which I teach is not the state's only major public university; some of my friends took years to understand that I wasn't teaching at Ohio State University.

In Nebraska, on the other hand, I felt centered. The state was at the center of the 48 contiguous states. My hometown of Scottsbluff was the center of activity in the Nebraska panhandle. My university was the central institution of higher education in the state. I always lived somewhere in the middle of town, on easily found streets such as Avenue E, North 25th, and P Street. In Ohio, on the other hand, I've lived on Monticello Drive, Brumfield Road, Briarwood Drive, and Warwick Lane.

I don't think my experience is unique. I think most of us, in some way, feel a bit out of sorts. Change happens, and when it does, we become disoriented. When we move, when family members pass on, when we get a new boss, when any significant part of our lifeworld changes in any significant way, we look at our internal compass and find its needle spinning rather than settling. We seek something to help us find our bearings. That something can come in all kinds of shapes and forms. We may well even have more than one something to help us orient ourselves amidst the ongoing changes that life brings us.

For myself and, I've discovered, many other people like myself, one of those somethings is Nebraska Cornhusker football.[6] This initial realization pointed me in the direction of an answer to "what makes us different?" For Nebraska fans, football is not just football; it's also about a way of being in the world. Nebraska football is how we experience, shape, and share our understanding of being a Nebraskan.[7]

I took quite some time to reach this conclusion—months, in fact, after I first struggled to answer Christie's question—but in looking back I had my first clue four years prior to our conversation.

After five years of living outside of Nebraska, I returned to Lincoln on Friday, October 28, 1994, to watch the Nebraska-Colorado game the next day. To be there, I got lucky. Back in August, one of my college roommates,

Tony Korth, had snagged a ticket for me through a guy he worked with. When I arrived that Friday in October, the agent at the Alamo Rental Car counter told me that tickets were being scalped for as much as $400, thanks to the buzz surrounding the 200th consecutive sellout of Memorial Stadium and the matchup between the #2 (Nebraska) and #3 (Colorado) teams in the country. I also got lucky because my absence of five years made me more perceptive and observant about the things that I had taken for granted during the first 27 years of my life. Despite being "at home," I was also keenly aware that I was a Nebraskan who now lived outside of the state. I cherished the conversations with friends the night before the game as we ate pizza at Valentino's and had a bottle of Rolling Rock at O'Rourke's. I reveled in the euphoria of the game, especially the sight of a Husker player wearing the number 47 and the name Aden on the back of his jersey (my cousin Matt). I soaked up the family atmosphere after the game when I met up with three sets of aunts and uncles, two cousins, a second cousin, and assorted significant others. At each stop, I gradually, if not consciously, must have realized that football, family, and home were somehow related to one another.

My Aunt Kay, a resident of Colorado and Arizona for most of her adult life, helped crystallize what I was feeling. That Saturday, as we talked about the place we both still considered home, she said: "There's something about this place that sticks with you." The photos in my mental scrapbook from that weekend remain vivid. But most of all, I remember my Aunt Kay's words, for they triggered my reflections on home, disorientation, and what it means to be a Nebraskan.

I realized that our homes are not just houses or even mere spots on a map, physical locations marked by "Welcome to" and "Thanks for visiting" signs. No, our homes are intertwined with our beings, burned deep into our souls—for better or worse—that serve as our lifelong companions to one degree or another. As Nebraskan Johnny Carson once noted, "In a sense, we're like a turtle. We carry our home with us wherever we go."[8]

Homes are thus not places where we hang our hat, but places where we orient ourselves to the world. "Places ... provide points from which to look out on life, to grasp one's position in the order of things, to contemplate events from somewhere in particular," explains rancher and scholar Keith Basso.[9] When other people share our place of orientation, so much the better. We appreciate the company, and we like the affirmation of others in knowing that we have settled in a good neighborhood. Our neighbors also help us recognize what binds us together. That's why Bob Kully, a retired professor who lives in Los Angeles (and who left Nebraska 10 years before I was born), and I could talk on the phone for over an hour about "being a Husker" even though we had never met prior to the call.[10]

Together, we collect, reconfigure, and enact all those remnants of home that we value. These reconfigured remnants, in other words, function as our moral compass, our tradition, our bedrock foundation.[11] "Most of us," writes Lucy Lippard, "are separated from organic geographic communities ... [and] most of us live such fragmented lives and have so many minicommunities that no one knows us as a whole. The incomplete self longs for the fragments to be brought together. This can't be done without a context, a place."[12]

The place where we Husker fans gather our fragments and become oriented is a place I call Huskerville.[13] You won't find Huskerville on a Nebraska map, for it is a place in our hearts.[14] We can be in Huskerville no matter where we find ourselves on the map. I realized this on November 13, 1999, while walking down Wabash Street in downtown Chicago.

I was walking with Tim Borchers and Susanne Williams,[15] two of my favorite undergraduate students from my days as a teaching assistant at the University of Nebraska. After completing their bachelor's degrees in Lincoln, Tim and Susanne were married and earned doctoral degrees at Wayne State University in Detroit. They settled in the Fargo, North Dakota–Moorhead, Minnesota, area and helped establish the Min-Kota alumni chapter there. We had just left a watch party[16] at a bar called McGee's. There we were joined by roughly 200 other red-clad Huskervillers to watch one of the 22 televisions showing the Nebraska-Texas A & M game.

"What struck me is that I felt I should have known them," Tim said.

"It's like what my sister was talking about," Susanne continued. "If you see somebody walking down the street with a Nebraska sweatshirt on or something, you just feel like you should go up and say, 'Oh, you're from Nebraska. Me, too. Where'd you live?' and swap stories. You'd never do that with anybody else."

We do that because we believe we're all from the same place.

You see, Huskerville is like a lot of small towns in Nebraska. It's a place where neighbors know each other well, work hard at what we do, and try not to think of ourselves as better than others. It's a place where local festivities bring people together to share and celebrate, rekindle ties, and draw attention to characteristics that might go unnoticed by those from bigger places. It's also a place where the winds of change threaten long-held and valued traditions rooted in an agrarian way of life.

But it's also something more. It's a place where ideas about Nebraska, Cornhusker football, and being a Husker fan converge to illustrate the power of place in our lives. That's what makes Nebraska football different. When we root for the Cornhuskers, we are cheering at once for the place we call home, our way of life, and our cultural roots.

This story, then, is a story about place as much as—or perhaps more than—it is about football. Many of us are deeply attached to the places we call home. These attachments, as Setha M. Low and Irwin Altman note in the introduction to their edited book *Place Attachment*, are not solely to the place itself but also to the experiences the place contains and the way of life it represents.[17]

Thus, the story of Huskerville that I tell in these pages is much easier to experience than describe—as I discovered when responding to Christie's question. What the team does, what we do as fans, what we do off the field, what our forebears have done—all of these doings contribute to the contours of Huskerville.

My hope is that you come to know these contours more intimately after reading about the experiences of Husker fans. Just as flying over the fields of Nebraska can provide one perspective on the fields below, the experiences of being in those fields offer an altogether different set of perspectives. As I share those experiences, I tell a particular kind of place story about Huskerville; actually, it is a story of many stories.

As you might have gathered, this story of Huskerville is also a personal one. I have long been interested in the pull of place, yet I could not explain the allure of the most important place in my life. At various points in this story, then, I share some of my experiences. These experiences are not neatly laid out in chronological order. Instead, they are memorable moments that helped me put the pieces of the puzzle together.

As I visited with other Husker fans, especially those who have moved outside the state and still—to the puzzlement of their neighbors—call Nebraska home, I learned that my story is not unlike theirs. Thus, this story of Huskerville is also a collective one. While Husker fans such as myself have no shortage of Husker books from which to choose (we can read about the history of the football team, about the players and coaches, and one or two fan autobiographies[18]), no one has carefully and thoroughly talked to us about why we care so much about a football team's performance. I've tried to rectify that shortcoming here by relying upon the insights, experiences, and stories of over 500 Husker fans. Although my voice may be the loudest one in these pages, I try to serve as more of a conductor than author, and attempt to arrange the voices of the Husker fans who talked with me into discrete harmonies throughout the chapters that follow; their solos (or, extended personal stories) are found in the Appendix.[19]

This story of Huskerville is also a cultural one. Huskerville is a place where what happens on the football field says something about what people do off the field. Husker football games are more than just games; watch parties are more than just a gathering of fans in a bar; being a Nebraskan is more than just having lived (or living) in a state with boundaries dictated by geography and political compromise. Being a Husker fan, as we'll see, is about being a Nebraskan.[20]

Finally, this story of Huskerville is one of memory. It is about collectively remembering who we are by enacting and performing our distinct us-ness through the vehicle of Nebraska Cornhusker football.[21] Scholars who examine this idea of collective memory have emphasized its enduring importance in how groups of people define themselves and respond to present circumstances, but they have not thoroughly explained how we—everyday people—keep those memories alive in what we do and how we do it.[22] Husker football is a means of re-affirming a way of life while providing us with a means of orientation in the midst of ongoing change. "Place attachments," point out Barbara B. Brown and Douglas D. Perkins, "clearly promote and reflect stability, signifying long-term bonds between people and their homes and communities."[23]

So, back to the question: is this some sort of nostalgia thing?

Well, it is sort of a nostalgia thing in that nostalgia is about selectively remembering, altering, and even inventing something in the past—and the story of Huskerville selectively references stories from the past.[24] Selectively remembering the past, observes historian and geographer David Lowenthal, is a charitable process of "fabrication" in which we borrow from history to create our "heritage."[25] The story of Huskerville that I tell in the following pages is just one of many that can be, and are, told about Nebraska, Nebraskans, and the University of Nebraska football team.[26]

This is also sort of a nostalgia thing, but not in the sense of wanting to go back to another time. Nostalgia, I've learned, can be conceptualized as being about place more than time, for its Greek root, nostos, means "to return home."[27] (That we tend to think of nostalgia in terms of time is likely a product of Western societies' privileging of time over place.)

But this is not at all a nostalgia thing either since Huskerville is not a physical location to which I, and others, seek to return. Nor does Huskerville emerge because of our disillusionment with the present, as nostalgia often does.[28] Instead, Huskerville is about remembering and enacting a way of being in the world, a way of doing things, a way of getting along with others—a way of orienting in the midst of inevitable life changes.

As I hope this description makes clear, I tell this story of Huskerville for a number of reasons. Initially, I wanted and needed to be able to think through—by writing—why I felt being a Nebraska football fan was so important to me. Similarly, I wanted to write for other Nebraska football fans who might have also labored to explain the appeal of Husker football to their friends, neighbors, and co-workers. When I asked Husker fans *why* they believed the Husker experience was different, they often struggled as much as I did when I first undertook this project. Like me, they were convinced that something was, and is, different, but explaining the uniqueness was difficult for most all of us.

At the same time, I want non–Nebraskans—sports fans or not—to understand what makes us Husker fans tick. Undoubtedly, the intensity of the Husker experience shares much with the passion exhibited by fans of other teams. Other scholars have thoroughly dissected this general experience of "sports fandom,"[29] and some of the experience of being a Husker fan can certainly be explained by their generalized conclusions: we fans like the reflected glory of a winning team, we like being part of a community of like-minded souls, we enjoy participating in the social rituals surrounding sporting contests, etc. Other writers have captured the experience of being a fan of a particular sports team,[30] and their insights about identity and culture have also helped me to remember that every group of sports fans is different. I hope that by the end of the book that I will have provided at least some insight into why we Husker fans genuinely believe that we are different—while recognizing that we also share traits with other devoted sports fans.

Finally, I wrote this book as part of my job, and so doing requires that I have something to share with other people who do my kind of work. I hope that scholars interested in issues of collective memory, cultural identity, and the everyday performance of those two ideas find something of value in these pages. For these readers, and for other interested readers, I have included most of my references to scholarly material in the endnotes, although I point to the most accessible and pertinent information within the larger print.

As much as I would like to think that I've written a book that seamlessly and elegantly addresses the interests of all these audiences, I'm sure that I have failed on occasion. Undoubtedly, some of you will find places where I write like a professor. I try not to, I really do, but sometimes I can't help myself. You see, as a professor, I believe that each and every one of us loves to learn; understandably, I hope, you may well find me teaching when I see an opportunity.[31]

More obviously, I am a Nebraskan and a Husker fan. I am writing about something dear to me, a topic that is so intertwined with my own identity that I ultimately gave up trying to sound neutral. In fact, I eventually removed references to words such as "them," "they," and "their" when referring to other Husker fans because, frankly, I felt more than a little strange trying to distance myself from people like myself.

What you're about to read, then, is by no means unbiased. I even thought about stealing a phrase from Nebraska author Mari Sandoz's history of Nebraska called *Love Song to the Plains* and calling this book something like *A Professor's Love Affair with Nebraska and Its Football Team*.[32] This book is most definitely *not* one professor's objective dissection of the unique interdisciplinary phenomenon of Husker football. No, what you'll read is a Nebraskan explaining just why—and now I will steal a phrase, this time from the University of Nebraska fight song—"there is no place like Nebraska." Will I be glossing over some less than positive elements about the state or the football program? More than likely. As in any loving relationship, you tend to overlook what is potentially bothersome about your other half. Of course, you sometimes confide in others when your other half really bugs you, so I'll whisper "on the other hand" a few times in the endnotes.

That said, my passion for the Huskers pales in comparison to that of some extremely dedicated fans. Although I have plenty of Husker paraphernalia on hand, I don't have a Husker room in my house. My car horn does not play the Husker fight song. I even remember wearing a green hospital scrub shirt to a Husker game when I was a student in Lincoln, part of some silly phase of non-conformity that I've since gotten over. I *think* my big-fan-but-not-really-super-big-fan status was a good thing as I wrote this book because it allowed me to bounce back and forth between my professor and Nebraskan identities.

PART I

Rooting

1

Rooting: Sugar Beets, Family, and Fans

One of my more vivid childhood memories is of seeing sugar beets scattered along the side of the road each fall.

In my youth, the North Platte (River) Valley in the Nebraska panhandle was home to Great Western (GW) sugar beet factories in Scottsbluff, Gering, and Mitchell. Each autumn brought not only cooler weather and Husker football, but also what seemed to me to be a never-ending convoy of trucks hauling sugar beets in from the fields. In Scottsbluff, the trucks dumped their cargo into ever-growing mountains of sugar beets outside GW's factory on East Overland and 21st Avenue.[1]

Today, those images of sugar beets, crops that are essentially roots, remind me of my own roots in ways other than my childhood. They also remind me of my family's roots in the North Platte Valley. My mother's side of the family is ethnic German immigrants from the Volga River area of Russia.[2] German Russians were largely responsible for the success of sugar beet farming in Nebraska, for they provided a lion's share of the labor needed to work the fields during the first part of the 1900s.

"Down endless rows of choking dust they crawled or stooped, planting beets, thinning beets, weeding beets, harvesting beets. There was no thought of daycare centers for the children; the entire family worked as a unit in the furnace-like heat," writes Nebraska historian Roger Welsch.[3]

As the descendant of those field workers, I feel a bit guilty as I sit in my nice house working at my computer—especially as I reflect upon a photo my mom shared with me depicting my Great-Grandmother Henrietta Seckinger, my Great-Aunt Marie Seckinger, and my Great-Uncle Jake Seckinger taking a break from their work hoeing weeds on May 30, 1938.

Their work reminds me of the work done by other Nebraskans, from the efforts of homesteaders to establish roots by creating dugout and sod homes, to the farmers and migrant workers who kept the roots of crops healthy by uprooting weeds, to the invention of the center pivot irrigation systems which provided water to otherwise dry Nebraska farmland.[4]

Our cultural and familial roots are also important in Huskerville. That's why I read with fascination a collection of stories, called *Memories are for Sharing*, written by former North Platte Valley resident Vivian Roeder.

When Vivian heard about my desire to write this book, she sent her collection of memories to me from her home in Sun City, Arizona. Enclosed with the book was a photo of Vivian on her couch, which was covered by a Nebraska Huskers blanket. Next to Vivian was an 8 × 10 photo of Husker coaching legend Tom Osborne. In her note to me, Vivian wrote, "I was born [in 1906] on a homestead in Bayard—also the home of the Osbornes. Charles—Tom's father—was in high school when I was. He graduated a year later and went to Hastings."[5] In Hastings, Tom Osborne went to college across the street from where my Uncle Larry, Aunt Judy, and cousins Jeff, Kelly, and Kristy later lived. From 2001 to 2006, Tom Osborne served as the congressional representative for the district in which my mother and grandmother live.

Vivian's note and photo signify the many ways in which rooting works in Huskerville. First, when we are rooting as fans, we cheer for our team. We might spend much of our lives keeping our emotions in check, but rooting gives us a reason to cut loose, to engage in behaviors that might otherwise seem excessive. We scream, we shout, we jump, we hug strangers next to us. "Sometimes, we even think we can help our quarterback find his receiver, our defensive ends beat their blockers, and our tailbacks slash through tackles. The feeling is hard to explain and even harder to quantify, but everyone who goes through the turnstiles wearing red knows how it feels,"[6] writes Husker fan Steve Smith in his fan autobiography. We also know, but often cannot adequately express, the indescribable exhilaration when our team wins and inexplicable sadness when our team loses.

Dedicated fans don't stop cheering when the game is over either. We wear our allegiances on our sleeves—and on our hats, walls, vehicles, mailboxes, etc. My wife calls my home office, for instance, "the Husker shrine." I have had relatives and friends decorate their bathrooms in "Husker." I wasn't too surprised, then, to see Vivian's Husker blanket on her couch. The cheering in Huskerville never ends.

Second, when we cheer, we are also rooting ourselves in a place. We indicate the depth of our commitment, the strength of our roots in that place. That Vivian still thought of her home as the homestead near Bayard where she grew up—despite physically residing in Arizona—means she had been rooting herself in Nebraska. Like Old Jules Sandoz, the protagonist of his daughter Mari's remarkable Nebraska novel, *Old Jules*, Vivian could be described much the same way: "His root is strong."[7]

The landscape of Nebraska encourages such rooting. As University of Nebraska historian John Wunder observes, the big spaces, wind, harsh climate, and small populations encourage Plains dwellers to stick together.[8] No wonder, then, that, as historian Donald Hickey notes, "Nebraskans are more likely to be aware of their ethnic origins than other Americans and are more likely to consider their ethnic background important."[9] (I am probably more likely to be sensitive to this issue given my German Russian background: "The Germans from Russia are the only German group on the Great Plains who actively and consciously cultivate their ethnic heritage," writes historian Frederick Luebke.)[10]

Not only that, but Huskervillers literally and symbolically plant Nebraska flags wherever we go. Chapters of the University of Nebraska Alumni Association make sure that their logos reflect their roots, even when their physical residences may be thousands of miles away from Nebraska. Alumni chapter Web sites typically work in a visual reminder of their allegiance to Huskerville. For example, the Seattle area alumni chapter includes an image of the Space Needle with the script "Huskers" to its left, the Memphis area chapter superimposes a red "N" and "Huskers" on the Pyramid Arena, the Atlanta area chapter uses a red outline of the state of Nebraska as a background for a peach with a superimposed "N," and the Arizonans for Nebraska chapter has a logo of a white "N" perched cloud-like above a mountaintop with a saguaro cactus in the foreground. In addition, the HuskerHysteria Web site offers another visual reminder of how Huskers in states outside of Nebraska remain rooted: it features pictures of Husker-related vanity license plates from 29 states other than Nebraska.[11]

Third, when we nurture these roots, we help them grow and spread while remaining connected at their core. "Another advantage of deep roots is that they store energy which can produce new growth."[12] This statement, borrowed from the visitor's guide at Homestead National Monument just outside of Beatrice, Nebraska, describes the prairie grasses that are native to Nebraska. Yet, it can also illustrate how the roots of Huskerville continue to grow far beyond the geographic borders of Nebraska. Vivian, for example, would be welcomed by the Nebraska Chapter of the Sun Cities in Arizona. Rooting in this sense means the process of spreading our roots; Huskerville is found in many geographic locations.

This sense of rooting, of strengthening connections across and beyond cultural and geographic borders, is interestingly discussed by French philosophers Gilles Deleuze and Felix Guattari. Like most philosophers, Deleuze and Guattari try to explain abstract ideas by using metaphors. In their book *A Thousand Plateaus*, they borrow the term *rhizome* from plant biology to explain how people in different places develop strong attachments to one another while forming a group.

Rhizomes, they remind us, are tubers with root systems that spread horizontally underground, their shoots emerging in many different locations. From the surface, the plants appear to be scattered about in many locations, but underground they share a common tuber. Rhizomes are essentially self-sustaining and can reproduce themselves; thus, even when roots or shoots are cut, the rhizome itself continues to grow. "A rhizome may be broken, shattered at a given spot," they explain, "but it will start up again on one of its old lines, or on new lines."[13]

Yet, as anyone who has tried to grow something knows, roots are also quite fragile. Forces of nature and acts of humans can weaken, expose, or even sever what otherwise might appear to be strong roots. One storm, one careless act, and countless hours, years, maybe even generations of hard work will all be for naught. Such is the peril of uprooting.

Maybe that's why my childhood memories of fallen sugar beets are still so vivid. As much as I cognitively know that they were grown to be harvested, and that those beets that had fallen off the trucks were already uprooted, I had some strange sort of emotional reaction to seeing the beets on the side of the road. Not only had they been uprooted, they had also been left behind while others moved on.

I know, I know, they're just crops. But they're also metaphors for what happens when roots are not carefully tended. So, when various forces tug at the roots of Huskerville, its residents dig in a little deeper. Like the sugar beets, they know that the loss of their roots might leave them lost and alone.

This is a story of Rooting. When the world around us rapidly changes, when every place begins to look alike and, paradoxically, familiar places begin to look unfamiliar, having roots firmly planted in a particular place is a *necessity* rather than a luxury. Home allows us to simultaneously deny the passage of time and the changes in places, while also providing us with the necessary means of adapting to the passage of time and the changes in places. The following three chapters explain how this process works in Huskerville.

2

Cheering Around the World

Let me begin with a word of advice to sports fans: never try to watch your team play from the press box.

Granted, not that many fans would have the opportunity to visit the press box during a game. Rather than wondering what happens up there, though, I say they should count their blessings. Here's why.

The kind folks in the University of Nebraska–Lincoln Sports Information office consented to my request for two media passes for the 1999 homecoming game against Iowa State. I had planned to recruit a university student as a research assistant, but had no luck. So, instead, I asked my mom, who was journalism major in her days at the University of Nebraska, if she would like to drive from Scottsbluff to join me. After visiting with a number of Husker fans before the game, we made our way to the media access area inside Memorial Stadium.

Given the rampant commercial influences in college sports these days, I was surprised to see that the press box was not sponsored by some entity like Lysol or Listerine because the place had what can best be described as an antiseptic ambience. The crowd noise, deafening in the stands, is barely audible in the box. The conversations, which are rare, are conducted in hushed tones—as if the group inside the box was watching the opera instead of a football game. Just in case newcomers don't pick up on the library-like rules of conduct, the press box announcer reminds the occupants at the start of every quarter to be quiet.

Initially caught off guard by this atmosphere, I remembered that I was working, so I should be professional like the other professionals in the press box. Of course, that's not so easy when my work is embedded in my status as a Husker fan.

Before the game even began, I felt the walls closing in and made a dash out of the press box. I asked for directions, then found my way out of the press facility and toward the field. After I emerged from the labyrinth, I discovered that I was at field level; not in the stands, not on the sideline, but in between.

I felt strange. This was much better than the press box morgue, to be sure, but I felt encircled by—not part of—the crowd. I began to get over it when, at precisely five minutes before game time, I heard the music for the "Tunnel Walk," the relatively recent, but fervently embraced, tradition in which the tune "Sirius" by the Alan Parsons Project accompanies a montage of computer-generated images of Nebraska icons displayed on the big screens inside the stadium. As the montage concludes, live cameras show the team making its way through the tunnel under the stadium as the players move from the locker room to the field entrance.

Thirty seconds elapsed before the team captains emerged from the tunnel. Another half minute passed and the rest of the team congregated at the mouth of the tunnel. With 3:32 left before game time, the team was lined up at the end of the tunnel ready to explode on to the playing field.

Ten seconds later, they charged. The band—half on the field, half in the stands—played, "Go Big Red" chants echoed through the stadium, and chills cascaded through my body.

Later that fall I was reminded of this moment when I read in Willa Cather's My Ántonia, "We turned to leave the cave; Ántonia and I went up the stairs first, and the children waited. We were standing outside talking, when they all came running up the steps together, big and little, tow heads and gold heads and brown, and flashing little naked legs; a veritable explosion of life out of the dark cave into the sunlight. It made me dizzy for a moment."[1]

I've tried to explain to non–Nebraskans the profound experience of being a fan inside Nebraska's Memorial Stadium. I asked other Husker fans to help describe the experience.

All of us have struggled.

We can explain that Husker fans have filled the stadium every single game since November 1962, and that the next longest (current) streak of consecutive sellouts—held by the University of Michigan—is 13 years shorter.[2] We can attempt to put the number of fans into some kind of context by noting that the filled stadium would easily be the third-largest city in the state (as of 2006, the stadium holds over 85,000 fans).

But while this information provides some sense of the intensity of the experience, it hardly does it justice. While later pages of the book tackle this topic in more detail, for now I want to offer an explanation of how the

Another sellout at Memorial Stadium in Lincoln, Nebraska (photograph by Gloria Strope).

energy, the force, the electricity—all of these words seem insufficient—is so powerful that it radiates literally around the world. The roots of the rhizome that is Huskerville stretch far and wide, emerging in all kinds of places.

The vast network of roots which connects Huskerville seems to spread underground, much like the unimaginable pool of one of the Western Hemisphere's largest sources of groundwater: the Ogallala (or High Plains) Aquifer that lies largely under the rock and soil of Nebraska's geographic boundaries. Lying under parts of eight states, two-thirds of the aquifer is beneath Nebraska's borders.[3] The aquifer can be found under 83 percent of Nebraska, which holds just over two billion acre-feet of the 3.25 billion acre-feet of water in the aquifer.[4] In all, more water than in all of Lake Huron lies under the Nebraska soil.[5]

The tremendous amount of potential energy stored in this water comes alive when it is pumped in and up from the aquifer to sustain the Nebraska's agricultural efforts.[6] Similarly, Nebraskans' potential energy is activated when the rivers of people pouring into Memorial Stadium each game day become what is often referred to as the "Sea of Red." Like the groundwater of the Ogallala Aquifer, the figurative waters in the Sea of Red nourish the ground from which Huskerville's roots spread and its shoots emerge.[7] These shoots emerge throughout Nebraska, outside the state's boundaries, and around the planet.

In Nebraska

"No matter where you go," says one traveler well-versed with the state of Nebraska, "whether it's Scottsbluff in the western part of the state or Omaha, almost every business has a Nebraska football poster or calendar or memento sitting around. It's amazing how pervasive the interest is."[8] That traveler, former coach Tom Osborne, should know since he spent a few decades getting to know Nebraska, its towns, and its people.

The intense devotion he encountered is not all that new. Consider, for example, this 1939 description of a typical Husker football game day:

> Football in Nebraska is more than a diversion for college students. A State [sic] university game is an event talked about and eagerly followed by rural and urban fans. If the day of a football game is not too cold or rainy, the streets of Lincoln are sure to be jammed with people and cars, brightened with pennants and chrysanthemums. The highways are crowded for miles around. Broadcasts of games are picked up in almost every store and gas station from Omaha to the western border; farmers sometimes neglect their cornhusking in the afternoon to hear the game over the radio.[9]

The more things change, the more they stay the same.

Ask a Huskerviller today to describe game day and the account won't be much different. For instance, if Husker fans in Nebraska are unable to attend a game at Memorial Stadium, they have the opportunity to tune in to one of the 32 Nebraska radio stations that broadcasts games.[10] Those broadcasts are heard nearly everywhere in the state. "On Football Saturdays," writes Husker fan Steve Smith in his book *Forever Red*, "you can go into any building, anywhere in the state and hear the Nebraska game on the radio."[11]

I'm not so sure he's exaggerating. I can still recall listening to Husker games called by radio announcer Lyell Bremser as my family would go shopping in downtown Scottsbluff on a Saturday afternoon. While my memory is a bit fuzzy, I felt as if the game stayed with us no matter what store we entered. Later, as a teenager working at the Jack & Jill grocery store, we would wrap masking tape around the talk button on the store intercom, then position a radio by the microphone so that we—and the few shoppers in the store—could stay in touch with the game. Similarly, a Husker fan living in Albuquerque recalls, "My first memories of Husker football are back in the late sixties and listening to the games on the radio at Finke's Grocery in Creighton as I cut meat."[12] A Husker fan notes on the HuskerPedia Internet discussion board, "When I was 5 in 1969, my job every Saturday was to take the trash out and clean the garage. The AM radio blared with Lyell [Bremser's] voice shouting 'man, woman, and child' and I was hooked."[13]

In 1977, about the time I worked at Jack & Jill, sociologist Michael Stein noted, "It is difficult to be in a public place during a [Husker] game and not be in earshot of a radio broadcast."[14] Heck, one can even be in the great outdoors and still be in earshot of the Husker game. Recalls Husker fan Curt Eurich, who now lives in Whitesboro, Texas, "I also remember being on a Cub Scout camping trip and all of us sitting around camp listening to Nebraska beat Army (I think) 77–0. Back then it just seemed the thing to do. I truly believe that only in Nebraska would Scouts sit and listen to a football game instead of hiking or fishing, etc."

For visitors to Huskerville, such devotion can be, well, a bit confusing. Curtis Olson, who moved to Lincoln as an adult, recalls his first experience in a mall as a Husker game was broadcast on the radio. He describes the shoppers as staring off vacantly into space as they listened to the game, "a lot of people bumping into other people, and all of a sudden, 'Oh, they scored 7 points!' Everyone kind of perked up and this woman literally grabbed me and said, 'Did they score or did we score?'"

Bruce Jensen of Connecticut explains his wife's reaction during her visit to Nebraska during a Husker game: "My wife grew up in Connecticut and knew that I was a little crazy with my love of the Cornhuskers. While on vacation in Nebraska during a game day she went shopping and came back with a very puzzled look on her face. She went on to say that every store she went into that day, regardless if it was the grocery store or a clothing store that the game was being played over the store intercom everywhere she went. That's when I said, 'Isn't it great to be a Husker.'"

In many ways, as these stories illustrate, Husker fans who are not inside Memorial Stadium act *as if* we were at the game. We follow the Huskers with an intensity that matches that of the fans at the game. Whether we are working on a ranch, a farm, or in town, Huskerville residents root for our team.

Barb Martinson, for example, told me about her early years growing up on a ranch where "it did not matter where you were or what you were doing, the game was with you. It's just so hard to describe that to people." Adds fourth-generation rancher L. Jean Gentry, "Even hard-working cowboys hurry to get their ranching jobs completed so hopefully they can either watch on TV or at least hear the action on the radio."

Another Nebraskan recalls her days working on the farm with her brother:

> I grew up on a farm near Columbus, NE. Football Saturday didn't change any of our farm chores that we needed to do daily. Usually, however, it was always a time of working in the field. After the crops were harvested, the soil needed to be disked. This was one of my jobs. On this particular Saturday, my older brother was home from college. Being older and bigger he got the tractor with the cab and radio, while I was relegated to the "open air" small tractor and disk. Of course, I had no idea of how the Nebraska game was progressing. I did, however, know when Nebraska scored because my brother would jump out of the cab and do cartwheels. It is such a vivid memory for me. I didn't seem to mind the "little" tractor, nor the brisk weather, because it was so fun watching him do cartwheels! That was a long time ago, yet it seems like yesterday. In fact, it is about the only thing that my brother and I have in common— Nebraska football!

The bond of Nebraska football is evident throughout the state, especially on game days. As one Husker fan recalls in a posting on the Husker-Pedia Web site, "Growing up in a small Nebraska town, I fondly remember that on game days on those sunny, crisp fall Nebraska Saturday afternoons, the streets literally emptied and folks were gathered around radios everywhere listening to the game."[15]

The same scene would greet visitors to darn near every small town in Nebraska. Three Huskervillers from small towns in different parts of the state illustrate how game days in small Nebraska towns produce astonishingly similar scenes.

Loren Wagner, a high school teacher and coach in the west central Nebraska consolidated school district of Hayes Center, reports that "Life gets pretty quiet in Culbertson if the Huskers are on TV, or at least I think it is. I don't know for sure because I seldom leave the house when the Huskers are on. If it is a home game I am most likely in Lincoln. Culbertson is 250 miles from Lincoln but people are diehard Husker fans. They fly Husker flags on game day and throw Husker parties for televised games. Many people wear red Husker clothing regardless of whether they attended the game or not."

Jeff Baier, who grew up in the northeast Nebraska town of Wayne, recalls:

> A Husker football game turned my hometown into a ghost town at game time. Sure there were people outside in the morning, but everyone went inside

to watch the game or listen to it on the radio (that was before almost every game was on TV). All the stores had the game on inside, mainly for the people that worked there or those who waited too long to go home. Most of the stores also had speakers outside so you could hear the game walking from store to store. I think the chamber of commerce did this so that people would still shop on football Saturdays. It didn't work so well. After the game the town would liven up if the Huskers won. A lot of people would come out to celebrate. People would go to dinner or to the bars. If they lost almost everyone stayed home to deal with their depression or went to bed early. Interestingly, this happened when I lived in a small town like Wayne and larger town like Lincoln. It was a lot more noticeable in Lincoln when we lost.

Tim Hindman, a native of Hay Springs in the Nebraska panhandle, remembers:

At one time (in the not-so-distant past), people in Hay Springs and so many other small towns across the state would keep right on working as any other day, except that they would make sure to have a radio handy tuned into the game. If one happened to be otherwise occupied (e.g., getting married), someone was usually designated to listen to the game and keep the others apprised of the score and any other pertinent information. Today most people will drop what they're doing and gather around the TV (in many cases at a location with cable or a satellite dish) to watch the beloved Big Red in action for themselves. The game and the team remain a staple of conversation in any coffee shop, bar, or other public gathering place in town.

These conversations continue, too, even when the Huskervillers in question do not reside within the borders of Nebraska.

Outside Nebraska

Just like our Huskerville brethren within the borders of Nebraska, Husker fans outside of the state are devout followers of our team. Our rooting helps us remain rooted. Matthew Grosz explains how he and his brothers, scattered across the southeastern United States, remain rooted in Huskerville: "Every football Saturday, regardless of where we are—New Bern, North Carolina (me), Tallahassee, Florida (Milt—a pilgrim in an unholy land!) or Savannah, Georgia (Dr. Mike), it's like pre-game. We're nervous, a little tight in the stomach, hope the boys play up to their capabilities, little bit of sweat on the forehead. Everything done that morning is done just to kill time until the game."[16]

Once the game begins, the Grosz brothers find a way to stay connected. Like other Huskerville residents outside of Nebraska, they can stretch their roots through phone lines, radio signals, Internet connections, television watch parties, and even road trips to Nebraska away games.

In Florida, Barb and Marty Martinson's son stays connected through the telephone. Says Barb, "We telephone each other back and forth during the ball game. I bet you, if he can't get the game or he can't watch it, he calls about every five minutes." Meanwhile, in Carmel, Indiana, Dottie Renner's phone line was typically tied up during game days. "On fall Saturdays, there's really no point in trying to call. The line's busy. That's because her 83-year-old mother, Hilda, who lives in Lincoln, tunes in the game, calls her daughter, and sets the receiver in front of the radio. Then her daughter and son-in-law, both Nebraska graduates, can listen to the game—all of it."[17]

Unfortunately for Dottie, she did not live in one of the 11 states outside of Nebraska—including Washington, Arkansas, Arizona, California, and Minnesota—where Husker football games can be found on the radio.[18] In many of these locations, Husker fans in the area raise the money to help support a local radio station's broadcast of the game. I still remember, for instance, my college friend and roommate Jon Johnston's glee when he and other Husker fans who lived in and around the Twin Cities area of Minnesota found a small AM radio station willing to carry Husker games.

In Colorado, a Husker fan named Bob observes that, with the possible exception of Notre Dame, "nobody other than that has their local hometown football team on the radio.... If [you're a Colorado fan and] you're back in Nebraska or if you're anywhere else, you're not going to get a Colorado football game [on the radio]." Listening to the Husker games on the radio, explains Bob, "brings you home."

No wonder, then, that many Husker fans go to great lengths to find radio broadcasts of Husker games. Dottie Renner, for example, used to travel a couple of hours from Carmel, Indiana, to Kentucky in order to find a radio broadcast of the Huskers.[19] "In Sacramento, there is a store on the edge of town. On a select number of Saturdays, the parking lot is often full—not with Californians picking up their weekly supply of bean sprouts, organic waffles and white wine, but with Nebraska fans tuned into the game. Seems that the store sits on a hill offering the capital city's best radio reception. And thus it is here where Big Red-starved Californians congregate, sitting in their cars, screaming and hollering, honking horns and whooping it up, occasionally confounding wary shoppers unaware of the fever from Lincoln."[20]

In Georgia, the Georgians for Nebraska alumni group would hold parties to listen to the game on the radio. Someone in Nebraska would find the game on the radio, call Georgia, then put the radio by the phone. Meanwhile, at the Georgia end, the phone would be put on speaker so that everyone in attendance could listen to the game.[21]

More recently, Huskerville residents have been able to see Nebraska football games, not just hear them, as the growth of cable and satellite television has increased the number of televised football games. From 1999 to 2004, the Huskers appeared on television an average of 10 times per year.[22] And, when the Huskers are on TV, Huskerville residents congregate to watch. From 2001 to 2004, figures reported in the *Nebraska Alumni Resource Guide* indicate that approximately 600 watch parties were held each year under alumni association chapter sponsorship and that approximately 38,000 people attended those watch parties. In 2006, these watch parties were held in 91 locations outside the state of Nebraska.[23] In Austin, Texas, 320 Husker fans gathered to watch the 2004 Pittsburgh vs. Nebraska game.[24] In Bloomington, Minnesota, "nearly 400 Nebraska alumni ... gather every Saturday to root on the Big Red" at Joe Senser's sports bar.[25]

No wonder, then, that Eric Baer of Oklahoma City says, "Oklahoma City, California, Oregon, no matter where they are you can find a Nebraska fan who will go to bars, go to the games, watch the games, just follow religiously."

Echoes John Troia of Gaithersburg, Maryland: "No matter what part [of the country] you're in, you can find [Husker fans]. There's always a group somewhere, California, NY, DC, everywhere, who get together on game day to keep 'it' alive and to celebrate Nebraska football."

From Leavenworth, Kansas, Fritz Gottschalk reports, "No matter where you go, you can always find a group of [Husker fans]. I have been in Yuma, AZ, Fayetteville, NC, and Monterey, CA—always someone to watch the game with."

(In fairness, I should note that you can't find fellow Huskers *everywhere* in the country, although John C. Craig of Denver notes that in the 1980s, "I watched several Big Red games from the Kuparuk oil field at the north end of Alaska, and I took great comfort and pride in realizing that I was probably the northernmost fan on those Saturdays.")

This ability to find Huskers *almost* everywhere is a sign that Huskervillers, no matter where we find ourselves, are so strongly connected to our roots that we sometimes feel as if we are literally *in* Nebraska when we attend watch parties. As Matt, a Husker fan from the Denver area, remarks: "You get the crowd cheering—it's sometimes just for a split second—you actually think you're in Memorial Stadium."[26]

To enhance the feeling of being in Nebraska, watch parties may combine the voices from home of the radio broadcast with the visuals of a television broadcast. As *Seattle Times* reporter Danny O'Neil discovered when he entered the Lucky 7 Saloon in Kirkland, Washington, the "bar sounds like Nebraska on game days every fall." He writes:

> The Lucky 7 Saloon's address is in Kirkland, but the sounds say something else.
>
> The play-by-play announcing is the radio call from Lincoln, Neb., complete with commercials for corn seed and fertilizer. Red-clad Cornhusker fans watch the Nebraska football game on the TV's at the bar, but hearing Brent Musberger or Keith Jackson wouldn't be like home. So the Washington Cornhuskers alumni club pays a Seattle-area radio station to broadcast the Nebraska radio call.[27]

This feeling of being in Nebraska, no matter where you are, is not limited to the U.S. The nourishment provided by the tuber that is Memorial Stadium feeds the shoots of Huskerville that emerge around the globe.

Huskerville International

You have to be a dedicated fan when you follow your college sports team from another country. But as former coach Osborne wrote in 2004, Husker fans embody the idea of dedication:

> Of course I'm biased, but I've always felt that the best college football fans in America reside in my home state. I was reminded of this when I traveled to the Middle East last December as part of a congressional delegation. While meeting with our troops in Iraq, I spoke with several soldiers who were Nebraska natives. Instead of talking about the war on terror, all these young men and women wanted to do was chat about the Cornhuskers. Like nearly all Big Red fans, they were knowledgeable and passionate about the team. One soldier even flew a scarlet-and-cream Nebraska flag above his tent. It really touched me that someone halfway around the world whose life was in constant jeopardy would find a way to show his loyalty to the school—but that's a Nebraska fan for you.[28]

You can find these fans in all kinds of places, from Taiwan to Haiti to Armenia. *Sports Illustrated* reports that people from approximately 25 countries log on to the Internet to hear radio Web casts when the Huskers play.[29] The popular Internet discussion group Husker List has drawn over 6,000 members from outside the United States.[30] In my efforts to hear from Huskerville residents far and wide, I received notes or messages from Huskers living in Italy, Armenia, Japan, Germany, Ireland, and Taiwan.

Their common refrain: to be in Huskerville is to be home. Scott Pagel reports that he follows the Huskers from Tapei, Taiwan, because so doing "keeps me in touch with family and friends."

Strat Warden, now a physician in Elizabethtown, Kentucky, tells this story about being in Huskerville: "When I was in the Navy and in Okinawa, Japan, I can remember when Nebraska was playing Clemson for the national title in one of the eastern bowls. I flew back on New Year's Eve because over there they didn't have any live television shows. I flew back on New Year's Eve just so I could see Nebraska play Clemson and had to fly back that following night. It's like a nineteen-, twenty-hour flight. And that's the kind of thing that people [do]; they have an identity for it."

Husker fans don't leave home, Strat reminds us; instead, we work to nourish our roots—no matter where we are. "I can remember sitting in a bunker during my year in Viet Nam listening to Armed Forces Radio," writes Bob Sklenar, "trying to get the latest score or with any luck listen to the Big Red play." Another member of the armed forces, Fritz Gottschalk, a native of Papillion, Nebraska, told me about running into two Husker fans while on assignment in Haiti in 1994:

> One day, right prior to Thanksgiving, I was returning from a patrol. As we approached the town, I saw two missionaries walking back from a roadside market. We (me and the other guys on the team) stopped off to talk to them. That was one of our habits, if you see a friendly face, stop off and talk to them. They were both Catholic missionaries and had been running a nursing school in the area for several years (15–20 or so). One was about 50, the other was 74. Both were happy as heck and we had a good time talking. After about five minutes of talking, the conversation turned to hometowns. They were from just south of Lincoln!
>
> I invited them to the base camp for Thanksgiving, but they had other plans. We had just had Armed Forces Network TV installed at the base camp, so I invited them down for the OU/NU game. They couldn't make that one either, but did take up my offer for the Orange Bowl that year.
>
> The older missionary was pretty much blind, but she more than made up for that in rowdiness. [During the Orange Bowl game] we all three were singing Nebraska songs, cheering every play. Awesome time. Middle of Haiti, combat zone, not the most pleasant of surroundings, sitting in an army tent, watching a fuzzy TV screen and the Huskers. It doesn't get any better, the surroundings kind of disappeared and we were just three folks from Nebraska sharing a good game.[31]

On a different kind of mission, Arthur W. Hudson has also shared the joys of Huskerville around the world. A former elementary school principal in Valentine, Nebraska, Arthur and his wife left their jobs in Valentine to begin teaching children in other countries. Their work, as Arthur explains, also includes teaching kids about the wonders of Huskerville.

> While we were teaching at the International School Singapore for three years, my wife had her 4th grade students trained to always make the principal happy on Monday morning by bringing in the Nebraska score. She had one

faithful little Chinese girl that always knew the Nebraska score on Monday morning. Her students also know which of the states in the United States is most important. They also know what a "CORNHUSKER" is and what we mean by a sea of red and white.[32]

So, we can find Husker fans inside Memorial Stadium, in the small towns and fields of Nebraska, throughout the United States, and around the world. Huskerville is a place where the city limits stretch far and wide.

But how deep are those roots?

In a word, *very*.

When the University of Nebraska football team plays a game outside of the state, you will find Huskervillers emerging in all corners of the stadium. (A number of rhizomes are weeds, so we understand if the fans of teams hosting the Huskers find our presence a bit irritating.) As writer Jeff Snook explains, "The famed Sea of Red can and will travel anywhere and turn another university's stadium into the site of a Nebraska road party."[33]

Apparently, this has been going on for quite some time. Husker fan Charlie Winkler, notarized in 1975 by *Sports Illustrated* as the nation's biggest fan, notes that he heard the story of 3,000 Husker fans traveling to Minnesota for a game in the early 1900s, well before cars were widely used for highway travel.[34]

In 1970, as Husker player Joe Blahak prepared to enter the playing field for the game against the University of Southern California (USC), "There was this big roar as USC ran out, and then we ran out, and I heard it get even louder. There was red everywhere and that's when I learned how well Nebraska fans travel."[35] The next summer, as the football coaches in the Big 8 conference gathered for their annual kickoff luncheon, Kansas State coach Vince Gibson told the assembled crowd, "I think we're all gonna be seeing a lot of red this year. The only thing I hate about Nebraska is that they don't have any road games. When they play on the road, so many of their fans follow them it's like a home game for them."[36]

Fourteen years later, I was able to experience a Husker road game. On September 9, 1995, I traveled to East Lansing, Michigan, to watch the Huskers play the Michigan State Spartans. Despite my awareness of the legions of Husker fans who attend road games, I was still a bit apprehensive about traveling to a stadium where I would be cheering against the home team. My concerns disappeared quickly as we pulled into the parking lot and I immediately noticed many other fans wearing red. Inside the stadium, I felt right at home among the thousands of Husker fans who sat and cheered together.

Four years later, as I chatted with Scottsbluff residents Barb and Marty Martinson outside the Nebraska Bookstore prior to the Iowa State game, my memory of visiting East Lansing returned when the Martinsons told me about watching the Nebraska at Iowa game on TV earlier in the season:

MARTY: "The first game this season with Iowa this year the stadium was red."

BARB: "And it was in Iowa and we watched it on television and Iowa fans are not red they are yellow."

TOGETHER: "But the stadium was red!"

The Martinsons' observations might help explain the following joke, shared with me by an Iowa native and resident, Todd Wolverton, who spent a formative four years as a student at the University of Nebraska–Lincoln:

A Texas fan, a Nebraska fan and an Iowa State fan were out riding horses one day. At one point, the Texas fan pulled out a bottle of expensive bourbon, took a long swig, threw the bottle to the ground, pulled out a pistol and shot it.

"What are you doing?" said the Nebraska fan. "That was perfectly good whisky."

"In Texas, we have more whisky than we need," said the Longhorn fan, "and bottles are cheap."

They rode along for a while, and the Nebraska fan was thinking. Then he pulled out a bottle of champagne, opened it, took a swig, threw down the bottle, pulled out his pistol and shot the bottle.

"What are you doing?" asked the ISU fan. "That was perfectly good champagne."

"In Nebraska," said the Husker fan, "we have more champagne than we need, and bottles are cheap."

They rode along for a while, and then the Cyclone fan pulled out a bottle of beer, drank the whole thing, put the bottle back in his saddlebag, pulled out his pistol and shot the Nebraska fan.

"What are you doing?" asked the Texas fan.

"In Iowa," replied the Cyclone fan, "we have more Husker fans than we need, but bottles are worth a nickel apiece."

The Iowans may have company. *Sports Illustrated* reports that in 2001 the Kansas stadium "was a sea of Nebraska red. In the third quarter, with the visitors well on their way to a 51–7 victory, the fans began chanting, 'Let's go Huskers!'"[37] Similarly, Innes Mitchell recalls, "As a graduate student in Kansas, I vividly remember Lawrence being flooded by this 'sea of red,' a natural phenomenon that no other visiting team's support came close to matching."[38]

In Colorado, a Husker fan named Bob reports that when he received tickets from a University of Colorado employee, he found himself surrounded by other Husker fans who had found their tickets the same way. "Almost everyone in the section was for Nebraska," he recalls. And, during the excitement prior to the 2002 national championship game in Pasadena, California, an estimated 8,000 to 11,000 Husker fans gathered on the Santa Monica Pier for an alumni association sponsored pep rally. Andy Washburn, the alumni association staff member in charge of the event, said, "We talked to the pier folks. They said it was the largest event the pier has ever held in its history."[39]

In one of the more surprising demonstrations of Husker fan commitment, an estimated 30,000 Husker fans attended the 2000 Nebraska-Notre Dame game in South Bend, Indiana, despite the fact that Notre Dame allotted only 4,000 tickets to Nebraska fans. "'That's what I will always remember from walking out of that tunnel at Notre Dame,' Eric Crouch said of the 2000 game in South Bend, Indiana. 'I expected to see all blue and gold, and all I saw was red. You can't imagine how good that feels for a Nebraska football player.'"[40]

Amazingly, another 20,000 Husker fans traveled to the game but didn't make it inside the stadium, according to the Associated Press.[41] That story quoted Notre Dame athletic director Kevin White as saying, "When I was on the field before the game I wish I was color blind.... Disappointing, very disappointing." Echoed a group of three Notre Dame sophomores in a letter to their campus newspaper, "[ESPN analyst] Lee Corso summed it all up the best when he said, 'It was an embarrassment for Notre Dame to see their stadium in a sea of red. I can't believe it happened.' Neither can we, Mr. Corso, neither can we."[42] A photograph taken inside the stadium that day has circulated among Husker fans via the Internet.

Undoubtedly, devoted fans of other sports teams can likely muster evidence indicating how their fan community is unique, too.[43] For example, Warren St. John opens his book about the Alabama football fan experience by mentioning that 90 percent of Alabama residents describe themselves as college football fans. In the next sentence, though, he inadvertently reveals a fundamental difference between college football in Alabama and college football in Nebraska: "Eighty-six percent of [the football fans in Alabama] pull for one of the *two* major football powers there, Alabama or Auburn, and 4 percent pull for other teams—Florida, Notre Dame, Georgia, Tennessee, and Michigan, or smaller schools like Alabama A & M or Alabama State."[44]

In Nebraska, the state's population is not carved up into different fan fiefdoms.

A former (and ongoing) teacher of mine, Tom Preston, who grew up in North Carolina as a fan of Wake Forest and the University of North Carolina before becoming a Huskerviller while attending graduate school in Lincoln, observes: "What continues to set the Big Red experience apart [from even Wake Forest and North Carolina] is the unity.... There are many 'villes in North Carolina and east coast fandom—each I suppose reflecting the values of each institution—but none representing an entire STATE such as Nebraska."[45]

This is one of the reasons why Huskerville is a little bit different. But it's only part of the story.

3

Anchored in Nebraska

The rest of the story begins with me waking up.

You see, I am not a morning person. You are much more likely to hear me grunt than to hear me say "wow!" anytime before noon.

Yet, there I was, saying "wow!" at dawn while I was checking out of the Nebraska Center following the 1999 homecoming weekend at the University of Nebraska.

Staring at me from a poster on the wall was the sower, the Lee Lawrie copper statue that adorns the top of the Nebraska State Capitol. I remember first seeing pictures of the sower as an elementary school child learning about Nebraska history. I remember visiting the capitol itself shortly after that as part of a family vacation. The view from the observation deck, just below the sower and more than a football field length above the ground, was stunning for a child who grew up in a town where only a few houses had two stories. I also remember working underneath the sower as an intern in then-governor Bob Kerrey's Policy Research Office. The peaceful walk from campus up Centennial Mall, past the fountains and shrubbery, helped give me a feeling that I was both growing up and moving up as I made my way toward the sower.

But in the very early morning of homecoming weekend, I was seeing the sower as I have never seen him before—larger-than-life, transcendent, almost floating in air—because the poster photo is an aerial view that features the sower and only a bit of the dome on which he is perched. I was startled by the new perspective and marveled anew at the amazing engineering feat that allowed the sower to balance atop the capitol for so many decades.

But perhaps the sower's amazing balancing act is not simply the work of astounding engineering? It's a question I chewed on as I thought and read more about the sower and his relationship to Nebraska.

The sower is an unusual figure, and not just because he sits atop Lincoln's tallest building. He is part Michelangelo's *David*, a classical figure with a stoic face and chiseled physique, and part Johnny Appleseed, a bag of seeds slung over his shoulder and resting against his waist. Raised to the dome of the capitol on April 24, 1930, the 19-foot tall statue has literally weathered the storms since that time. It has been struck several times by lightning, yet the copper melted and filled in the holes caused by the strikes, leaving dents but not destruction.[1]

In this respect, the sower—or what the Fall 2001 issue of *Nebraska Magazine* calls the "Sentry on the Plains" and the "state's tallest citizen"—"symbolizes all of Nebraska," says 1948 University of Nebraska graduate Patrick Sano.[2]

I agree.

Packed within this inanimate statue are the characteristics that embody what Nebraskans hold most dear: a stoic determination to produce something from land dismissed as barren; a commitment to independent, hard work; an appreciation for applying the rules of life fairly and consistently; a recognition that, just over the horizon, others like you face similar joys and heartaches; and, above all, a quest for holding these values in balance while being buffeted by natural and cultural winds of change.

While the sower miraculously stays rooted to the top of the capitol dome, Nebraskans remain rooted to our shared values and traditions. We attempt to live the words of Paul Gruchow: "To inhabit a place means, if one is attentive to the idea from which it comes, not simply to occupy it, or merely to own it, but to dwell within it, to have joined oneself in some organic way to it; it is the place to which one's heart as much as one's body is attached."[3]

Places like Huskerville gather histories, experiences, ideas, and memories, then contain them within their borders while simultaneously keeping out those that do not belong.[4]

This merger of people, place, and practices is not unique to those of us in Huskerville. It can be found anyplace where people take their roots seriously. In many Native American cultures, for example, the land is considered to be literally a part of the people who live with it. Kiowa author and Pulitzer Prize winner M. Scott Momaday calls this process "reciprocal appropriation"; we give something to the place, and the place gives something to us. We are *in* it, and it is *in* us.[5] We are rooted.

To be rooted is more than simply feeling at home in some place. After all, many of us may feel at home in any number of locations. To be rooted is to have such a profound attachment to a particular place that we use those roots as something of a moral guide in our daily living.[6] Our expectations of others, and of ourselves, derive from these roots. These roots, moreover, are not merely bound to a geographical location; they are connected to the physical place *and* to the activities, people, values, and experiences that are embedded in that place.[7] To be rooted, then, means that our attachment to a place has depth. The winds of change cannot easily erode the land that surrounds those roots.

This condition is both literal and metaphorical among Nebraskans. Quite literally, the roots of Nebraska's prairie run deep. University of Nebraska–Kearney biology professors Harold G. Nagel and Marvin C. Williams explain that "prairie plants are usually credited with having at least half to as much as two-thirds of their total plant growth present as roots."[8]

They suggest that, up to a foot below the earth, a chunk of prairie sod contains "a root hair in every visible portion of the soil."[9] As a result, prairie grasses in particular have "survive[d] weather extremes, mowing, grazing, and fire."[10] They were also used to help the state's early homesteaders survive by providing shelter in the form of sod houses, dugouts, or a combination of the two.

The strength of these roots was reflected in both the somewhat facetious name for sod ("Nebraska brick") and by its prevalent usage (historian Everett Dick points out that in 1876, approximately 90 percent of the residents of Butler County, Nebraska, "had at one time or another since their arrival lived in homes constructed of earth").[11]

Metaphorically, as Momaday explains in his discussion of reciprocal appropriation, the depth of attachment to a place develops when both the land and the cultural history of the people in that land merge.

Sports, in particular, provide the vehicles for such a merger. Michael Novak, author of *The Joy of Sports*, explains that sports offer us a means of rooting ourselves through, well, rooting. He writes, "A team is not only *assembled* in one place; it also *represents* a place."[12] And, since we live in those places, they represent us, too. That makes them mighty important, which is why some of us read the sports pages before the front pages—and not just in Nebraska.

Robert Ruck, lecturer in sports and urban history at the University of Pittsburgh, argues that "sport as much as steel has cast the image of Pittsburgh to the world. Pittsburghers have used sport to tell a story about who they are both to themselves and to others. It's about tough, hard-working, gritty people who struggle and win and lose and win."[13]

Not surprisingly, then, North Carolina native Will Blythe explains that the outcomes of North Carolina-Duke basketball games speak to more than simple wins and losses. He writes, "Issues of identity—whether you see yourself as a populist or an elitist, as a local or an outsider, as public-minded or individually striving—get played out through allegiances to Duke's and North Carolina's basketball teams."[14]

In Wisconsin, Governor Jim Doyle told *Sports Illustrated* in 2003, "The [Green Bay] Packers are more than just a state team.... They determine the state's mood. They throw this state into a depression if they lose. Productivity is affected. It's been like that forever."[15]

Same thing in Nebraska.

Almost. Or, at least we like to think so.

Those of us who live in Huskerville believe that our roots run a bit deeper. Now I wouldn't be surprised if all devoted sports fans felt the same way about their teams. We all like to think that our group is special. Rather than try to conclusively *prove* that we Huskervillers are different—and I've had fans of other sports teams rightfully tell me that I really can't prove to them that we are different—I'll try to explain how and why we *believe* we're different.

First, the testimonials. Ehren Mitzlaff, a Colorado-based Husker fan, asserts, "I've lived in many states since leaving Nebraska and never have I seen such a statewide love for its team."

Trev Alberts, who grew up in Iowa, played football at Nebraska and in the National Football League, then became a national sports commentator, concurs, "I've yet to experience the depth of feeling in any other place. Football as played right here in this place [Memorial Stadium] is unlike any other in the country."[16]

Joe Starita and Tom Tidball, authors of the book *A Day in the Life: The Fans of Memorial Stadium*, proclaim: "In the world of collegiate athletics, there are fans. And then there are those who follow Nebraska football. Two distinct, discernible species. Mutually exclusive. Separate and unequal."[17]

These guys are all a bit biased, I know. So, I turned to see what non–Nebraskans say about Huskervillers. *Kansas City Star* writer Joe Posnanski claims, "Nowhere, not in the Tuscaloosa, Ala., humidity, not beneath the Dome in South Bend, Ind., not among the swamps of Florida, not in the corner bars near Camden Yards, not along Tobacco Road, not in the rafters at Allen Fieldhouse, nowhere are there fans like the ones who fill Memorial Stadium in Lincoln.... They are simply the best, no question."[18]

Lee Corso, an ESPN college football analyst who spent years coaching college football, knows the college football scene as well as anyone in the country. He, too, says Nebraska fans stand out. "If somebody wanted to go one place and watch a game, I'd tell them to go to Lincoln.... It's the best. Nobody compares. The fans are the most knowledgeable and fair and love the game of college football more than any place I've ever been."[19]

I also not so humbly offer historical testimony from those without bias. Writing in 1975, the year of my first visit to a filled Memorial Stadium, author David Israel assures us:

> I can't say I wasn't warned. They were friends from North Platte and Omaha, and they told me all about it before I left for the airport and my first football weekend at the University of Nebraska in Lincoln.
> We had all gone to a Big Ten school, and I was sure that Lincoln couldn't be any different from Columbus or Ann Arbor or West Lafayette or South Bend. There is tradition at all those places. They reek of tradition.
> They told me Columbus, Ann Arbor, South Bend were all minor league compared to Lincoln. I insisted that couldn't be; they insisted I would see football madness like I had never seen it before. And they told me that this madness occurred as a matter of course. They told me it didn't take a special event such as Oklahoma-Texas. If the Cornhuskers were playing Yankton College, the madness would be just the same in Lincoln as if the opponent were Oklahoma....
> My friends were right; South Bend was never like this—could never even hope to be like this.[20]

While we take great pleasure in the unsolicited testimonials of others, we Huskervillers also like to point to statistics to reassure ourselves that we are different from other fans. Numerically speaking, Nebraska football fans say they root harder than other fans. A 2004 *Sports Illustrated* magazine poll reported that, on average, Nebraskans declared that our state's passion for sports was 89.1 on a scale of 100. No other state's residents ranked their enthusiasm higher.[21] No wonder, then, that over 60,000 Husker fans show up for the *scrimmage* that marks the end of the spring practice season—compared to 15,000 for the University of Southern California, 11,000 for Florida State University, and 6,000 for the University of Colorado.[22]

An additional statistical comparison comes from Mike Nolan, manager of the online discussion group Husker List. He observes, "We've all heard the line about how the population of Memorial Stadium would make it the third-largest city in the state. Somewhat more impressive is that when the Huskers are playing at home, one out of every 25 Nebraskans is there to watch. It's hard to imagine one out of 25 Californians doing anything together."[23]

Huskervillers do things together outside of Memorial Stadium, too. I decided to compare Nebraska with a few other prominent college football programs to see how we Huskervillers stacked up against them in our watch party attendance. By visiting alumni association Web sites for the University of Southern California (USC), the University of Texas, the University of Alabama, Ohio State University, and Miami University, I was able to compare the number of alumni association chapters located outside of each state and the number of watch parties listed for each program outside of the state.

Let me begin by saying that Nebraska's information was by far the easiest to access, an initial indication that knowing where one goes to watch the Huskers play on TV is very important to Huskerville residents. In addition, the same Web page that lists Husker watch sites also provides information on where we can set our radios to hear broadcasts of Husker games. Now, on to the comparison.

Nebraska's alumni association Web site identifies 54 alumni chapters outside of the state and 91 locations where Husker fans can gather outside of Nebraska to watch our team play on television.[24] Compare those numbers to the other schools'[25]:

School	Chapters Outside the State[26]	Watch Parties Outside State
Nebraska	54	91
USC	31	21[27]
Texas	40	14
Ohio State	112	62
Alabama	19	10
Miami	21	23[28]

These comparisons can be taken with a proverbial grain of salt, of course, because each university—including Nebraska—will find its fans gathered in any number of unofficial watch parties.

Nonetheless, I think the numbers are striking when one considers both the ease of accessing this information and the disparity in enrollments (and thus alumni) among the schools.[29] Consider, for example, that the Nebraska Web site lists 19 watch parties in California alone—more than the total listed above for Alabama and Texas, and just a few below the total numbers for Miami and USC.

Moreover, Husker fans host nearly twice as many watch parties as they have chapters, while the closest competitor on this list—Ohio State—has about half as many watch parties as chapters. This means that some Huskerville chapters need multiple locations to host parties. For example,

Coloradans for Nebraska needs six locations in metropolitan Denver, and Californians for Nebraska spreads out into 12 locations across the Los Angeles area.

Bob Sklenar, who heads up the Pennsylvanians for Nebraska alumni chapter, explains this difference by arguing that the deep roots of Huskerville are tied to the state of Nebraska, not just a team or university. "People [in Pennsylvania] may have an attachment to Philadelphia or Pittsburgh or the Eagles or the Steelers," he says, "but they do not have that attachment to the state."

With apologies to the devoted fans of other sports programs, then, I think the Nebraska difference is this: while other teams, to use Michael Novak's word, *represent* a place and its people, we believe that the Huskers *are* Nebraska and its people.[30]

Let me try to explain the difference. When sports fans see their team as *representing* them, they take seriously what the team does for it is a *reflection* of them. Reflection is the key word in this understanding of representation. When we look in the mirror, we see our reflection, but the reflection is not us—it is a representation of us. The image in the mirror is flattened, and we are separated from it by the distance between ourselves and the mirror.

When the team *is* us, however, we are joined, not separate. The team is not merely like us, it is us. As former Husker football player and assistant coach Turner Gill explains, "When you're describing the people of the state of Nebraska, you're also describing the Nebraska football team."[31] The players on the team are our kids, friends, and neighbors.

Observes Chuck Love of Louisville, Kentucky, "A good share of the team every year are local Nebraska-raised young men.... It's such a small state, such a small population, that a lot of these young farm boys have a lot of meat on them, they come in as these linemen, and a lot of local Nebraska people [and] playing Nebraska football."

In particular, we see the Husker players as coming from the same rural areas as the rest of us. Harriett Aden, my mother, points out, "The Huskers are largely an in-state product—players come from little towns with 8-man football teams." The Huskers come "from all over, towns like Wood River, Elm Creek, Hyannis," adds my childhood friend Craig Embree.

When we compare ourselves to other places and teams, Pat Ferguson of Lakeland, Minnesota, says, we believe "a larger percentage of the Husker squad is actually from Nebraska than at most schools (or at least we think so)."

No wonder, then, that former University of Nebraska sports information director Don Bryant fondly remembers his interactions with Nebraskans who saw the team as just like them. "You'd be out recruiting around the state, driving through the state, and you see a farmer in the field or something, plowing and you stop and get out and walk to the fence and walk out to the field and talk with the guy," Bryant says. Recalling the ensuing conversation, Bryant continues, "'Hi folks.' [Responded the farmer], 'How's our boys going to do this year?'" Bryant shakes his head in amazement, and concludes, "[That farmer] was no more a Nebraska alum, he's just a farmer out there plowing his field, but by God, it was his boys—'how are *our* boys going to do?'"

The results of the 2003 telephone poll bear witness to this merging of team, fans, and place. Of the 80 Nebraska residents who indicated agreement with the statement, "I closely follow the Husker football team,"[32] only 13 of them, or 16 percent, *disagreed* with the statement, "The characteristics of the Husker football team match the characteristics of Nebraskans generally." Only 17 of them, or 21 percent, *disagreed* with the statement, "A true Nebraskan is a Husker fan." Even more tellingly, only *one* of the 80 self-identified fans *strongly disagreed* with the "true Nebraskan is a true fan" and "match the characteristics" statements.[33]

The poll also asked the Nebraska residents to explain the difference between a Nebraskan and a Husker fan.[34] Their responses illustrated how Husker fans see "being a Husker" and "being a Nebraskan" as equivalent; non–Husker fans do not make the same connection between the team and the state.[35] Two non-fans, for instance, noted that "A Nebraskan cares about Nebraska and not just the football team" and "There are a lot of people who don't follow football who are good Nebraskans."

On the other hand, Husker fans responded to the question with statements indicating their belief that a "Husker fan" is simply another name for "Nebraskan."

> All the same thing.
> There is no difference.
> There is none.
> If you're a Nebraskan, you're usually a Husker fan. They are pretty much the same.
> Not sure how to separate Nebraskan from a Husker fan.
> Hell if I know.
> No difference.
> Don't know.
> Nothing.
> They're one and the same.
> Pretty much the same.
> Should be none.

Or, as one fan responded, "A Husker fan is a Nebraskan that uses Husker football to express their unity with other Nebraskans."

Huskervillers who live outside the state of Nebraska echo these sentiments.

Cory Osborn of Tempe, Arizona, says, "I think of Nebraska, I think of the Huskers. They are one and the same." Kerianne Kluge of Louisville, Kentucky, adds, "Huskers is a synonym for Nebraska." John M. Harrington of Lantana, Florida, proclaims, "The Huskers and the state are indivisible in my mind."

This is a bit puzzling to folks who are not from Nebraska. Bob Kully of Los Angeles, California, recalls, "I have one friend saying 'You didn't even go to the university, how come you became such a fan?' I used to say this to people 'You don't understand. There is no the University of Nebraska football team. It's a State of Nebraska football team.'"

Mike Nolan, who manages the popular Husker List internet discussion group, eloquently articulates this blending of team and state identity in a 2002 column in the *Lincoln Journal Star*. Headlined, "The Huskers Just Aren't Important to Nebraska, They ARE Nebraska," Nolan's column is instructive:

> Nebraskans have run for president, written books considered classics, entertained us on film and TV and created products recognized around the world. But those accomplishments are usually not tied to the image of the state. They may have been from Nebraska, but the Huskers are Nebraska....
>
> The Huskers are a state consciousness, a state identity. New York has the Statue of Liberty, Nebraska has the outline of a football helmet with a red "N" on it....
>
> The late Roone Arledge coined the famous phrase: "the thrill of victory and the agony of defeat." Nebraskans understand. Our emotional cycles are tied to the successes and failures of the Huskers nearly as much as to our families.

What the Husker football players do on the field is important, but what we do as fans is also important, for we are the same people from the same place enacting the same principles in doing what we do. This vague language takes a more concrete form in the chapters that follow. For now, I want to emphasize that "being a Husker" is an identity that envelops both fans and players, and that "being a Nebraskan" is its equivalent. "For many Nebraskans," adds Darren Carlson, "University of Nebraska football is not a sport, pastime, hobby or thing of interest. It is truly a part of their identity."[36]

Perhaps these roots run so deep because, as St. Louis resident Matt Shurtliff writes in a posting to the Husker List Internet discussion group, "if you grew up in the state, the very tapestry of your life's experiences is interwoven with the history of the football team." He continues:

> Other things are woven into that tapestry that is "growing up in Nebraska," too, like the Blue Streak Sports section, Fort Robinson, Chimney Rock, the license plate numbering system, dirt section roads, the Sandhills, apples in Nebraska City, the Niobrara Valley, county fairs, and my personal fave, the Sandhill Crane migration. But the football program has been an absolute constant, for all of us. Not all of us are into fishing at the Harlan County Reservoir, but we are all into the football team. Our memories, hopes, dreams, joys, loves, fears, and sadnesses are all linked, if only in some small way, to that constant.[37]

Matt's observation that being a Husker involves an interweaving of football, place, and life experiences is reaffirmed by other Huskerville residents in different parts of the United States. Their words evoke Momaday's notion of reciprocal appropriation:

ERICA BOTTGER OF SEATTLE: When you grow up with it, Nebraska football becomes part of you.

JEFF WALZ OF DENVER: If it's part of Nebraska, it's part of you.

BOB SKLENAR OF AMBLER, PENNSYLVANIA: You can take the boy out of the country, but not the country out of the boy.

ALISA BREDENSTEINER OF CHICAGO: There is a strong feeling of attachment. I belong to them and they belong to me, so it doesn't matter where I live or where I'm at.

These explanations of rootedness are also not unlike those that the main characters in Willa Cather's novels My Ántonia and O Pioneers! experience. Jim Burden, the narrator of My Ántonia learns, through his interactions with the novel's title character, that to be intimately, indivisibly connected to your land is perhaps the ultimate definition of happiness. In an excerpt that includes part of what became Cather's epitaph, Burden describes his feelings as he sits in his grandparents' garden: "The earth was warm under me, and warm as I crumbled it through my fingers.... I was entirely happy. Perhaps we feel like that when we die and become a part of something entire, whether it is sun and air, or goodness and knowledge. At any rate, that is happiness; to be dissolved into something complete and great."[38]

Similarly, Alexandra Bergson in Cather's O Pioneers! seems to be most content when she is at one with the land: "You feel that, properly, Alexandra's house is the big out-of-doors, and that it is in the soil that she expresses herself best.... There were certain days in her life, outwardly uneventful,

which Alexandra remembered as peculiarly happy; days when she was close
to the flat, fallow world about her, and felt, as it were, in her own body the
joyous germination in the soil."[39] At the conclusion of O *Pioneers!* Alexandra's process of reciprocal appropriation is confirmed by her friend Carl:
"'You belong to the land,' Carl murmured, 'as you have always said. Now
more than ever.'"[40]

In some ways, Carl's observation is reflected in the sentiments of Husker
fan Robert W. Thorpe. The first person I interviewed on my trip to Lincoln
in 1999, Thorpe—coincidentally, I discovered, a native of Scottsbluff—
remarked, "as Dostoevsky once said, you scratch a Russian you find a peasant, you scratch a peasant you find the soil. I think when you come back to
Nebraska you have some of that similarity." Or, as my college friend Todd
Wolverton observed, "I define a Nebraskan as someone with roots in the
state. In a way connected to the land."

Thus, just as Alexandra belonged to the land, Huskers belong to
Huskerville.

To be sure, sports fans of all types identify with their teams and players.[41] In Huskerville, however, we use language to describe our relationship
with the team that suggests a connection beyond identification. First, we
describe ourselves as having Nebraska "in our blood" or as somehow a part
of our physical make up. Second, we define Nebraska as "home" no matter
where we reside.

In the Blood[42]

Invoking the metaphor of biology, Huskervillers suggest that being a
Nebraskan and Husker is a natural process in which the place enters the
body. Husker fan Ann-Marie Duffy wrote to me from Ireland, "The Cornhusker team really binds Nebraska together. The spirit they exhibit is transmitted to the entire state, absorbed and becomes part of us." This process
of absorption, of taking in the spirit of Nebraska, was frequently described
by Husker fans in terms of a merger of body and soul. John Lynch, a Husker
fan in the Seattle area, explains, "It is in our bones."

The most frequent phrase used to describe this connection, perhaps
because of the symbolic power of the color red, was "in the blood." Explains
Ryan Gray, "There is an aura that oozes out from Nebraska and seeps into
our blood forever. Whether it is football or something else, Nebraska finds
us ... and unifies us to 'Stay Red.'"

After visiting a Kentuckiana Huskers watch party, my friend Alena

Amato Ruggerio suggested that I title this book "It's in Your Blood" because she heard Donna Love, Dan Koleski, and Kerianne Kluge all refer to their Nebraska connection as being "in your blood."

When Huskervillers move out of state, they remain anchored in Nebraska because of this biological bond. Kevin J. Bourn, whose family moved from Nebraska to Iowa when he was nine, recalls: "I remember when my friends [in Iowa] used to give me a hard time about being a Husker fan. I would just tell them, 'You just don't understand, I have Big Red blood flowing through my veins.'"[43]

In Lincoln, I visited with Nevada resident Rocky C. White, who proudly explained that—even though he had not lived in Nebraska since 1970—he continued to follow the Huskers while sending his kids to school at the University of Nebraska–Lincoln. "It's just something that gets into your blood ... and you keep going with it," he says. Chris Tradewell, of Hartford, Wisconsin, affirms this notion: "Being loyal to the Huskers is in my blood.... It feels innate."

Perhaps it is.

Stew Price suggests that being a Husker is genetically coded. "There is an unwritten code that says, 'once a Husker, always a Husker,'" he writes. "It gets built into your genetic code, similar to a salmon that innately knows that it must swim upstream."

No wonder then that Huskervillers speak of their connection to the state and football team as something that they are born with. Walt Fulton of Maryland notes, "Once a Nebraskan, always a Nebraskan, from cradle to coffin." University of Nebraska–Lincoln student Stephanie Dagerman told me, "I've been a Husker fan since I was born," and Columbia, Missouri, resident Kelly Hendricks explains, "The Huskers are as much a part of being a Nebraskan as being neighborly and friendly. It comes with your birth certificate."

Husker fan Erik offers his theory about how this process unfolds:

> It began in September 1958. My mom was 3 months pregnant with me. In those days women in a "delicate condition" didn't attend sporting events. While my dad drove from Omaha to Lincoln for each home game, mom sat in a rocker and listened to "the game" on the radio. Whereas it is now vogue for expectant mothers to listen to Mozart, hoping for the next great genius, my mom hatched a die-hard Husker fan....
>
> Throughout my life, my birth, my youth, my loves, my sorrows, my service to my country and the deaths of loved ones, Nebraska football has always been there.... I can't explain my devotion to their cause other than to say it is, and always will be, a part of me.[44]

As Erik concludes, the depth of Huskers' commitment means that our connection to Huskerville is permanent, much like our biological make-up remains unalterable. No matter where we go, Huskers are always in Huskerville; we are always home. Anthropologist Keith Basso's observation of the Western Apache could just as easily apply to those of us in Huskerville: our homes are "eminently portable possessions to which individuals can maintain deep and abiding attachments, regardless of where they travel."[45]

Always Home

Dennis Kelly, an Ohio resident, explains a Husker is "a person with deep roots—some always planted in Nebraska." Atlanta area resident and Husker fan Ed Vinton proclaims, "The Huskers are like home. It doesn't seem to matter how far away from Nebraska that I live, watching the Huskers always seems like being at home in Nebraska."

The names of alumni association chapters also illustrate this kind of rootedness. While you might encounter a few formal sounding chapter names, you will also find Nebraskans around the country who define their groups in terms of their Nebraska roots: Alaskan Nebraskans, Idaho Huskers, Hoosier Huskers, Las Vegas Nebraskans, North Texas Nebraskans, and National Capital Cornhuskers.[46]

Individual Husker fans also describe ourselves as Nebraskans or Huskers, even when we live outside of the borders of Nebraska. Here are a few examples:

GERALD L. MELVIN: I never tell anyone I'm from South Dakota; I'm a Nebraskan living in South Dakota.

MARSHALL WIDMAN: The Kansas City area is where I live, but Nebraska is and will always be where I call home.

DAVID MAX: I have lived in southern California for half of my life and whenever someone asks me where I am from the answer is and always will be "Nebraska!"

MATTHEW G. GROSZ: I live in New Bern, NC. I graduated from Florida State University, University of South Florida and Stetson University in Deland, Florida. I have not lived in the state for 19 years, but I take the state with me wherever I go.

MIKE AND CINDY LENZ: We moved to Nebraska in 1980 and we lived here for eight years. We've since then been in Texas and we live in Kansas right now, but we got to be Husker fans and we carried that.

SAM ELDER: I'm in Husky country [Washington state], but I'm still a Husker fan.

Home, for these Husker fans and for others like them, is where we are rooted. Explains Colorado resident John A. Wilke, "When I say 'I'm going home,' my co-workers all know that means I'm going to Nebraska, not to my house." Conversely, when he leaves Nebraska to return to his residence in Los Angeles, Bob Kully notes, "I don't say, 'I am going home.' I do this without thinking about it. I say, 'I am going back to LA next week.'"

This feeling of being always at home, or in Nebraska, is not limited to Husker fans. Listen to what these former Husker players—who played from the 1920s through the 1990s—told writer Jeff Snook in his book *What It Means to Be a Husker*:

GLENN PRESNELL: I live in Ironton, Ohio, now, but I love Nebraska very much. It was always home to me.

FORREST BEHM: You know, I have lived in New York State since 1944, but my heart is still back in Lincoln. When people ask me where I am from, I just say, Nebraska.

FRED MEIER: I've lived in California now most of my life since leaving college, but let me tell you that I have corn in my blood.

VIC SCHLEICH: I remember this secretary from the alumni association who used to travel with us to all of our games. I heard him make speeches a number of times, and he always ended them with this: "Once to be a Nebraskan is always to be a Nebraskan ... in the deep down constitution of your soul!" I think that says it all.

STEVE TAYLOR: I still fly my school flag on game days and I will always consider myself a loyal Cornhusker.

AARON GRAHAM: I left Texas to go to a foreign place, and now that place has become my home.[47]

That Nebraska is home is acknowledged in other ways by Huskers scattered around the country. The 1999 Arizonans for Nebraska directory, for example, listed the hometowns of each member, while the March 5, 2001, electronic newsletter from the Washington Cornhuskers group recounted an activity at that year's Founders Day dinner: "We had a Nebraska map mounted on a board so the attendees could locate and place a pin on their home town. It was fun to see where all the transplanted Nebraskans called their 'real' home!"

The orientations of Husker fans can best be summarized by Jerry Henderson of Cle Elum, Washington, who told me: "We are Huskers no matter where we live." Or, as Deb McChane, a member of the Kentuckiana Huskers, proclaims, "Once a Husker, always a Husker. That is how it works and that's the way we like it."[48]

Frank Solich learned this after he was unceremoniously fired as the head coach of the Nebraska football team (more on this in the next chapter). Strangely, he ended up in—of all places—Ohio University. This was big news in Athens—but also in Nebraska. *USA Today* sportswriter Christine Brennan explains:

> The staff at College Book Store on the brick-paved main street in this little college town [Athens] was minding its own business on a quiet mid-December day, preparing for the holidays when the orders started mysteriously streaming in.
>
> A half-dozen website requests came into Ohio University that day, all from the same place: Nebraska. "Omaha ... Lincoln," said Andrew Stout, the store's licensed products buyer. "My assistant said, 'What's going on in Nebraska?'" ...
>
> Within minutes, a call came with another order. Once again, it was from Nebraska. Stout happened to pick up the phone and take the order, so before hanging up, his curiosity piqued, he said, "I have to ask you, we're shipping all these orders to Nebraska and we're wondering what's going on?"
>
> The answer was swift, and direct: "You hired our coach, dummy."
>
> Our coach. Even then, one year after being fired as head coach of the Nebraska Cornhuskers, Frank Solich was "their" coach, at least to some Nebraska fans.[49]

Adds Ward Jacobson, a morning host on Lincoln radio station KFOR, "There are still so many old-school Nebraska fans. If you have ties to this university, they'll stick with you.... You're one of us. You'll always be one of us."[50]

Apparently so.

Just over one month later, Scottsbluff resident Bill Coleman wrote a letter to one of my local newspapers declaring, "As a long-time football season ticket holder and fan of Nebraska football, I'd like to tell you just how sad we are to see Coach Solich go, and how happy we are for him to be where he wants to be ... Ohio University! ... I am, as of this day, a big fan of Ohio University football. But I will also cheer on the Huskers."[51] The next day, I stopped at the post office to mail an Ohio University Bobcats sweatshirt to my grandmother in Scottsbluff. I was not alone in my shopping. Local newspapers noted that bookstores in Athens, Ohio, had been continuing to receive requests for Ohio University Bobcats clothing from people in Nebraska.[52]

Later, a group of Nebraskans living in Athens developed a Web site, "Huskers for Ohio,"[53] and created a half-Ohio, half-Nebraska flag. Bookstores in Athens designed shirts proclaiming "Got Frank!" (which my thoughtful wife purchased for my birthday!). I found myself coaching the children of Ohio coaches Keven Lightner and Tim Albin, a former player and coach for the Huskers respectively, on my daughter's kindergarten soccer team. Suddenly, Nebraska had come to me.

If only things were that easy.

4

Winds of Change and the Threat of Being Uprooted

Things aren't easy because they change. Once we figure something out, we can count on it changing—leading us back to square one. Perhaps that's why we nurture the roots of our traditions with such care; they provide us with the necessary illusion that some things never change.

Since I started working on this book I have changed houses, added a daughter to my family, sent another daughter away to college, lost a father, seen my mother retire, said good-bye to my childhood home, experienced dramatic changes in my work environment, and watched the Huskers play in a national championship game—and also experience their two worst seasons in the last 40 years.

That's just a short list of the changes in my life. No doubt you have a list that's similarly long. All of us, in addition, are very familiar with how our larger world has changed since the turn of the century.

So as much as we may want to remain rooted, our physical and social surroundings are buffeted by winds of change. Dealing with these gusts is no small matter. Our very identity, both as individuals and as communities, is entangled in our roots.[1] What do we do when these roots are weakened by the eroding sands of time, the shifting winds of cultural change?

Like the sower, we try to stay anchored—but that's not so easy when our foundation is weakened.

Over the course of the 20th century, the number of farms in the United States dropped from six million to two million, and the number of people living on farms dropped from 30 million to five million.[2] The percentage of the population made up of farmers dropped from 38 percent in 1900 to less than 2 percent in 1999.[3]

Notes farmer and professor Victor Davis Hanson, "There has not been a single month since the early 1950s when the number of genuine American farms has increased or even stayed the same."[4] The erosion in the number of farmers across the nation, Hanson continues, has been so substantial that the Census Department announced over a decade (now two decades) ago that it would no longer count the number of American farmers. "Those still making a living by working and living on their own land," Hanson observes, "were dubbed 'statistically insignificant.'"[5]

This trend shows no signs of reversing since the number of young people entering agriculture is also declining. In 1985, 25 percent of all farmers were under age 35. In 2000, only 15 percent of all farmers were under 35—while the average age of those farmers increased from 49.4 in 1987 to 52.5 in 1997.[6]

All these numbers are not terribly surprising in some ways; farming, after all, is not exactly a glamorous profession. The 2002 version of the *Jobs Rated Almanac*, in fact, rates farming as one of the worst jobs available in the United States,[7] while the Web site careerbuilder.com predicts that farming and ranching will lose a quarter of a million jobs between 2005 and 2012.[8]

These changes aren't exactly news to Nebraskans. It all started during the Dust Bowl days of the 1930s. In 1935, the number of farms in Nebraska hit the historical peak of 133,616; today, only about 50,000 farms remain.[9] Seventy-two of the state's 93 counties reached their population peak in the 1930s or earlier; today, 40 percent of the state's counties have less than half of their historicall peak population.[10]

While the state's overall population does continue to grow, Nebraska's rural population steadily declines. For example, the populations of Douglas, Sarpy, and Lancaster counties—the main population centers for the Omaha and Lincoln areas—collectively grew by 160,000 people between 1980 and 2000. Yet, in 73 of the state's 93 counties, the population declined during those two decades. In many cases, those drops in population were significant; 56 counties had more than 10 percent migration between 1980 and 2000. Not surprisingly, then, according to the 2002 Census of Agriculture, Nebraska lost 18,000 farms and nearly 270,000 acres of farmland between 1974 and 2002.[11]

The University of Nebraska–Lincoln's Bureau of Business Research predicts that significant population losses in the state's smallest counties—the 34 smallest counties have lost about one-third of their residents since 1960—will continue in the next two decades.[12] This prediction is underscored by 2002 Nebraska Rural Poll results that show farmers and ranchers are much more concerned about their livelihoods than are other rural Nebraska residents.[13] "You don't have young people taking over the farms, and you don't have businesses staying," says Jon Bailey of the Center for Rural Affairs, "Even the parents are telling the kids to get out. There is very little to keep many of these [small] towns going."[14]

Even in 1995, *USA Today* reporter Rae Tyson observed, "Schools, hospitals, fire and police departments and once-thriving businesses are shutting down. Churches are closing, consolidating or being forced to share ministers with another congregation. Professionals are bailing out, leaving many towns without lawyers, doctors and dentists."[15]

If this trend is not reversed, warns John Allen, a rural sociologist at the University of Nebraska's Institute for Agriculture and Natural Resources, "many of our counties will consolidate, the rural life will fade away, young people will increasingly leave the state."[16]

Allen's dire prediction omits what I think is the most frightening consequence of these developments: Nebraska's cultural identity will be shaken.[17] The state is, perplexingly, at once becoming more urban and more desolate— and, thus more disconnected from its traditional mooring in an agrarian lifestyle. The result, as a turn-of-the-millennium story in the *Grand Island Independent* proclaimed, is simple: "Nebraska faces identity crisis at start of 21st century." In that story, reporter Phil Rooney quotes Creighton University economics professor Ernie Goss, who says, "It's a transition period, really.... We're now an urban state."[18]

Nebraska's rural areas are becoming so sparsely populated that many of them now meet census officials' definition of "frontier," or fewer than six residents per square mile. For example, in Page, Nebraska—the hometown of Husker football player Adam Ickes, a walk-on turned starting linebacker in 2005—enrollment at the K-8 school dropped from just under 100 in the mid-1990s to eight in 2005.[19]

Laurent Belsie of the *Christian Science Monitor* observes that "in 1950, you could still drive from Omaha, Neb., to Denver without passing through a frontier county. No longer.... This semiarid territory now contains two-thirds of the 377 frontier counties in the contiguous US—up from half in 1950. The land in this depopulating region is still owned and mostly farmed. But it feels as though it's moving backward in time and space."[20]

Moving backward in time and space. Those are chilling words for people whose identity, in large part, stems from the belief that our lifestyle generates progress. By progress, I don't mean simply a better standard of living. No, this progress is also, perhaps primarily, moral.[21]

The books of Nebraska novelists Willa Cather and Mari Sandoz are populated with characters endowed—like the sower—with larger-than-life determination and physical abilities. Their goal, like those of countless Nebraskans who enacted those same qualities in their daily living, was to make something out of what others saw as nothing. Making something out of nothing is a moral victory, but not in a hollow "nice try" way. Instead, argues Cather, "Attainment of material prosperity was a moral victory, because it was wrung from hard conditions ... [it] was the result of struggle that tested character."[22]

In other words, these numbers mean that Nebraskans fear losing a way of life that has provided a cultural identity, a sense of who we collectively have been, continue to be, and hope to be. As scholars who study the notion of "collective memory" emphasize, who we remember ourselves to be, in many ways, determines who we continue to be.[23] In this respect, Huskerville is about remembering more than it is about nostalgia.[24] Without relevant roots, we may blow about the cultural terrain aimlessly, like some kind of cultural tumbleweed.

Laurent Belsie's words elegantly capture this fear of losing our roots: "Even more broadly, the spreading frontier is challenging America's [and Nebraska's] sense of itself. After all, this is the place where the local barbershop and corner drugstore still exist, where neighbors really do look out for one another, and people cling to small-town values of hard work and keeping one's word. While it's easy to romanticize these places, they nonetheless represent a bedrock of American character—a bedrock that's eroding away."[25]

Thus, even if the state continues to grow in total population, something vital will be weakened, perhaps lost: a sense of who we are and the faith in what we can accomplish in the midst of naysayers.

That's why small Nebraska high schools, faced with declining enrollments, will field eight- or even six-man football teams rather than give up their football programs. Speaking of these programs, Bill Heffernan, chair of the rural sociology department at the University of Missouri, says, "We are talking about institutions that define our sense of identity, our sense of place."[26]

That's why we take changes involving the Cornhusker football team so seriously. And that's why we Huskervillers have been more than a little worried lately.[27]

When head coach Tom Osborne announced his retirement after the 1997 season, we were a little worried. After all, he had been the head coach since 1973 and with the program as an assistant coach since 1962. His presence had been a constant in Huskerville for decades.[28] Our unease was mitigated by the fact that another long-time Husker coach, Frank Solich, was named to replace Osborne (Solich had been unofficially designated the heir apparent for quite a few years prior to his formal promotion). Things would remain pretty much the same we thought (and hoped).

They did. And they didn't.

While Solich had a great deal of early success, the team also struggled through some lopsided defeats and, in 2002, the worst season in the previous 40 years: an unheard of 7–7 record. Following that season, Solich did something that was also unheard of in recent decades: he fired a number of long-time assistant coaches. This was shocking news; our impression was that assistant coaches left the staff only to pursue better opportunities (often as head coaches) not because they failed. We were a little nervous.

So was new athletic director Steve Pederson.

Perhaps he sensed what the spring 2003 telephone poll conducted for this book demonstrated: only one-third of those who responded agreed that "this past fall's [2002] Husker team represented real Nebraska football."[29] At the end of the next season, Pederson fired Solich following the completion of a 9–3 season. Pederson justified the firing by implying that the previous season's 7–7 record and the severity of the three losses in the 2003–04 season[30] meant that the program was in danger of sliding "into mediocrity."[31]

Some Husker fans were pleased with Pederson's decision; others were upset. Others, like me, were just plain nervous. Yes, things had changed: we don't lose seven games and we don't get blown out of the games we lose. But we also don't reward 25 years of hard work and a 9–3 season (which 90 percent of college football programs would love to have) by firing someone. Who *are* we if we fire someone like that?

The questions were just beginning.

When Pederson announced the hiring of Bill Callahan, a National Football League head coach who had recently been fired by the Oakland Raiders, more questions arose. Did Callahan, who had no ties to Nebraska, really understand what Husker football and its fans were all about? How would he treat valued traditions in Huskerville? How would he change the program, and would it be for the better?

While Callahan professed his admiration for Nebraska and its traditions, he also repeatedly spoke of "flipping the culture" as part of his new job as head coach of the Cornhuskers.[32]

When you're a Huskerviller already uncertain about cultural changes occurring on and off the field, you can bet that a non–Nebraskan's flip comments about "flipping the culture" won't go over very well. When those comments are followed by flippant behavior, well, some of us get a little worried. More on that in a minute.

First, to be fair, I heard that people in Huskerville also grumbled when Bob Devaney, a person with no ties to the state, was hired as head coach in 1962. I know that some Huskervillers also grumbled when Devaney's successor, Tom Osborne, tinkered with offensive schemes early in his tenure as head coach. I know that at different points in their careers, both Devaney and Osborne were the targets of criticism about their perceived lack of ability to run the football program.[33] In this respect, Callahan's arrival in Huskerville had parallels with his predecessors—both of whom came to be warmly embraced by the time they stepped down as head coach.

In other important ways, however, Callahan's arrival was different. He scrapped an offensive system focused on running the football, a system that Osborne had called a necessity given the sometimes nasty Nebraska weather that could limit an offense that relied more heavily on passing the ball.[34] As Husker fans know, running the football—or, in football parlance, the ground game—was appealing to people who make their living working the ground.

Not only that, but Callahan also replaced the ground game-oriented offense with something called the *West Coast* offense.

West Coast?

Nebraska?

As the 2004 season began, *Sports Illustrated*.com writer and Hastings, Nebraska, native Albert Chen described Callahan's change of offensive systems in less-than-glowing terms: "New Nebraska head coach Bill Callahan has brought his West Coast offense to Huskerland, where he quickly torched three decades of tradition and a system that produced three national champions in the past 10 years."[35]

Maybe we could grow to appreciate this system, despite its name. But one of Callahan's other early culture flipping moves hit a bigger nerve: he significantly reduced the size of the team's fabled walk-on program.[36] The depth of our devotion to this program becomes clear a couple of chapters down the road, but for now let me offer this brief description of the program: begun by Devaney and embraced by Osborne, the program allows small-town Nebraska boys who are not offered scholarships the opportunity to earn their way onto the team through hard work and dedication to improvement.

"Those kids are our backbone," declared Osborne when he was coaching the Husker football team.[37] "If we didn't have the walk-ons come here," he later added, "I think it wouldn't be long before we became a second-rate program. They're very, very important to us."[38]

Although walk-on players may come from anywhere in the country, especially if they are encouraged to walk-on by the coaches, we Huskervillers think of the walk-on program as something that has been primarily provided as an opportunity for small-town Nebraskans who may not have been noticed during the recruiting process.

Steve Glenn was one of those kids. He's a former Husker football player, a two-year letter winner, who came to the University of Nebraska from the small town of Pawnee City, Nebraska. He didn't have a scholarship, but he did have a dream: to play football for the Huskers.

A lot of Nebraska boys grow up like Steve. They go to school in one of the hundreds of small towns scattered across the state, play high school football (sometimes with only six or eight boys to a side), and wonder if they might, someday, be able to carry on the Cornhusker tradition and make the folks back home proud.

Sounds a little schmaltzy, I know, but it's true—which is one of the reasons why Steve Glenn is worried. He's also worried because Callahan's reduction in the walk-on program seemed to be coupled with a belief that small town Nebraska boys did not deserve scholarships. In Callahan's first recruiting class, for example, only two Nebraskans accepted scholarships and both of them were from the Omaha area. Four Nebraskans—three from Omaha and one from Lincoln—accepted scholarships in his second recruiting class. In his third recruiting class, only three of the 28 scholarships went to Nebraska high school students (one from Omaha, one from Cozad, and one from Norfolk). In three years of offering scholarships, a total of nine Nebraskans accepted—and only two of them were not from Lincoln or Omaha.

We notice these things.

"I am worried about the disenfranchisement of the state from the program," Steve Glenn told me in a December 2004 phone conversation. "When you don't recruit walk-ons, when you don't recruit very many Nebraska players, or the recruits that you do—like this year—are just from Omaha, the rest of the state is disenfranchised.... The question I pose to people is this: if Nebraska wins a national championship and there are no Nebraska players on the team, does anybody really care?"

Steve's concerns are not unfounded. In 2000, 53.7 percent of the players listed on the team roster graduated from Nebraska high schools as did 50 percent of the players on the two-deep depth chart (the first and second teams on offense and defense, excluding the punter and kicker). In 2005, though, 42.6 percent of the players on the team roster were from Nebraska; in 2006, the percentage dropped even more, to 38.3 percent. In both 2005 and 2006, only 36 percent of the first-and second-string players had graduated from Nebraska high schools.[39]

"The critical element that I don't think is being acknowledged anymore," Steve emphasized, "is that tie to that small town. That has been the reason why this whole state glued around the university. If and when that changes, the glue will no longer be there. I think that glue is that walk-on, is that recruited athlete from North Platte, Grand Island, Scottsbluff."

Steve's thoughts were echoed by former Husker quarterback Scott Frost, who underscored that former players were not upset by recruiting out-of-state players (a practice common to all college football programs). "I'm all for going to California and Florida to recruit great players," he explains, "but I also wish we wouldn't stop making the effort to bring home-grown athletes along as Huskers."[40]

Steve and Scott's point is simple: when we Huskervillers are implicitly told that the young men from our small towns are not good enough and that the team cannot win if these young men form the nucleus of the team, we can't help but take this culture flipping stuff a bit personally.

That's why Steve Glenn and some other former Cornhusker football players formed the Cornhusker Tradition Coalition. News accounts quoted former Husker players as saying, "I don't know how many people are in the coalition, but I know a lot of people are of the same mind,"[41] and "A lot of ex-Nebraska players are very true and hard to this tradition, and I think some of them are feeling maybe it's falling away from the tradition it used to be."[42] Tradition, you see, is a mighty important thing to hang on to when your culture is changing.

This general sense of unease was coursing through Huskerville during and after Callahan's first season as head coach—especially since the team, composed of players recruited to play a different kind of football, struggled to a 5–6 record. The season marked the end of the Huskers' NCAA record streak of continuous appearances in a bowl game and the team's worst record since 1961.

We were not used to losing—and we did not like it. But the frustration we experienced during this change is more about a perceived severing of cultural roots, of traditions, than it is about winning and losing.[43] As lifelong

Huskerviller Loren Wagner explains, it's about shifting from "the right way" to "just like everybody else's way":

> How I feel about this whole deal has very little, if anything at all, to do with winning and losing.... It was a sad day when Solich got fired. It was the end of "NEBRASKA" football. Now it is just Nebraska football. We are just like everybody else. We run the same trendy offensive schemes. We hire and fire coaches on a whim. There is nothing any different than anybody else in the country. We were DIFFERENT and we were DOMINANT for 42 years because of it. We will never see the likes of that again, EVER! It is over, it is gone and there is nothing we can do about it.[44]

Perhaps the most frustrating aspect of change, as Loren concludes, is the frequent feeling that we have no control over changes that affect us. When those changes eviscerate the roots of our cultural beliefs, we are left uneasy about the future.

A Huskerviller using the online name of BlueCreek expresses such unease in his Internet posting. He recalls that the lessons his late father taught him were reinforced by the Huskers:

> The Husker program was the epitome of stability, loyalty, honor, and integrity; the last major bastion against what has become the NCAA status quo. No other program matched Nebraska in these regards.... But now we have sold out these values for wins....
> And I am left now, with a son, mere weeks old, who will never have his grandpa there to teach him. I have the daunting task of raising him to be a Husker as my father raised me. Not just a fan, but also a true Husker as it meant to him. But in the likely revolving door of high paid head coaches and assistants always in search of a better job that we have succumbed to like everyone else, what do I point to, to show my son the true meaning of being a Husker? Where will my son's pride in the program come from? Just winning seasons, or something deeper than that ...
> As always and forever, Go Big Red, but may the pendulum swing back by the time my child is the age I was when my father taught me one of life's most valuable lessons: the path you choose to victory is infinitely more important than winning itself.[45]

The feeling of loss that permeates the comments of these Husker fans and players is shared, too, by the former head coach of the Cornhuskers. After a period of remaining quiet or diplomatic, Osborne finally spoke out, albeit indirectly.

Although Osborne and his wife, Nancy, initially agreed to have their name put on the university's athletic complex facility, Osborne—while still expressing support for the university and the athletic program—asked the university to seek a corporate donor willing to have its name placed on the complex instead. Amidst all the changes in the football program, Osborne said, "We lost something in the process."[46]

What we have lost, I think, is the belief that the team is "our team." When people with Nebraska connections and roots took care of the football program, when the way things were done seemed consistent with the way we did things ourselves, and when the coaching staff went out of its way to treat the team as belonging to us, we could honestly and genuinely believe that the team was ours.

As Osborne observed, "Nebraska fans have always had quite a bit of ownership in the team and have been very loyal and felt in some way that the team belongs to them."[47]

Now we're not so sure.

In addition to the actions we have witnessed, we also hear words that don't ring quite true. When Callahan assures us, "I love Nebraska and what it stands for and what it means to the people out there,"[48] we notice the distinction he makes. We are "the people *out there*," distant from himself and the team that we have long thought of as part of us.[49]

We've tried to bridge the divide because we want the coaches and team to succeed—and to do so while recognizing that we see the team as ours, too. Huskerviller Darren Carlson, for instance, wrote an open letter to Callahan at the beginning of the coach's first season.[50]

Wednesday, September 01, 2004
Letter to Coach Callahan
I was born on the prairie and the milk of its wheat, the red of its clover, the eyes of its women, gave me a song and a slogan.
—From "Prairie," a poem by Carl Sandburg (1878–1967) in his book *Cornhuskers*
Dear Coach Callahan,
I thought the allusion above an appropriate way to open this letter for a variety of reasons. Carl Sandburg is arguably the most important poet from your home state of Illinois, and the poem "Prairie" is a part of his appropriately named book, *Cornhuskers*. Most importantly, that portion of "Prairie" speaks to the way a person's place of origin forms their identity. This sense of identity is why I write to you today.
I want you to truly understand that for many Nebraskans University of Nebraska football is not a sport, pastime, hobby or thing of interest. It is truly a part of their identity. Collectively, those individuals make Cornhusker football an indelible part of the state's identity....
I genuinely wish you the best for the upcoming season. Make us proud.

As Darren's letter emphasizes, we want Callahan and the team to do well, but we want to be part of—not merely audience to—that success. We want, as we always have, the team's actions to honor what we value. We want the coaches to see "us" as part of "them" rather than as two distinct groups.[51]

That's what we want. But how do we make it happen? The same way that Nebraska farmers and gardeners have done for years when the seasons changed and the food was in danger of being lost to the elements: we preserve.

While the stuff that we store into the container of Huskerville is not so discrete as a tomato or a pickle, we act in much the same way that Alexandra Bergson's mother acted in O *Pioneers!* As Willa Cather writes, "Alexandra often said that if her mother were cast upon a desert island, she would thank God for her deliverance, make a garden, and find something to preserve. Preserving was almost a mania with Mrs. Bergson."[52]

When Husker fans seem manic to outsiders, well, they are right. The mania is in large part the hard, intensive, vital work of preserving a way of life—of keeping it from being uprooted.[53]

Remaining rooted in Huskerville allows us to preserve the connections we value, in short, to preserve our presence in our homes. As Marty Howell of Lenni, Pennsylvania—who was not born or raised in Nebraska—explains:

> Like so many people who go away to college, I fell in love with the environment in which I placed myself during early adulthood. When I first discovered NU football in '71 (age 13), the state represented a mystical, faraway place of which I knew little. The very name "Nebraska" had an earthy, robust sound to it. I admired the scarlet and cream colors as well as the basic uniform design and simple helmet insignia "N." A poor high school student, I eventually enrolled at NU to get far from home in pursuit of ill-defined dreams in a perceived dreamland: Nebraska. Viewing my present surroundings (greater Philadelphia) as inferior in many regards to Nebraska, I maintain loyalty to Nebraska football because it enables me to keep my life there in the present tense, not just a memory.

Marty's words echo those of Willa Cather, who once told an interviewer that, although she was living on the Atlantic coast, "I was always being pulled back into Nebraska.... My deepest feelings were rooted in this country."[54]

When we preserve, we do not lose that which would otherwise wilt on the vine. We also remind ourselves that preserving means taking care of everything that we have given roots. John Troia of Gaithersburg, Maryland, elaborates: "My wife said last week, 'I'm surprised you are still such a fan. I thought you would forget about them after living here a few years.' Some folks just don't get it. Football allows me to stay connected to those memories of times together years ago, with family, watching football."

Even if we are, at some level, profoundly aware of the changes around us, rooting ourselves in Huskerville allows us to somehow overlook these changes. Instead, we remember consistency; the way things were seems to be the way things are.

Prior to the changes in the football coaching staff, for example, Cory Osborn of Tempe, Arizona, said: "You can look at the football staff, or the staff for most of our major sports for that matter. There is consistency. Years and years of very little change in them. I think of the state the same way, not much changes. Things just keep moving in the world around them, but Nebraska always seems the same."

So, as we navigate the personal, social, and cultural changes that inevitably disorient us, our roots in Huskerville provide a compass that we use to re-adjust our course or, perhaps more accurately, to stay on course despite the turbulence we encounter.

As Annette Frain wrote to me upon hearing about this project, "It was really nice to read that I am not the only one that has a need to connect with Nebraska. Sure my family and friends are there, but so is the spirit of being a Nebraskan. That is imbedded deep within me and no one will ever be able to take that away."[55] Tim Hindman eloquently summarizes why and how Nebraskans remain rooted in Huskerville: "For many of us, though, Nebraska is home, a place we carry in our hearts and memories, wherever we go and whatever we do."[56]

As Tim and Annette demonstrate, a culture's history provides us with strong roots. The stories we tell about ourselves and our way of life provide what Kenneth Burke calls "equipment for living" with life's changes.[57]

Research into organizational change, in fact, reveals that these "identity stories" provide groups with stability in times of change by reminding group members of their enduring values.[58] Such stories are vitally important to those of us who tell them and hear them because "a primary challenge of human being is living in the present with the awareness of an uncertain future."[59]

To be sure, these stories selectively remember and highlight parts of the panorama of a culture's history—we are, after all, reluctant to remind ourselves of those less-than-admirable moments from our pasts. But in this respect our stories are also revealing, for they point to characteristics that we believe most embody our character and our community—the two core characteristics of any culture, according to agricultural philosopher Wendell Berry.[60]

The next part of the book, then, identifies and explores the qualities that we Huskervillers, in our words, say most embody our character and community—and how we attempt to enact them in our rooting performances as well as how we like to see them embodied in the performances of the Cornhusker football team.

II

Homesteading

5

Homesteading: "They Know How to Plow"

How can we locate ourselves if not by the things we live by.[1]

"*'They Know How to Plow.'* That's what you can call your book," Sam Elder told me. "You got to stay in that furrow. You got to stay centered."

I was in the back part of the Lucky 7 Saloon in Kirkland, Washington, a suburb of Seattle. Sam and I were joined at the long table—really a collection of tables—by eight other Nebraskans living in the Seattle area as well as some of the professors and graduate students who had helped me with interviews in other parts of the country. We were talking about Nebraska, Nebraskans, and Husker football.

Tony Joyce, owner of the Lucky 7, and Bob Paine, then president of the Seattle area alumni association chapter, had graciously worked with me to make this conversation happen. The academics in the group were in town for a conference, while the Huskervillers were at the bar prior to a watch party for the 2000 Nebraska-Kansas State game. The academics were telling the Huskervillers what they thought about the parts of Huskerville they had visited (Portland, Louisville, Denver, Austin, and the virtual community of Huskers online). The Huskervillers were telling the academics what they thought about their ideas. I was listening, asking questions, writing down notes, and audio recording the conversations.

As the group shared stories, memories, and insights, I thought more about Sam's phrase, "they know how to plow." He emphasized that the phrase didn't mean just expertise; it also encompassed the idea that Huskers know "a right way" to do things. "Right" means correct, of course, but it also implies "should"; that is, *if* you want to do this the right way, *then* you should do it this way. The "right way" is rarely, if ever, the fast way, the easy way, or the selfish way.

The "right way" also implies the existence of a moral code known by those who understand "how to plow." Sometimes referred to, in softer language, as "a way of life," a moral code provides a behavioral compass of sorts. While formal moral codes, such as those outlined in holy religious books and professional codes of ethics, clearly articulate what counts as right and wrong, the more informal versions found in a way of life are compelling because they illustrate the moral code *in action*. Huskerviller Wayne Hastings, for example, moved out of Nebraska in 1961, yet when asked why he still followed the Huskers, he simply said, "The team projects a way of life that I am very comfortable with." Similarly, when asked to describe Nebraska and its people, Doug Bottger of the Seattle area observed, "It's more than a state, but a state of mind and a way of life."

So, what exactly is this way of life?

As I asked Husker fans questions about how to define a Nebraskan, what characteristics a Nebraskan possessed, and how these characteristics are evident in the football team's performances, the implied shoulds emerged.

Donna Love of Louisville identified these shoulds in terms of what Nebraskans do: "They're very hard-working, very up-front, who you see is who I am, very honest, very loyal, very friendly people. They're very caring, everybody works together. If you move into the state, you're just like somebody that's lived there forever. There's no little cliques or anything. Nebraska people are just very hard-working, down-to-earth people."

Perhaps this way of life is best described in the words of the University of Nebraska fight song. Written in the 1920s by homesick ROTC commanders Deitrich Dirks and Harry Pecha,[2] "There is No Place Like Nebraska" offers these observations about Huskervillers:

> There is no place like Nebraska
> Dear old Nebraska U.
> Where the girls are the fairest,
> The boys are the squarest,
> Of any old school that I knew.
> There is no place like Nebraska,
> Where they're all true blue.
> We'll all stick together,
> In all kinds of weather,
> For Dear old Nebraska U!

As unfashionable as the lyrics of the song might seem, they provide a moral guide for Huskervillers. "When I think of a Nebraskan," notes Strat Warden of Elizabethtown, Kentucky, "I think of a lot of the corny stuff that's in the Nebraska fight song. It's honesty and simplicity, and truth and those kind of things. Now that might be a little hokey, but I've lived all over the country and all over the world, and I've found that to be true.... I think that's manifest in the fans." Confirms C. Bair Van Dam of Washington, DC, "'true blue' as well as 'square' get to the heart of what it means to be a Nebraskan."

Importantly, adds Walt Fulton of Lexington Park, Maryland, Huskervillers "live the creed of doing the right thing, 'even if no one is looking.'" Enacting the moral code, in other words, depends less upon fear of what others might think and more upon following what you know to be right. Not surprisingly, the shoulds outlined in "There is No Place Like Nebraska" are rooted in the agricultural orientation suggested by Sam's phrase "they know how to plow," for in the fields often no one is looking.[3]

This is a creed planted by the state's first homesteaders, led by Daniel Freeman. Freeman, who was said to be on leave from the Union Army, claimed a parcel of land near the present-day town of Beatrice, Nebraska. Today, that land is recognized as the site of the nation's first official homestead and now serves as the site of Homestead National Monument.[4]

Over the remainder of the 19th century, almost 69,000 people followed in Freeman's footsteps and claimed land in Nebraska under the Homestead Act; no other state in the country could claim more homesteaders.[5] During this period, the population of the state exploded. During the 1880s alone, Nebraska's population more than doubled, growing from 452,000 to just over one million. During that decade, the number of farms nearly doubled as well, from 63,387 to 113,608, and the number of acres devoted to farming increased from just under 10 million in 1880 to 21.5 million in 1890.[6]

Yet, even at the turn of the century, a large portion of the state was still unsettled. The parcels of land allocated under the Homestead Act were simply too small for farmers and ranchers in the more arid parts of the state. The land there required more work, more water, and more hope than the land in other parts of the state. So, in 1904, after numerous attempts, Nebraska representative Moses Kincaid succeeded in pushing into law the Kincaid Act, which allowed homesteading on 640-acre parcels in 37 counties in the northwest portion of Nebraska.

These homesteaders, known as Kincaiders, joined the hearty settlers who had already moved to the area, including one Jules Sandoz, the subject of his daughter Mari's book, Old Jules. Between 1900 and 1920, the number of homesteaders in these 37 counties grew from roughly 136,000 to over 251,000; in addition, corn production nearly doubled, and wheat production quadrupled.[7]

This success was certainly not instant or easy—nor was it enjoyed by all who attempted to homestead. Historians note that a number of boom and bust periods, many of them weather related, occurred within the homesteading era. For example, the crash of 1890 occurred after farmers who had mortgaged much of their property during the boom of the 1880s experienced yet another drought. "In the year 1891," notes the Federal Writers Project's history of Nebraska, "eighteen thousand prairie schooners trundled over the Missouri River and out of Nebraska. Only the most hardy, determined farmers remained to fight the hard times of the nineties."[8]

Those hardy, determined farmers had to work hard, watch out for their neighbors, and keep their heads about them. Their legacy of working hard to turn a fair chance into realized potential is cultivated by contemporary Huskervillers—even if some of us no longer work in the fields.

Huskerviller Jack McHenry, who now lives in New York City, remembers what he learned from his grandfather:

> My grandfather was a rancher that built up two ranches 40 miles outside of Valentine, NE. His relatives were homesteaders that first pioneered Nebraska staying in sod houses and living off the land. His sons and grandsons still run the ranches today. His word (as well as theirs) was his bond. If Bill Fisher said he'd do something—that was it—he'd do it, no questions asked, no follow up needed. He was an honest, blunt, stubborn, hard working, good man. I can't say enough about him and the values and ethics he left engrained in everything and everyone he came into contact with.

He has company.

Overwhelmingly, respondents to the 2003 telephone survey conducted by Ohio University's Scripps Survey Research Center acknowledged the special importance of agriculture in the life of Nebraska. In particular, over 80 percent[9] of those surveyed agreed with the following statements:

> The family farm must be preserved because it is a vital part of our heritage.
> Agriculture is the most basic occupation in our society and almost all other occupations depend on it.
> Government should have a special policy to ensure that family farms survive.
> A farmer should be proud if he can say that he owes money to no one.

As part of this agricultural legacy, Nebraskans tend to embrace the values initially enacted by the state's homesteaders. The 2002 Nebraska Rural Poll, for example, found that 74 percent of rural Nebraskans indicated that they possessed "commonly shared values."[10] Among those values were being work-oriented, self-sufficient, tough or resilient, and friendly.[11] In particular, farmers and ranchers—even more than other rural Nebraskans—espouse the values of working hard and being friendly.[12]

Additionally, if you ask Nebraskans to describe themselves, as I did in my questionnaires, you will hear answers that sound much like the terms used to describe homesteaders. The most popular responses to questions that asked for definitions characteristics of a Nebraskan were, in order: hardworking, friendly, loyal, honest, and having good values.[13]

In Huskerville, these characteristics are also associated with the football team. When I asked Husker fans how the characteristics of the state were apparent in the team, they most frequently mentioned that the Huskers were hardworking, dedicated, proud, and loyal.[14] Thus, in Huskerville, the homesteading continues, albeit in slightly different forms.

"We've always been pioneers," claims the University of Nebraska in a recent marketing campaign. You won't get much argument from the fans who fill Memorial Stadium.

As Starita and Tidball observe in their book about the fans of Memorial Stadium, "Descendants of people who didn't blanche at breaking sod on a frozen prairie, Memorial Stadium fans are oblivious to howling winds, harsh conditions and hardship."[15]

The folks behind the scenes at Memorial Stadium undoubtedly recognize this connection, too. The Husker football team and the state's agricultural roots are intertwined in the HuskerVision show that plays on the screens in the stadium as the team prepares to enter the field. Although the show has changed slightly over the years, the following description of one version highlights the football-agriculture relationship:

> [The show] starts with a tractor spelling out a victory message in a wheatfield, an overhead camera zooming across the state starting in the west with Chimney Rock—which has "Go Big Red" carved on its base, a flock of geese forming an "N" in a bright blue sky, zooming on to the Capitol Building in Lincoln, where "The Sower" statue on top of the golden dome does a "raising the roof" motion with his arms (last year, he was holding a football and charging).... Everything about the wordless "HuskerVision" video seems designed to say "We're tractor-pulling, beef-eatin' machines who will show you who's the boss."[16]

If any doubts remain about the connection between homesteading and football, the roar from the crowd that accompanies this show puts them to rest.

To try to make the Huskerville way of life more tangible, I have thought about the relationships between the homesteaders and contemporary Huskers. I sifted through the results of the various surveys and questionnaires, reviewed what people told me in interviews, and reflected upon what

I had read. I have concluded that Huskervillers, above all else, believe that one should work hard, be neighborly, and remain down-to-earth.[17]

Each of these shoulds points to a way of *doing* something. Working hard refers to what individuals should do on our own. Being neighborly tells what we should do in our interactions with others. Remaining down-to-earth reminds us of what we should do as we live our lives. These doings generate our collective memory of the ways things have been, and continue to be.

These collective memories are not necessarily true from an outsider's perspective; that is, they may be incomplete, selective, even inaccurate. But they are treated as true by those who adhere to them, for the memories highlight what the collective considers vital to its sense of group identity. In fact, the collective memories of groups are perpetuated *because* the groups continue to enact those vital beliefs in their contemporary interactions. "What is accepted in society as tradition is the result of a rhetorical process," writes performance scholar Jean Haskell Speer. "Tradition has no *a priori* existence in the past, but is created through communicative processes in the present."[18]

In Huskerville, then, the doing of values such as working hard, being neighborly, and remaining down-to-earth, revitalizes the collective memory of homesteading (and the cultural identity of contemporary Huskervillers). Anthropologist Keith Basso's words about the Western Apache apply equally well to Huskervillers: "Like their ancestors before them, they display by word and deed that beyond the visible reality of place lies a moral reality which they themselves have come to embody."[19] No wonder, then, that Judy Tonjes of Omaha claims, "These values are the 'roots' to life."[20] Homesteading, then and now, keeps us rooted.[21]

In the chapters that follow in this section, I explore what Huskervillers believe we should do and how we try to do it—in other words, how we attempt to stay anchored amidst the forces of uprooting by enacting what we have traditionally valued.

"As Nebraskans," observes Husker List manager Mike Nolan, "we are survivors. We have overcome the limitations of geography, of weather, of past failures. We experience a periodic re-energizing of the spirit of the pioneer that is in all Nebraskans. And since sport offers an annual metaphor for the rest of life, we know the Huskers will do the same."[22]

This is a story of Homesteading. In it, Nebraskans live the moral code of Huskerville: work hard, share, and don't get too full of yourself. These fundamental ideas are rooted in the performances of Nebraska's homesteaders, who enacted them as much out of necessity as of choice. Yet they endure through the game day, and everyday, performances of Husker fans, players, and coaches. These contemporary acts of homesteading at once make, or construct, the home of Huskerville and seek to preserve the legacy of the state's earliest homesteaders. At the top of the list of shoulds is working hard.

6

Working Hard and Walking On

I failed. And, as failures tend to do with humans, it has stuck with me.

I was 10 or 12 years old, something in that neighborhood anyway, and like most kids of that age range, I was hungry for money. As winter approached, I eagerly knocked on neighbors' doors, trying to line up a few jobs shoveling snow. I found only one house on the street willing to take me on: an elderly couple named Mr. and Mrs. Baggs.

I can recall my joy at finally seeing the first snow of the season begin to fall. I eagerly tromped down the street and began shoveling the Baggs's driveway. At first, the visions of dollar signs dancing in my head allowed me to overlook the fact that this snow was deep, wet, and heavy. Eventually, as I reached about the halfway point of their driveway, my cold spaghetti arms gave out on me.

I quit.

I walked back home and told my parents that I could not do the job.

Even today, as I write these words, I feel the shame in quitting, in not following through with what I said I would do and in realizing that my parents had to finish the job for me. I'm especially chagrined as I think about the German Russian kids my age who couldn't have quit working in the beet fields when their arms gave out.

I would like to say that this lesson about working hard and not giving up immediately sunk in, but I was a slow learner.

A couple of years later, I eagerly embraced the opportunity to deliver the morning newspaper, the *Star-Herald*. After a couple of weeks of rising at 4:30 A.M., I first learned that I am not a morning person. My younger brother, Chuck, agreed to split delivery duties with me and, together, we made it through the school year before quitting.

Yet, I showed signs of promise. I did not quit the paper route during the winter when the bitter cold and fierce winds left my hands so numb that I needed to run them under warm water after spending a couple of hours collecting payments from customers on the route. I did not quit delivering the paper during a couple of early morning blizzards that made walking such a struggle that my dad came to find me because I was still out of the house an hour after I usually came home.

What I know now, of course, is what other adults—and a lot of kids—in Huskerville know: working hard is a bedrock principle of the community. When I quit shoveling the snow that day, I failed to enact this bedrock principle. The Huskerville work ethic is simple: when hard-working, dedicated people are given a fair chance to prove themselves, they will succeed. If you quit, you can never succeed.

This work ethic allows, perhaps even expects, individuals to overcome obstacles while they transform raw potential into a polished product. The idea of self-sufficiency is also embedded in this work ethic, for if someone does not succeed, it is his own fault. Rural living, in fact, demands self-sufficiency since rural residents must "be capable of doing pretty nearly everything [themselves] as the price of continued existence in the country."[1]

Neighbors may—and should—offer help, as the next chapter illustrates,[2] but asking for help is a sign of weakness. Complaining, whining, and giving up all demonstrate a lack of character. Not even trying denotes a near absence of character. On the other hand, when failure is met with a re-dedication to more, and harder, work, all things are possible.

This work ethic is perhaps best described by Huskerviller Beth Townsend of Colorado Springs, Colorado: "The Huskers work hard, very hard. When they win, they attribute it to their hard work, when they lose, they will tell you they need to work harder next time. It's never about whining or name calling. It is that mindset, if you will, that is so typical Nebraskan: the belief that hard work will get you just about anywhere and if you aren't succeeding, it's probably because you aren't working hard enough."

The Huskerville version of the work ethic is rooted in the practices of Nebraska's homesteaders.

On January 1, 1863, the first of what would be tens of thousands of Americans staked their claims for free land under the auspices of the Homestead Act of 1862. Called "one of the truly epochal laws of American history"[3] in a document celebrating its centennial anniversary, the Homestead

Act offered a 160-acre section of free land[4] to adults willing to live on, and improve, the land for five years.

Upon completion of the five years, homesteaders were said to have proved up their claim.[5] While the phrase "proved up" lacks grammatical elegance, it effectively captures the transformation from potential to success embodied in the idea of homesteading. As farmer and professor Victor Davis Hanson claims, "Farming involves deed, not mere word, reality over theory, substance over brag and big talk."[6]

For recent immigrants, and those with relatives still living in Europe, the Homestead Act's opportunity to earn your land through what Nebraska folklore historian Roger Welsch called "sweat and courage"[7] was a dream come true. Your bank account did not matter. Your family history did not matter. Your connections did not matter. The only thing that mattered was your willingness to work hard and to persevere.[8]

Homesteading, as Huskervillers know, was not for the timid. Welsch tries to envision what early homesteaders encountered upon reaching Nebraska:

> Imagine the despair of traveling 10,000 miles—or even 1,000 miles—to make a new start. At last the pioneer reached the selected land on the Nebraska plains. He had a wagon drawn by two horses, a few supplies, an axe, a plow, a shovel, a barrel or two, a canary, a wife, and three kids. With this he had to build a home. There was not a tree to be seen—in fact, none had been seen for three days. There were no rocks, no stone outcroppings. There was absolutely nothing but sky and grass.[9]

Welsch's words echo those of Jim Burden, narrator of Willa Cather's *My Ántonia*: "There seemed to be nothing to see; no fences, no creeks or trees, no hills or fields…. There was nothing but land: not a country at all, but the material out of which countries are made."[10]

Given the harshness of the land, the one sure route to success was working hard. As Mari Sandoz writes in her essay "The Homestead in Perspective," every member of the family was expected to work. "Almost from their first steps, the homesteader's children had to meet new situations, make decisions, develop a self-discipline if they were to survive."[11] They would learn, she notes, that when their arms were sore from using a spade to plant corn, "the remedy for that was more work."[12]

Such tireless effort not only transformed Nebraska into a state where 95 percent of the state's land is used for farming and ranching, it also became part of a learned moral code that permeates Huskerville.[13] As Cather's characters illustrate, for example, the homesteaders' values provide a moral foundation, a way of being in the world and with others.

"Nebraska, Cather saw, was not simply territory or one homesteaded place on the American continent, but a universal symbol of suffering and hardship overcome by the indomitable immigrant spirit."[14]

That spirit is embraced even today. In the 2002 Nebraska Rural Poll, almost two-thirds of the rural Nebraskans who responded believed that people like them were "work-oriented, self-sufficient, and tough/resilient."[15]

Interestingly, farmers and ranchers seemed to embrace many of these characteristics more than other rural Nebraskans. For example, farmers and ranchers are more likely than laborers to believe that rural Nebraska is work-oriented (72 percent to 54 percent).[16]

Similarly, a survey of University of Nebraska–Kearney students revealed that they scored higher on the Protestant [Work] Ethic Scale than did students from other parts of the country. Moreover, Nebraska students from small towns scored higher than those Nebraska students from cities. Concluded the study's authors, "It is almost axiomatic in central Nebraska, and especially in smaller towns, that the way to get ahead in this life is to work harder than the day before."[17]

Huskervillers, too, claim to notice a difference between a Nebraska work ethic and work ethics in other parts of the country—even in states with a strong agricultural base. Todd Roenfeldt, of Montrose, Colorado, says, "The work ethic seems to be different in Nebraska. They seem to have more of a never quit attitude." Fellow Colorado resident Matt Ridder confirms this. "The state's a lot different than say here in Colorado," says Matt. "Like we were a lot more self-sufficient, you know, growing up on a farm." In Topeka, Kansas, Jill Hayhurst notes, "I know that I only live 200 miles away from Nebraska, but Kansas has a different environment and atmosphere. Nebraska has strong farm families and the Husker fans are derived from the same backgrounds."

From the fields of the homesteaders, to today's farms and ranches, to the football field: work hard and you will succeed. James Bandy, of Sugar Land, Texas, explains this connection between homesteading, contemporary agriculture, and Husker football:

> The settlers of this vast plains state [Nebraska] were a hardy people. Those who survived passed along to their descendents an appreciation and respect for hard work. And this value, which is pathetically absent in many parts of the country, is clearly manifested in the citizens of Nebraska today. Perhaps the Nebraska football team is simply a microcosm of this manifestation.

Adds Mark LaMalfa of Portland, Oregon: "We're an agricultural community, working hard. We expect that in the football program and we praise the players who work extra hard."

When the players work as hard on their fields as the farmers do in their fields, and as the homesteaders did in theirs, Huskervillers are confident that the team will be successful.

Listen again, for example, to Todd Roenfeldt: "The hard work and dedication it takes to have a consistently winning program epitomizes the farming mentality of Nebraska." And Pat Ferguson of Lakeland, Minnesota: "Work ethic. We all know the team works very hard to be successful on and off the field and farming is hard work as well, so there seems at least to me, a natural affinity to associate the two." Ehren Mitzlaff of Denver, Colorado, continues, "The characteristics of the team's core that remind me of the state are the dedication and hard work they put into each and every game. The farming industry is what comes to mind most, since most of our boys come from small towns which thrive on the hard working farmer's determination and risk taking. It all comes back around when they get on the field."

And off the field as well, for we Huskervillers believe that the players work as hard in the classroom as they do on the field. Observes Marty Howell of Lenni, Pennsylvania:

> The transformation of farm boy to Outland Trophy winner or Academic All-American is a modern example of the Puritan work ethic. Instead of baling hay, running dad's tractor or detasseling corn, the infamous walk-on dedicates himself to blocking drills and Boyd Epley's hallmark strength and conditioning methods. Or, he might excel in the classroom. Does academic discipline lend itself to the achievement of athletic excellence, or vice versa? The average Husker fan asks not the distinction. What we know is that our school has produced a prohibitive number of success stories. We still live by myths, some of which contain more than just a "kernel" of truth.

Statistics provide us with some of those kernels of truth. During the period from 1989 to 1999 (the most recent period measured as of January 2007), 93 percent of Nebraska student-athletes who completed their eligibility earned their degrees.[18] Moreover, Nebraska leads the nation in the number of Academic All-Americans in all sports as well as football in particular. (As of August 2006, Nebraska student-athletes had earned Academic All-American honors 235 times since the award's inception in 1962; Notre Dame is a distant second with 178, while MIT is third with 129 and Penn State fourth with 126.)[19]

Some Huskervillers can quote statistics like these—Terry Pedrett of Aurora, Colorado, knows that Nebraska football has produced "three times" as many academic All-Americans as any other university—while others, like Jan Lightner of Seattle, know that inside the athletic department the photos of the academic All-Americans are "much larger" than the photos of the athletic All-Americans.

But we all know that "it's not just football" where hard work pays off, notes Kevin Popp of Louisville:

> I'm amazed about how many athletes that go there that are in postgraduate work, not just graduating, but you know are going after their master's and all that, that's really something very special. Where other teams in today's world, they don't graduate or have high graduation rates and all that.
>
> But their academics with their football program, that's second to none. Yeah, Penn State might have it, Notre Dame might have it, but not like Nebraska. If you look at the GTE All-Americans, the academic All-Americans, and you put that list up, it dwarfs the list of other schools like Stanford, Notre Dame, Ohio State, other really good academic institutions. And that's something that people out there in the world really don't understand about Nebraska. It's not just football.

The belief that the team's success, on and off the field, is rooted in the work ethic of the homesteaders and their descendants has also been shared by both coaches and players in the Husker football program. Tom Osborne remarks, "Our players, for the most part, always had a really good work ethic. Many of them grew up in small towns or on farms, and they knew what hard work meant."[20] Former Husker player Tom Ruud, whose sons have also played for the Huskers, amplifies this sentiment: "The one thing I know is that Nebraska football players always played hard. Even when they weren't successful in the early days, they played hard in every game. It is because hard work is the staple of the state of Nebraska. Nobody works harder anywhere than the farmers and the ranchers in this state."[21]

In fact, Fred Meier, who played Husker football from 1939 to 1941, credits his football success to his teenage farm work. He explains:

> In the summertime, my dad farmed me out to a cousin for work. I went to work at the age of 13 on my cousin's farm, taking care of the horses. We would hook them up to a cultivator and cultivate the corn and pitch hay on the rack by hand. When I was 16, my cousin took his family on a vacation and I ran the whole farm for two weeks. There were nine cows to milk twice a day. There were horses, hogs, and chickens to take care of. We had a walking plow. I made a dollar a day, plus I got room and board. Now that taught me about hard work and how to withstand suffering.[22]

As Meier suggests, homesteading means not just working hard, but also being tough.

Toughness is manifested in a determination to persevere, no matter what the circumstances. Like the work ethic in general, toughness is a quality that has been passed along from generation to generation, beginning with the state's homesteaders. As University of Nebraska student Elizabeth Merriman told me one fall evening on the Lincoln campus, "You know, we are all about being tough.... A lot of people [in the state] are farmers. They work really hard and that's what they like to see: people working hard."

Consider, for example, the remarkable similarities between the stories of Old Jules Sandoz and former Husker player Forrest Behm. Both suffered injuries so severe that doctors initially suggested amputation. "But when [Old Jules] was prepared for the operation he sat up, his gaunt cheeks flushed a violent red under his beard, his bloodshot eyes glittering. 'You cut my foot off, doctor, and I shoot you so dead you stink before you hit the ground.'"[23] Similarly, Forrest Behm's father told the doctor, "No way. You are not amputating my son's leg. He's going to walk again, he's going to run again, and he's going to play sports someday."[24] And, in both cases, painstaking and painful treatments helped Old Jules and Behm recover (though Old Jules was plagued by a lifelong limp).

The homesteaders' determination to succeed in the face of adversity— Old Jules didn't immediately seek medical assistance because "even now [as he was injured] the land came first"[25]—likely played a role in the development of one of the football team's early nicknames, the Bugeaters. Huskerviller David Max notes:

> The early nickname Bugeaters might have had a negative connotation to outsiders. But, to those in the state it meant something different. I think the reference was to a time when the state was devastated by a drought, yet people were so determined, they were willing to eat bugs rather than give up. Presumably, in most cases that was figurative. But the point is, those people were battlers, not easily defeated by the elements. Nebraskans have always had those qualities. And I think they have been exemplified by the university football teams.

Brandt Mackey, of Arlington, Virginia, agrees. "We have a lot of pride in where we come from and who we are," he says. "The Huskers play a hard-nosed physical football game, just like farming is a tedious and very physical occupation." Even in the 1930s, "many Nebraska players were tough young men who had grown up on dirt-poor farms and small towns."[26]

Another part of the Huskerville work ethic is determination. While toughness is both physical and mental, determination is entirely mental. No matter how tough people are, they will fail if they are not determined to succeed.

Al Dedrick of Laurel, Maryland, defines a Nebraskan as "someone that knows what hard work is and doesn't back down from it." Such dedication is both learned and taught to Huskervillers as we grow up. Explains Rhonda Johns of Aurora, Colorado, "As a Nebraskan, that's just how we were raised. To work hard, to have the strength to keep working no matter how hard it is and to never give up." Adds Matthew Grosz of Cherry Point, North Carolina: "It's a feeling that you know you can get the job done because of the hardy brand of people who came before you would rather die than give up."

Examples of this determination in action abound. Let's look at just three, shared with me by Huskervillers from across the United States. Tony Gevo of the Philadelphia area tells a story about his grandfather's tenacity, and how it continues to inspire him today. Tonya Cross of Roxana, Illinois, praises her father's dedication as he works on his ranch near Arthur, Nebraska. Jan Lightner explains how her husband doggedly continues to work and help others despite losing his ability to speak. Here are their stories:

TONY GEVO: One of the factors that pulls strongly on Nebraska natives, even though we have been removed from the state for so long, is the heritage of our families. My grandfather, Oscar Peterson, left Sweden when he was 16 because of a disagreement with his father over how the horses were being taken care of and came to America. Talk about a guy with an attitude! On the boat, he made friends with a guy that we only know as "Big John" and after landing in Boston they decided to go to the Pacific Northwest to do some lumberjack stuff. After a few years he ended up in the Wayne, Nebraska, area and really toughed it out. The stories I was told are almost not able to be believed; except that I know my grandfather and know that they're all basically true. One that has always made me proud of my Nebraska heritage and the self-sufficiency I learned concerned a border dispute Oscar had with a German farmer whose land adjoined his. As the story goes, each spring this German would plow a couple of rows in Oscar's land. He never said anything, but after the third year or so, Oscar simply waited at the point for the guy to show up. My mother and the rest of her brothers and sisters became worried when it got past dinner time and he didn't show up. They took the horse and wagon to look for him and they found both of them, Oscar and the other farmer, unconscious. Apparently they had gotten into a fight and pretty much beaten the shit out of each other. My mother simply loaded Oscar into the wagon, left the German lying there, and took him home! The boundary issue ended there; no police, no lawyers, no whining! That's the grit, determination and courage that we came from and it's very, very good to be able to draw upon that strength today.

TONYA CROSS: To illustrate the strong work ethic, here's a story of one fellow Nebraskan. My dad, who grew up on a ranch in Arthur, NE, has always been a hard worker. About six weeks ago [written June 3, 2004], he hurt his back—which was inevitable with all the hard work he had been doing—and he needed to have surgery. But seeing as he had "stuff to do," he couldn't just sit back and let others do it. Even while injured, he was out mowing the lawn because "it needed done." Even after the surgery, he tried to help out with things as much as possible even though my mom told him to take it easy. That's the kind of hard-work ethic that seems to embody the Nebraskans I know.

JAN LIGHTNER: My husband is a Nebraskan—he lost his ability to speak about five years ago. Instead of being depressed and feeling sorry for himself, he went back to research and has had three patents issued in that time and another five applied for. He is working with UNL and the Foundation to share the patents—all to do with biomass as burnable fuel. It's his way of returning something to the University and the state.

As each of these stories demonstrates, we Huskervillers believe that hard work, fortified by determination, will generate success—no matter what the obstacles.

So, where does one find toughness and determination?

I know that I sure couldn't find it when I was attempting to shovel my neighbors' driveway. The answer is simple: faith, tempered with patience.

Homesteaders who eventually proved up had to wait for five years to make that claim. A good number of them suffered mightily in their first few years. In fact, many of the early homesteaders failed in their efforts to make a home in Nebraska. Nebraska historians James C. Olson and Ronald C. Naugle report that only 52 percent of the original homestead claims were proved up after the required five-year settling period.[27] The Kincaiders had about the same amount of success in northwestern Nebraska.

On the one hand, these figures can be used to point to the failings of the legislation that encouraged homesteading.[28] Or, as Mari Sandoz points out, the numbers can highlight the work ethics of those who failed and those who succeeded. Her words about the Kincaid homesteaders are telling: "Once more the shallow-rooted left and the rest turned into combination farmers and stockmen."[29]

Remaining rooted means being faithful and patient. The successes of the homesteaders—accomplished in the face of stubborn land, inhospitable weather, and a lack of resources—were reflected in the faith and patience of Old Jules Sandoz, who remarked, "'The country's bound to grow,' he had said from the start. The various booms and their dying echoes agitated him little. A community can't be planted like a potato patch, all in a day; a wilderness can't be tamed in a year.... His optimism for the Panhandle was unshakable."[30]

I was reminded of this patient faith at many times, and in many places, as I worked on this book.

As I was flying into Lincoln on a beautiful October afternoon in 1999, for example, I discovered that one of my fellow passengers was former Nebraska governor Norbert Tiemann. He graciously agreed to visit with me for a few minutes in the airport terminal. As we talked about his time in Nebraska, he recalled his first campaign for governor, in which he was running in the primary election against a former three-term governor, Rob Peterson. "They said, 'Well you don't have a prayer, there's no chance you can win—somebody from a town of 600 people [Wausau]—against a former popular three-term governor.' ... But then I made my one hundred campaign speeches a day ... I out-campaigned him—that's what it takes to win the election."

Overcoming. Making something of yourself. Transforming raw potential into a polished product. That's what Huskervillers, from former governor Tiemann to players who don the red and white of the Husker football team, try to enact.

Underlying it all, of course, is faith and patience. "It's in the moral fabric of the state," says Don Bryant. "I repeat, boy, Nebraskans have had to be optimistic. If you tossed in the towel every time something went bad, you were dead.... Because no matter how bad things look if you keep plugging and keep going for it, something good might happen.... I think there is a lot of that in that Nebraska work ethic and positive thinking."

Thus, when the Huskers seemed on the brink of winning a national championship at the 1984 Orange Bowl, only to heartbreakingly lose the game (and the championship) to the University of Miami when a two-point conversion failed, Huskervillers did not proclaim "woe is us" or "if only we had gone for the tie."[31] Instead, as Kevin Popp of Louisville (a Huskerviller who has never lived in Nebraska) explains:

> The perfect example is when Nebraska lost to Miami by one point. How the state rallied behind one man [coach Tom Osborne]. Then ten years later [January 1995], they were down I forgot, I think it was like 17–7 or something[32] [in another national championship game against the University of Miami], and you know they scored the last two touchdowns in the last ten minutes, and that is like, it's the people of Nebraska saying to the world, "You can't keep me down, I'm still going to keep striving through the snow, through the corn, through all that, I'm going to keep striving, just going to keep winning."

The football team's successful enactment of the Husker work ethic—be tough, determined, faithful, and patient—provides us Huskervillers with additional evidence that this part of our moral code should continue to be embraced. "The football team," notes David Max of California, "gives validity to the Nebraska work ethic."

We take pride in the accomplishments of individual players whose exceptional work ethics have contributed to the team's historical success. Antone Oseka of North Platte, Nebraska, elaborates: "We work hard, and that's why we appreciate the Huskers as much as we do. They work hard on the field all the time. It represents who we are. We aren't flashy, like Florida, or have the most talent, like Tennessee or Michigan. We just work harder than anyone else. That's why 'There's no place like Nebraska.'"

Echoes Matthew Grosz, "There's a pride involved knowing that they aren't the most talented team around, but they develop the players through practice and game experience to toughen out the worst of storms the world of college football has to offer. FSU [Florida State University] and Florida will always be more talented, but they don't have the history of a hard state behind them to build up their young men and have them look to compete for the best program in the country."

In what might seem, to non–Nebraskans, to be a strange bit of reasoning, Huskervillers take pride in pointing out that—compared to other successful college football programs—not many Husker players succeed in the professional ranks.[33] Explains Mick Messbarger, one of my graduate school roommates, "Our success is based on the tradition of hard work and dedication. Year after year we can see other programs who send many more players on to the NFL and who have many more players that are even better in the pros than they were in college. That is a very rare event for a Husker player. Many great Husker college players don't come close to the same level of success in the pros."

Mick goes on to note that Husker players tend to peak while in college because the dedication and commitment expected of them at Nebraska brings out their best. "A Nebraskan," he observes, "believes that you win by working harder than your opponent, being in better physical condition and being stronger mentally." These qualities, he believes, are not as apparent among professional football players.

Osborne also noted that the work ethic among his players helped overcome some differences in natural ability. "I've often felt that our players have outworked opponents more than they have outshown them with talent," he writes. "New coaches on our staff have marveled at how hard our players work during the off-season compared to players at other places they've been."[34]

The Huskerville work ethic is perhaps most apparent in the stories told about the University of Nebraska football team's legendary walk-on program. It recognizes that players without the exposure of playing in bigger cities, and players who have yet to reach their potential, may have something valuable to offer the team. It embraces the possibilities of transformation, believing that a young man who may not currently have the abilities of others has the potential to outplay others in the future—if he works hard by being tough, determined, faithful, and patient.

As Paul Davie of the Seattle area explains, "Well, the walk-on program at Nebraska has always been the biggest mainstay at the university. It gives the average kid a chance to come on and play. He may not make first string or second string or third string. He may not even make the fourth string but he will go out there and he will stay on that team because you have the opportunity that one day you may crawl out of that lower position and be on that team."

In many ways, then, the walk-on player is the contemporary manifestation of the homesteader. Just as the early homesteaders in Nebraska saw the possibilities for an agricultural haven in the midst of what others called the great desert, walk-on athletes do not see themselves as others see them.

Instead, they see themselves as they *can* be. They believe that they can work harder than others and, ultimately, overcome others in competition— "if they are willing," writes reporter Malcolm Moran in language that recalls the work of Old Jules and other early homesteaders, "to endure years of unrewarded effort."[35] (Some walk-ons may earn scholarships after a couple of years on the team; others may spend their entire undergraduate careers on the team and rarely, if ever, get on the field during a game.)

Not surprisingly, the innovative champion of the walk-on program sees a direct relationship between the work ethic of the walk-ons and the state's agrarian roots.

"The inception for that work ethic [found in the Husker football program] was essentially the walk-on players," Tom Osborne says. "Most of them are from small towns and rural areas and they knew something about working hard and they would come here and just try to work so hard that they'd get a chance to play."[36]

The idea of "the field" as a great equalizer was even suggested by a young Willa Cather, when she wrote about football as a University of Nebraska student in the 1890s: "The field is the only place that some young men ever know of anything of the rough and tumble of life.... Neither his bank book nor his visiting list can help a man on the eleven, he has nothing to back him but his arm and his head, and his life is not any better than any other man's."[37]

A century later, Huskerviller Sam Elder underscored Cather's point:

"That farm boy makes a real good offensive tackle because he has been conditioned first. He works his butt off out on the farm and when he comes to town to play football, they bring a lot with them."

Former walk-on Joel Mackovicka recalls Osborne telling him that walking on would give him the same opportunities as scholarship players had. "I played 8-man football and was from a small school.... [Coach Osborne] said as far as me walking on, it was a great place to come and play. It's a place where they don't treat walk-ons any different. You're part of the team and they give you a fair shake."[38]

In practice, the walk-on program has been primarily an opportunity for people like Mackovicka, graduates of small Nebraska high schools, though a good number of young men from outside the state's borders have walked on to the team as well.[39] Huskervillers are well aware of this history and embrace it as an enactment of what we practice—hard work—on the fields that cover the state.

As Huskerviller Chris Kelley observes, "I guess a lot of our players are from Nebraska and I think the coaching staff gives all the players a fair opportunity even if they're from a small Nebraska town."

If the walk-ons make the most of their fair opportunity, they are awarded with a scholarship. In the language of the homesteaders, walk-ons who earn scholarships have proved up their claim. The claim, in their case, is not a land claim but a claim that they could transform themselves into top-notch college football players.

Huskerviller Jeff Jackson explains: "You know a lot of guys from the state of Nebraska, you know most of them are walk-ons, it's a tradition. They choose to stay there. They grew up their whole lives, you know, wanting to be a Husker, and that's why we're so good because a lot of the guys choose to stay at home. They might not get that scholarship, you know, one, two, maybe three years but you know hard work pays off. But that's why we have one of the best programs in the country."

Rather than feeling entitled to play football for the state school, Husker boys treat the walk-on experience as both a privilege and an opportunity to show what hard work can produce.

Kerianne Kluge of Louisville, Kentucky, says, "Most of the players are Nebraska high school athletes: they walk onto the program and bring with them the hard work ethic that is characteristic of people who make their living farming. Having grown up in the state and realizing how many would like to be NU athletes, but so few actually make it, they understand just how much of a privilege it is to wear the Nebraska jersey."

In short, notes reporter Malcolm Moran, the walk-on program "appeals to the farmers and ranchers whose conservative principles are based upon the worth of an honest day's work."[40]

For example, Matt Schroeder, the son of a Belden, Nebraska, area farmer and a walk-on member of the 2004 Husker football team, said his father and grandfather both told him to "work hard and see what happens" after coach Callahan announced that the number of walk-ons in the program would be reduced by about 50.[41] Accordingly, Schroeder observes about his work in the weight room, "When I know I didn't give as much effort as I should have, I get mad at myself.... If I'm there, I might as well be working as hard as I can."[42] Adds Adam Ickes, a walk-on who became a starting linebacker in 2005, "We small-town guys know we're going to have to work for it."[43]

As expected, Huskervillers take great pride in those walk-ons who succeed. Derrie Nelson was a fan favorite during my early years as a student at the University of Nebraska because he had transformed himself from a walk-on from the small Nebraska town of Fairmont to an All-American defensive end. As Nelson emphasizes, "You have to recruit the heart, not just the size and speed and those things."[45]

Tony Felici was a walk-on with heart. One of only four walk-ons to twice earn all-conference honors as a Husker, Felici fondly remembers the difference the walk-on program made in his life: "Look at where I came from: I was a walk-on with poor grades, a guy who nobody really wanted. If I was in this generation today, I would have been kicked aside as small, dumb, and too slow. But the main thing is that I persevered and things fell into place for me."[44]

Other Husker walk-ons have experienced similar success. Six walk-ons eventually earned All-American honors. Between 1990–2004, an average of four of the 22 starting positions on the team were held by walk-ons.[46] In 2002, seven of the starters were walk-ons.[47] One of my brother's high school classmates—whose abilities were questioned even by some of his high school peers—transformed himself from a walk-on to the Huskers' starting quarterback.[48]

These statistics point to the results of the desire to succeed as well as the discipline needed to achieve such success. These characteristics, notes Todd Wolverton of Creston, Iowa, are developed in rural Nebraska in particular: "Young kids in these towns want to grow up to be the next guy from that town to take the field in the Husker uniform." For example, my friend Mick Messbarger told me about a young man named Matt Plooster from

Mount Michael Benedictine High School; Matt turned down an academic scholarship from Harvard in order to walk on at Nebraska.

Walk-ons like Matt are no doubt inspired by the successes of those who preceded them. For example, former coach Osborne recounts several "rural kids to Husker starters" success stories in his book, *More Than Winning*, including Mike Tranmer, "a 180-pound walk-on noseguard from Lyons, Nebraska," and Brian Heimer, "a 180-pound walk-on from David City, Nebraska."[49]

Heimer was even cut from the team in the spring of his freshman year, but "pleaded with us during the summer to give him another chance," writes Osborne. "I remember his saying, 'I think I can work harder.'" Heimer eventually became the Huskers' starting tight end because, as Osborne notes, "He worked harder. A lot harder."[50]

When walk-ons like Heimer succeed, Huskervillers know that our work ethic has been validated. Even if the work done in the fields of Nebraska is not always respected outside of the state's boundaries—more on this later—we know that a larger audience witnesses the successes of the walk-ons.

As Huskerviller Loren Wagner of Culbertson, Nebraska, proclaims: "Young men, who may not have as much skill or God-given talent as many Division I players, work their tails off in the weight room and on the football field just to be a part of Husker football. They are over-achievers that succeed because of their dedication and desire. I think the rest of the people in the state feed off of that. It is a source of encouragement to them."

At the least, Huskervillers use the success of the walk-on program as a means of comparison. Longtime Husker fan Leon Englebart told me before the 1999 Iowa State game that he believes the walk-on program speaks to what kind of people Huskervillers are: "They [the coaches] will give them [the walk-ons] a chance. A lot of schools really don't give a person a chance; they just kind of ignore them." Similarly, the early Nebraska homesteaders were largely people looking for a chance. In both fields, those who succeed are those who work hard and transform potential into product.

Former Husker player Trev Alberts tells the story of Gerald Armstrong, just one of the many Husker players who earned starting positions and scholarships by transforming themselves through hard work:

> The first year I was really getting beat up on the scout team, and I really wanted to quit. One time I was sitting in study hall with Gerald Armstrong, who was a walk-on tight end. I was venting about everything going wrong for me, and how this was so difficult, and all of a sudden, Gerald said, "Man, I don't feel sorry for you one bit. You scholarship guys don't have a clue!"

Gerald told me his story of how he grew up on a farm, and his parents had no money—just enough money to send him to school for one year. If he didn't get a scholarship after that, he would have to come home. Now try playing with that burden. But that made Nebraska football so special—those kids from Nebraska grew up with it in their blood. And no kids in the country are tougher than they are.[51]

This bond between life as lived in the fields and life as lived on the football field is the primary reason why coach Callahan's decision to reduce the size of the walk-on program generated much concern in Huskerville. As *Omaha World-Herald* reporter Elizabeth Merrill describes the reaction in Matt Schroeder's hometown area: "The news hit Laurel, Neb., and reverberated through grain bins across Cedar County. Bill Callahan, Nebraska's new football coach, was reducing the number of walk-ons. What would this mean to Matt?"[52]

Steve Glenn was especially upset by Callahan's decision to reduce the size of the walk-on program because he calls the walk-on program the glue that binds the team to the state's residents.[53] "I think the key [to Husker football] is Nebraska kids," he told me. "The Nebraska kids and the hard work and the determination that...." His voice trails off before he finds the words to continue. "This was their team. There was an identity with the team. And that's what's made it strong. And also, historically, Nebraska just outworked people. Talk about a blue-collar team. We were about as blue-collar as it gets."

So we're faced with a bit of a dilemma in Huskerville. We're supposed to have faith and be patient, but the current coaches of the team seem not to have that much faith in Nebraska boys nor do they seem to be all that patient, having brought 19 junior college players into the program in their first two years ("by far [the] most over any two-year period" in the team's history, notes sportswriter Rich Kaipust.).[54]

How do we have faith and patience in these circumstances? But, on the other hand, what if we do not have faith and patience? What does that say about us?

So we look for events and commentary to help us work through this dilemma. When walk-on Adam Ickes blocked a potential game-winning Pittsburgh field goal early in the 2005 season, for example, you could almost hear the symbolism ringing throughout Huskerville. Radio play-by-play announcer Jim Rose gushed about it on the air. Omaha *World-Herald* columnist Tom Shatel described the block with such reverence that we Huskervillers couldn't mistake its monumental statement about the way things should be.

"In an otherwise ugly display of football," Shatel wrote, "the beauty of Big Red football returned. A walk-on saved the day.... Thank you, Adam Ickes. Thank you for sticking around five years. Thank you for not going to UNO [University of Nebraska–Omaha] or South Dakota State. Thank you for coming from little Page, Neb., a burg of about 156 located an hour northwest of Norfolk, to pursue the dream of the walk-on."[55]

I.M. Hipp, one of the Nebraska football program's most legendary walkons, underscores the sentiment that seeps through Shatel's words: the walkons provide a link to tradition. "Walk-ons have been part of the essence of tradition and winning at Nebraska as far back as I can remember," asserts Hipp. "It proves that even though sometimes you're looked over and not given the blue-chip label, you can still play for whoever. If you have an aspiration or a dream you can make it. I was a walk-on, and I'm still a walk-on, and I carry it with me in my heart."[56]

Huskervillers carry this work ethic with us, too. As I learned years ago, and as the children of Huskervillers learn today, hard work is not something to be praised as an extraordinary accomplishment; it is simply expected. My college friend Todd Wolverton, who lived in Nebraska only during his college years, observed this phenomenon while a student in Lincoln. "Hard work," he says, "is not something that players on the team have to rise to the occasion to perform. It is accepted as the way things should be done."

"The way things should be done." This statement reflects our balancing act: we toe the line between disillusionment with the present and remembrance of what we want to continue to be. It also underscores just how tightly we hold on to working hard as a bedrock belief of Huskerville. At the same time that we work hard as individuals, though, we also need to look out for one another.

7

Being Neighborly

> In my town everyone knew each other's business. If someone got a new car, it was time to celebrate. If someone did well fishing, he displayed his catch out on his front lawn. We knew what our neighbors had for dinner, what their favorite TV shows were, what time they went to bed. There must have been comfort in knowing all this. We wanted it that way.[1]

In August of 1980, I loaded up my 1970 Chevrolet Monte Carlo and began the 400-mile drive from Scottsbluff to Lincoln. The 400 miles was made even longer by the fact that I was entering a different world.

I was leaving a town of 15,000 people and moving to a university campus where the student population alone easily outnumbered the number of folks in my hometown.

I was moving into a 10-story dormitory—a structure three times as tall as anything in my hometown—that was home to nearly three times as many students as I had in my entire high school class.

I was feeling a bit overwhelmed. Then I met Danny Hayes.

Danny was the first person I met as I hesitantly, and cluelessly, moved into my dorm room. He was ironing his clothes in an alcove and called out, "Hi," as I trudged past, looking for my room. He introduced himself, told me how to get a cart to carry my belongings, and warned me that I should move my car if I didn't want to get a parking ticket.

Danny and I were from different worlds—he was from the big city of Omaha and I was from the town Scottsbluff, he is African American and I am white, he was confident and I was not—yet he immediately helped me feel at home in my new, overwhelming environment.

A large part of feeling at home, I know now, means that you know, and have faith in, your neighbors. Before I even opened the door to room 628 of Schramm Hall, I knew that I had a neighbor.

In many ways, as I reflect, Danny was a lot like Mrs. Collopy, the woman who lived with her husband next to my family on Avenue E in Scottsbluff.

She welcomed us to the neighborhood, endured the frequent forays of my brother and I into her backyard to retrieve foul balls from our whiffle ball games, gladly purchased a few of our garden vegetables at the end of the summer, and—every once in a while—gave us a few extra pieces of candy when we stopped in the small store she and her husband ran across the street from the neighborhood elementary school.

I don't know that Danny Hayes and Mrs. Collopy were ever considered my friends, but they were something just as important: my neighbors. Neighbors are friendly even if they are not friends. By their actions, which I'll talk more about in this chapter, they help us to become part of a collective. Both Danny and Mrs. Collopy have helped me to recognize another bedrock principle of Huskerville: we share the world with others.

Not a terribly profound observation, I know. But when you grow up, and live, in places where not many of those others are near you, you can either become overwhelmed by the seeming emptiness of the area or you can embrace your opportunities to be with others.[2] This was especially important for the state's early homesteaders. As Mari Sandoz notes in *Old Jules*, "Jules's dugout attracted more and more settlers, for news or to escape the need of living with themselves for an hour or so."[3]

Even today, when you see someone in these parts, it's a somewhat novel experience, and novel experiences are to be appreciated and treated as special. I recall learning the "one finger wave" (more on this later) from my dad as we traveled the nearly empty highways in the Nebraska panhandle. I remember driving to and from college on Highway 26 and not seeing another car on the road over 10, 20, even 30 miles of highway. "The Nebraska I know and love," writes a Huskerviller using the online name of Calla, "is people who don't even know each other, wave at each other when they are driving down a gravel road."[4]

Think about this approach to sharing the world with others in comparison to how people in some parts of the world interact with each other when they share the road. I'm talking about road rage. When you're in competition with others, when sharing the world with others means you think you have to fight to get what's yours, even if it's an insignificant piece of concrete amidst hundreds of miles of concrete, you enact "sharing the world with others" much differently than folks in Huskerville do.

In Huskerville, on the other hand, the essence of being a Nebraskan is enacted through being neighborly, or what Mari Sandoz observed among the homesteaders as "the hospitality of the frontier."[5]

Explains Loren Wagner, "I believe caring and hospitality are two words that go a long way in defining the 'essence' of Nebraska. Nebraska is a place where people will still go out of their way to make you feel at home; a place where people will stop to offer help if you are stranded on the side of the road. For the most part we are people persons who care about people and try to lend a helping hand."

For example, during World War II, Nebraskans from 125 communities participated in the operation of the North Platte Canteen, a place where each day thousands of soldiers traveling by rail would stop for 10–15 minutes and be treated to drinks, snacks, magazines, and friendly conversation.[6] These helping hands were, and continue to be, lent because being relatively alone generates an awareness that you may have to depend upon others for help— and that they may depend upon you for help. In short, you need each other.

While the Huskerville work ethic encourages self-sufficiency, neighbors know to look out for one another without being asked. Notes poet Charles Fort of the University of Nebraska–Kearney, "The land and its open spaces force one to work harder at finding other people to work with and to live with. That effort, though, gives these relationships more meaning."[7]

Thus, being neighborly might, in some ways, be a more profound experience than being friends. What, in particular, gives these neighborly relationships more meaning? I believe that their meaningfulness derives from what is done through the performance of being neighborly. Specifically, Huskervillers enact neighborliness by: (1) being friendly; (2) being helpful; (3) being loyal to one another; and (4) being respectful of visiting neighbors.

Being Friendly

Perhaps I had been away from Nebraska too long when I returned for the Iowa State game in 1999. On the morning of the game, I sat on the steps of a sidewalk near the Nebraska Center of the university's east campus. My mom was showing me photos and postcards of her summer trip to Germany, the country where her ancestors were born.

As we looked at the pictures that spoke to our biological and cultural roots, players and coaches from the Husker football team walked past us on their way from the Nebraska Center to pre-game meetings. I had forgotten that the team stayed at the Nebraska Center the night prior to home games.

I had also apparently forgotten my Nebraska roots, for I felt an awkwardness that I could not quite understand—until my mom, without seeming to give the matter a second thought—began to casually say "hi" and "good morning" to those players and coaches who passed by us.

As we continued to look at my mom's photos, and as my mom continued to acknowledge the presence of the people passing by, I realized that I had forgotten a simple lesson of Huskerville: be friendly.

What my mom reminded me of, other Huskervillers remember and enact on a daily basis. As Bob Estey of Colorado explains, "If you're walking down the street, you know, in the morning and you pass somebody on the street and you say 'Good morning.'" Sam Elder of Federal Way, Washington, concurs, "You can walk down Main Street in almost any Nebraska town and have people on the sidewalk smile and say, 'hello.'"

In his alphabetically arranged list of reasons why he likes Nebraska, University of Nebraska–Lincoln English professor Gerald Shapiro recounts the uniqueness of such an orientation to others:

> H is for "Hello," which is what people in Nebraska say to one another when they meet on the street. Sometimes they say, "Hi," instead, but that starts with "H" also, so it doesn't count. To native Nebraskans, this business of saying "Hello" doesn't seem like much. It's just a normal, decent thing to do. But I have news for you: the world at large does not say hello. The world at large, in fact, doesn't say much of anything. In Massachusetts, for instance, when people see each other on the street they look down at their shoes, as if eye contact would turn one or both of them into pillars of salt.[8]

Huskervillers are supposed to be so friendly that "you [can] call the wrong number by mistake and talk to the person for an hour anyway." This humorous line, borrowed from a "you know you're from Nebraska" list shared with me by Candy Hodge, is nonetheless treated as an exemplary enactment of Husker friendliness—as Dan Koleski of Louisville indicates in his description of a Nebraskan: "Somebody you could meet on the street and still have a good conversation with without worrying about being snubbed. You can drive down the streets of Nebraska, any street in any town, and wave at anybody and it's just like you've known him. One guy said one time, you know you're in Nebraska when you can make a wrong call and still talk for fifteen minutes. People are just really friendly out there."

Back in Nebraska, Ashley Smith agrees. She told me during my visit to Lincoln that "everybody is so nice here and we always welcome everybody with open arms." Monty Seidler concurs, recalling his first visit to Nebraska: "I went down to the mall [in Omaha], down there by Old Mill, Westroad. People were so friendly, I couldn't believe it. I have never experienced it at any place. I was walking down the mall [and] people were so overwhelming, so friendly."

Monty's surprise at the friendliness found in the usually-not-so-friendly experience of shopping was also noted by Gerald Shapiro when he moved to Nebraska. As he notes in his exposition of the letter "I": "I is for Ideal—the Ideal Grocery, in Lincoln. It's not only the best grocery store in Nebraska, it's the best grocery store in the world. Trust me on this. The people who work there are friendly in a way you have to see to believe.... The guys in produce act as if there's nothing on earth they'd rather do than weigh your onions."[9]

Both Gerald and Monty learned about Nebraskans' friendliness after they spent some time in the state. Their experiences reflect not just the general friendliness that Huskervillers attempt to enact, but also a more specific version in which non–Huskers are greeted and treated as friends (more on this idea at the end of the chapter).

Even the World War II prisoners of war who were held in camps located across Nebraska, including my hometown of Scottsbluff, came to understand Huskerville's version of friendliness. "During the holidays, it was common for people from nearby towns to send cookies and other food to the [POW] camps."[10] Said one prisoner of war, "Farmers usually showed us prisoners a wonderfully natural hospitality and friendliness."[11] Following the war, a number of the former POWs returned to Nebraska, not just to visit but to live.[12]

Similarly, Dr. R.H. Kobayashi points out that "the University of Nebraska made a generous and heroic effort to accommodate Japanese/American college students (Stanford, UCLA, Berkley, USC, etc.), who were relocated from the concentration camps" on the west coast of the United States. Dr. Kobayashi, who practices medicine in Omaha, writes, "I am continually asked by my friends in Hawaii as well as California and elsewhere, 'You are still in Nebraska? Why?' I believe the answer is quite simple, really. In my opinion, the most decent and honorable people in the United States live in Nebraska."[13]

No wonder, then, that Ed Vinton of the Atlanta area claims, "A Nebraskan is someone who has never met a stranger." Nebraskans "would share their supper with you if you, a total stranger, asked them to" (Fritz Gottschalk of Leavenworth, Kansas) and "say hello to you ... even if you are a stranger" (Thomas D. Miller of Topeka, Kansas).

That's the way I felt when Danny Hayes greeted me on the sixth floor of Schramm Hall in 1980. Coincidentally, 20 years after our introduction, I had the pleasure of reading the story of our resident assistant on Schramm Six, Jack Clarke, who wrote in Nebraska Magazine about his realization that Huskerville knows no strangers:

As the miles rolled away from my upstate New York home, I had no idea
what was in store for me. I was about to live my lifelong dream by attending
the University of Nebraska. My parents had met there and my grandfather was
also an alumnus. Now it was my turn. I also was trying out for the Cornhusker
Marching Band....

One afternoon I found myself walking alone downtown. A young man in
his early 20s was coming toward me on the same block. He gave me eye contact
and said "hello" as he kept walking. I was stunned. I was raised where strangers
didn't speak to each other, let alone give you eye contact. It was then I realized
I was in Nebraska, a place I would grow to love. I will never forget that
moment.[14]

Not surprisingly, Huskervillers extend this same embracing of strangers
as not strangers to football fans visiting Nebraska, too. For example, as
espn.com reporter Jim Caple reports, father and son Greg and Jeff Kohnel,
respectively, from Shelby, Nebraska, hold "a tailgate party before every game,
arriving as early as seven hours before kickoff to set up their tent.... This
being Nebraska, everyone is invited to stop by, especially opposing fans.
When Washington played Nebraska a decade ago, a Husky fan dropped by
and joined the party, repaying the Kohnels by sending a school cap a couple days later."[15]

Wrote one Southern Mississippi fan after attending the September
1999 game against Nebraska in Lincoln: "We were delighted by the generosity of the Husker fans. Several folks stopped us as we walked the tailgating
area to say hello, ask about our team, and even offer us food and drink. We
did not have one time where Nebraska fans said anything derogatory or
unsportsmanlike during the entire visit. I was quite impressed with the hospitality of the fans."[16]

When *Sports Illustrated* online reporter Lars Anderson visited Lincoln
during a home football game, he left thinking that Huskervillers "are some
of the friendliest people on the planet. Ask a Nebraskan for directions and
don't be surprised when he draws you a map and hands you his phone number, insisting that you give him a ring to let him know you arrived 'all super
safe and sound.'"[17]

Even outside of Nebraska, Huskervillers seem to know no strangers.
My friend Alena Amato Ruggerio and her husband Brad visited a Kentuckiana Huskers watch party in Louisville on my behalf. After the experience,
she wrote to me:

Everyone at the watch party was welcoming and kind to me and Brad.
They bought us sodas, introduced us to the organization leaders, and
announced our goals to the group. Not one person declined an interview, and
several didn't wait for me to approach them. They embodied much of what

they said about Nebraskan people. They were definitely warm and friendly people.... When I told John Strope [of the Kentuckiana Huskers] that we were ready to leave, he again made an announcement to the group, and they all actually applauded as we left. My gosh, I've got to go to Nebraska.

This commitment to hospitality has been nurtured since the days of Nebraska's homesteaders. "Hospitality was one of the cardinal virtues of the West," notes historian Everett Dick. "Even utter strangers were welcome to the settler's table and bed. Though it might be supplied at sacrifice, the settler's hospitality was always extended."[18]

It's also practiced today.

Nebraska, notes Ned Criscimagna of Annapolis, Maryland, is "a place where our agricultural heritage affects even the cities, making them friendlier and more open than most." Former Nebraska governor Frank Morrison echoed this idea, observing in 1963 that the "word 'welcome' means a lot of things to a lot of people in a lot of different places. But here in Nebraska you find the handshakes a little firmer, the smiles a little warmer and a little more sincerity to that 'hello.'"[19]

In some cases, we don't even need to communicate verbally to show our friendliness. On the rural roads of Nebraska, for instance, the one-finger wave is a common greeting. Before you get the wrong idea, let me say that the one-finger wave is the signature greeting of drivers passing each other on rural highways throughout Nebraska. With one hand on top of the steering wheel—two hands are relatively unnecessary when the road is fairly straight and the sides of the road so open as to preclude unexpected animal crossings—drivers simply raise their index finger in a "we're old friends, no need to get all excited about it" kind of greeting, no matter whether they know one another or not. On occasion, in what passes for exuberance, the driver may lift all fingers in salutation, while keeping their thumb wrapped around the steering wheel just in case.

This friendly greeting is performed by rural Huskervillers in particular, for in those sparsely populated areas each oncoming vehicle may well be a neighbor. Mark Harris, who grew up in McCook, remembers that his "father would always raise a finger or hand to wave at every car he met on the road.... 'I don't know if he knew everybody he passed, but he knew they might know him.'"[20]

Huskervillers Jim and Kim Carmen compare the reactions of drivers in Nebraska and Colorado as a way of illustrating Huskervillers' friendliness. Says Jim, "You wave at them [Coloradoans] and they think that you're doing something obscene to them or something. Just being friendly and waving and that's just the way we do it out here in Nebraska." Adds Kim, "[In Nebraska], you know everybody, if you drive by, you wave. I mean everybody waves. As opposed to Denver, they think you're flipping them off or something!"

Things *are* different in Huskerville. Walt Fulton of Lexington Park, Maryland, notes, "I have lived around the country from coast to coast. I've never met more cordial, polite, and pleasant people to be around." Walt's sentiments are shared by other Huskervillers:

> SHARON JAROSZ: I travel all over and ran into other fans and they just don't seem to be as hospitable as Husker fans.... I just think Nebraska is such a happy state. Everywhere I ever traveled around Nebraska, I ran into people that are the most congenial, happiest people that I ever met.
>
> DAN KOLESKI: I've lived all over the United States and all over the country, and I just find the people in Nebraska are just extremely friendly.
>
> MARK SAYRE: I've been to seven countries and thirty-five states, and they're some of the friendliest people I've ever met.
>
> AMY HIGA: The people are friendly here more than other places that I've been throughout the United States.
>
> ROBERT DAVIS: They are friendly, friendliness of the people. I have traveled, I have been to every state all over United States, people in Nebraska are friendly I think more so than other states.

Huskervillers trace the roots of this friendliness to our small-town and rural upbringings, frequently noting that our experiences in bigger cities have helped to convince us that being a friendly neighbor is more likely to occur when you have rural roots.

Explains Eric Baer of Oklahoma City, "[Nebraska is a] rather small state. I mean the city of Dallas has more people than the whole state of Nebraska on any given day. There is a small town feeling ... to the state. It is just small, friendly; you will get that, even in Lincoln and Omaha, a lot [more] friendly than especially Oklahoma City or Atlanta or Kansas City. It is just [a] small town feel for the whole state."

When we Huskervillers find ourselves in bigger cities, we clearly see the difference between Huskerville and our larger surroundings. Explains Bob Estey of Denver, "But, a lot of the people who are here, you know, they're kind of lost because it's, it is, it's kind of hard for a typical Nebraskan to fit in to this city. Denver's a very cold city, although it's not as bad as San Francisco or L.A. or somewhere like that."

Similarly, Darren Seidler notes, "In Nebraska when you walk down the street you acknowledge somebody coming towards you, and in Virginia that was one thing that blew me away when I first started working in the Pentagon. I would be walking down the hallway and somebody would come towards me and I would say 'Hi' and they would look at me like, 'what do you want?'"

Even Huskers who would be more likely to be acknowledged by their non–Nebraska neighbors encounter this lack of friendliness elsewhere. For example, former Husker football player Pat Fischer, who was a mainstay of successful Washington Redskins football teams and now lives in the DC metro area, observes, "Nebraska people will say 'hello' to you or share a smile every day. It is a place you get to know your neighbors. I have lived here in northern Virginia for a long time, and I hardly know my neighbors."[21]

Perhaps, paradoxically, the distance between neighbors in Nebraska produces a closeness that is absent among people who live only short distances apart. Perhaps those who live close to others, in terms of distance, take neighbors for granted.

At any rate, being friendly is an integral element of performing neighborliness in Huskerville, and these performances serve to make relationships among geographically scattered people meaningful. As Conal Furay explains in his article about neighborliness in small towns, "A good part of the communication that went on was aimed not at exchanging information but at reinforcing one's sense of relatedness."[22] Such reinforcement, Furay notes, also includes offering assistance to neighbors in need.

Being Helpful

Huskervillers take pride not just in being friendly, which could be taken by outsiders as a superficial type of neighborliness, but also by enacting our commitment to others through helpfulness.

When people need help, Huskervillers provide help—no questions asked. Our friendliness, in other words, is marked by a genuine caring for others. As Tracey Welshans Elmshaeuser notes, "Everybody really cares about each other and takes care of one another." Echoes Kathryn Martin, "People generally look out for each other, not just for themselves."

A commitment to helping your neighbors is part of what Michael Fletcher, of Marble Falls, Texas, calls the Husker tradition. "I grew up in the Husker tradition," he says. "My family taught me to be helpful and give a hand when someone needed it."

This tradition has its roots firmly planted in the efforts of Nebraska's homesteaders. Writes historian Everett Dick: "Neighborly helpfulness was manifested on every hand. If a prairie fire burnt a man's hay, a neighbor sent a load over to him. If he lost his crop by some accident, the neighbors donated a few bushels to tide him over the winter. When sickness prevented the head of the house from putting in his crop, the whole neighborhood turned out with tools and in a day or two put the more unfortunate neighbor on the way toward economic stability and opportunity."[23]

Mari Sandoz's *Old Jules* offers many illustrations of how the early Nebraska homesteaders offered each other a helping hand, including their collective efforts to protect their claims from those who wanted the land for other purposes. Ultimately, Sandoz observes, the differences among the homesteaders blurred as they became one people, collectively looking out for one another: "Common need knit them closer. It was no longer the Americans, the Hollanders, the Germans, the Slavs, the Swiss."[24]

The homesteaders' legacy of watching out for your neighbors continues in contemporary Huskerville. Claims Huskerviller Lisa Steward of Littleton, Colorado, "Only in Nebraska will you find people who are gracious, friendly and always willing to step in and help someone in need. Whether it be a friend or a stranger, they will always be taken care of and treated like one of the family."

Adds longtime Huskerviller and former University of Nebraska Sports Information Director Don Bryant, Huskerville residents "rise to the occasion of crisis and help people.... They take food into somebody's house if they're sick.... You have that small town 'pull together' atmosphere, where you got to all pull together."

This commitment to pulling together is recognized by younger Huskerville residents, too. Adds Michele Lueders, who was a student at the University of Nebraska–Lincoln when she visited with me, "Everything that we do here, we all help each other out whenever there's any kind of a problem and anywhere in the state people come together to help each other out."

Writing from Idaho, John Bruns offers an example of what Michele and Don identify: "Just read any news article following a personal or community tragedy. The out-pouring of support from people who don't even know those affected. Most recently [in 2004], the tornado devastation in Hallam, Nebraska. I personally witnessed the same type of support in Lawrence, Nebraska, in the late 1980s after a March tornado severely damaged their town."

Huskervillers try to enact this helpfulness in all situations, not just in crises such as natural disasters. Consider Jack Kovacs' experience shopping for furniture, for example:

I'm not a native Nebraskan, but was stationed at Offutt Air Force Base from 1968 through 1970 and again from 1972 through 1975. I graduated from UN-O through classes at Offutt at night. My first positive impression was when shopping for furniture for our new house. Montgomery Wards didn't have what we were looking for, but the clerk (now associate, I guess) actually told me the name of a competitor store where I could probably find it. To me, that meant she wanted to really help us. We found this tendency in several other stores in Omaha.

Jack's experience seems to illustrate Maxwell, Nebraska, resident Aub Boucher's definition of a Nebraskan: "A 'Nebraskan' is someone who will go out of their way to help anyone."

Importantly, being helpful in Huskerville also means that you keep an eye on your neighbors. Knowing each others' predilection for self-sufficiency, Huskervillers recognize that someone in need of assistance may be reluctant to ask for help. So, instead, you pay attention to others, not just yourself, and offer help *before* it is sought.

Ed Vinton of the Atlanta area points out that Huskervillers "will do things for people without being asked." Adds a Husker fan living in Connecticut, people in Nebraska have "no need to worry about having your car break down—because someone is guaranteed to stop and help you in just a few moments."

Darren Seidler, a Nebraska native living in Washington, DC, remembers her husband Monty's surprised reaction when he was provided with offers of help when his car was in the shop. As the three of us talked in the Nebraska Union one night, Monty—who has never lived in Nebraska—and Darren talked extensively about what they appreciate about Nebraskans. Of the car incident, Darren recalled, "Monty's car was in the shop at the time and three or four people came up to Monty and said, 'You can use my car.'" Turning to Monty, she asked, "Do you remember that? It was shocking to you."

Monty's initial shock was perhaps also due to the fact that when Huskervillers provide such help, we expect nothing in return. Instead, we provide help because we believe that doing so is simply the right thing to do.

Jeff Jones, of Ocala, Florida, who both wore the Harry Husker outfit on game days in Lincoln and was commissioned into the Army's Big Red Battalion, explains that Huskervillers are people "who will lend a hand and not expect a return!" Adds Dennis Lindquist, of San Antonio, Texas, a Huskerviller "will always assist those in need, without thought of payback."

Brian Sharp testifies to the accuracy of their statements. "I worked a summer over in Ogallala—got [my] car stuck in sand at Lake McConaughy. I walked one or two miles to a guy's house—he left dinner, drove out and pulled me out. It took about an hour or so. I asked what I owed him and he said to return the favor for someone else or to stop if he is stranded some day on the side of the road."

Tracey Welshans Elmshaeuser also experienced some of this Husker helpfulness, no payback expected.

> I was supposed to be flying back to Lincoln after visiting a friend on the West Coast. The flights into Lincoln had been cancelled. There was still a flight going to Omaha, so I got on it thinking it would at least be better to get that close than spend the night in the airport. On the plane, I started talking with the two girls next to me. As it turned out, they also lived in Lincoln, but had flown out of Omaha. I asked them if they knew of any shuttles or buses going to Lincoln. They said there was one I could take for $65, but not to worry about it, that they could give me a ride. They took me back to Lincoln, right to my front door. I asked them if I could send them gas money, and they said no. I never got the chance to ask their names, but it was six years ago and I don't think I will forget the kindness they showed me when they didn't even know me. I really think that it wouldn't have happened anywhere else.

As Huskervillers like Tracey attest, this type of commitment to others isn't always found outside the borders of Huskerville. Mike and Cindy Lenz, for example, told me, "You know, we've gone other places and you really don't find that [helpfulness] anywhere else. People are willing to help you [in Nebraska], they are willing to reach out to you; they are friendly."

Bruce Jensen illustrates this notion as he talks about his Connecticut-raised wife's reaction when visiting the grocery store in Lincoln:

> The people of Nebraska are very friendly. My wife grew up in Connecticut and knew that I was a little crazy with my love of the Cornhuskers. While on vacation in Nebraska during a game day she went shopping and came back with a very puzzled look on her face. That is when she knew there was no place like Nebraska, especially on game day. She first told me that after she had paid for the groceries someone grabbed her cart and started to push it out of the store. She was startled to say the least and asked the employee just what he thought he was doing. He replied by saying that he always helped the customer to the car with the groceries. This was news to her because in Connecticut where she grew up she said that you could be laying in the middle of the aisle in the store and people would just step around you; this help to the car was very much a new idea to her.

Similarly, a Huskerviller now living in Germany reports that he notices the difference between the performance of helpful in Germany and Huskerville:

People [in Nebraska] that you meet at work, on the street, etc. are usually very willing to help you find your way, to include you in their activities (invite you to their home or their church, etc.). I have also noticed, since I moved to Germany, that people will more readily take advantage of other people here than in Nebraska. For example, when a sales clerk in Nebraska gives someone back too much change, my experience is that the customer corrects the mistake. Here, I have seen people almost literally "take the money and run!" There are also many stories, both published and unpublished, of fans from the guest team having car troubles in Lincoln on a game Saturday or needing a doctor or some other mishap. These people were helped by Lincolnites out of their trouble, and the guests usually state that they were treated as "guests."

In one of the more extreme instances of helpfulness shared with me, my old college roommate Jon Johnston reminded me that—as Iowa State was upsetting Nebraska in Ames, Iowa—he was sharing tips with Iowa State students on how to properly tear down the goal posts to celebrate their victory. "Make sure you all get over the fence at once," he told them, "otherwise the cops will pick you off if you go one by one! Make sure not to go onto the field. Stand at the edge of the field, but don't go on it!"[25]

Now, not every person who lives in Nebraska enacts helpfulness in an exemplary manner, but those of us who consider ourselves residents of Huskerville attempt to enact the distinction between living in Nebraska and being a Huskerviller.

Mike Nolan, who manages the Husker List discussion group on the Internet, tells a story that highlights the differences between the two groups: "I've heard bad stories about Nebraska fans, too, including the year that someone who had recently moved from Colorado to Nebraska and was parking downtown on the day of the CU game had 'GO HUSKERS' scratched into the side of her car. To complete that story, several auto body shops in Lincoln offered to repair the damage for free."

Perhaps this commitment to helpfulness stems in part from a practical belief, namely that neighbors need to be responsible for one another, especially when we are separated by vast distances. Perhaps it stems in part from a moral belief, the idea that we are all in this world together. Maybe it's a bit of both. But no matter what its origins, Huskervillers believe that neighbors should stick together.

Being Loyal

"We'll all stick together in all kinds of weather."

This wonderfully rich line from the University of Nebraska fight song reflects a number of sentiments rooted in the homesteading practice of being loyal neighbors. It promotes a type of collective dedication, similar to the individually oriented dedication found in the Huskerville work ethic. It references Nebraska's weather extremes and, by extension, how neighbors from the past, present, and future have and will continue to watch out for one another. It also implies a preferred type of fanhood, for fans who are not dedicated are termed fair weather fans; they support their team only when the weather—the skies or the team's season—is good.[26]

This collective orientation, the Huskerville version of the Three Musketeers' motto of "One for all, and all for one," is historically rooted in Nebraska. Prior to the passage of the Homestead Act, homesteaders formed claim clubs that would run off those who attempted to claim jump, or steal the land already claimed by a homesteader.[27] After the Homestead and Kincaid Acts brought a more formal process to homesteading, pioneers continued to help neighbors in need. Notes Mari Sandoz, "Every spring [Old Jules] gave away wagonloads of shrubbery, sucker plums, asparagus, horseradish, and pieplant roots to anyone who would promise to care for them."[28]

In addition, as historian Everett Dick details in his fascinating book *The Sod-House Frontier*, the early homesteaders looked out for their neighbors when they left home for a stretch. "While the men and possibly some of the women from a given community were gone on the long trip," Dick writes, "those left behind in the settlement looked after their families and stock."[29]

Today, this type of loyal neighborliness manifests itself in how Nebraskans support one another in our everyday lives, how the Husker football team approaches its work, and how we Husker football fans describe ourselves. Let's start with a look at how Huskervillers stick together in our everyday lives.

Rod and Deb Weitzel argue that Nebraska's agricultural orientation has much to do with this loyalty. They told me, "Nebraskans stick together and they are loyal to one another.... I think because it is a farming community so families always stuck together and you know generations have stayed in Nebraska so I think that is just the loyalty and the family. You know in other states, in bigger states, bigger cities families don't stay by one another as they do in Nebraska."

Cristine Miller, of New Albany, Indiana, agrees. She sent a letter to me in 1999 explaining how Huskervillers' collective orientation was exemplified in her small hometown of Shelby, Nebraska. She writes, "My mother has recently (three years ago) had a stroke. This event has left her disabled in physical ability and judgment. The community has rallied around her and my father to make sure that she is rarely alone."[30]

Cristine's experience in Shelby has, not coincidentally, much in common with the experience of Husker football players who find themselves embraced by, and ultimately embracing, this stick-together attitude.

For example, *New York Times* reporter Malcolm Moran observed in 1988, in words that still hold true today, "It does not seem to matter that the quarterback, a wingback and the kicker are from California, the left outside linebacker is from Houston, the cornerbacks are from Kansas City and Colorado Springs, and the New Jersey pipeline remains important. 'When they're here,' said Allen Swanson, a rancher from Arthur, 'they're Nebraskans. That's the way it is.'"[31]

Within the team, former coach Osborne said, "We tried to cultivate an attitude of unselfishness, to realize that if the team won on the field, then we all won. We tried to move players from a self-centeredness to a team-oriented concept. We tried to teach that if you sacrificed personal goals for team goals, it would benefit everybody in the end."

Husker fans integrate these historical practices, these everyday experiences, and this team orientation as we enact our support of the Husker football team. As Huskerviller Holli Beadell Van Valkenburg explains, Huskers "stick with their friends, spouses, their home state and NU football their whole lives. [We're] consistent and dependable." Affirms Mike Henningsen of Phoenix, Arizona, "A Nebraskan is someone who will stick with you no matter what." Adds Lori Parker of Lincoln, "Nebraskans are dedicated and loyal to their football teams and to their state."

Such support, Huskervillers emphasize, does not depend upon the team's success. Notes Bill Hancock, "Husker fans are more loyal. Most sports fans are loyal as long as the team's winning. But Nebraska fans are out there when losing and they'll be right back home on the following weekend." Nor does our support depend upon the weather. "Many people," observes Sam Elder of Federal Way, Washington, "have gone to the games when the weather was horrible."

As Bill's and Sam's observations indicate, Huskervillers' loyalty to one another is manifested in our support for the Husker football team. We define ourselves—especially in relation to others—as *not* fair weather fans. In so doing, we reference Nebraska's historical roots, the university's fight song, and the language of sports fans in general. Nebraska has "really few fair-weather fans," asserts Chris Kelley of Denver. He continues, "No matter if we have a really bad season or a really good season, there's still a sellout crowd at every one of their games, and people watch them all throughout the country."

This commitment, Huskervillers explain, is rarely found among other sports fans. As Rhonda Johns of Aurora, Colorado, claims, "I think what's really unique about Nebraska fans is that we're not those fair weather fans. We've gone through a lot of wins, a lot of hard wins, a lot of losses. But you know we've always been really strong fans."

Huskervillers pointedly compare our loyalty with other sports fans, in fact. Says Pam Hanson, "I could go to probably any college stadium in the country and not see the true blue fans like I do here. I mean we don't have very many fair weather fans." And, as several Husker fans noted, the phrase "fair weather fan" can be easily applied to other teams' fans. Here are a few examples:

> KYLE TONJES OF OMAHA, NEBRASKA: When we lived in the [San Francisco] Bay area the fans were very fickle and many switch allegiances if their team was losing. Also, they were not near as knowledgeable about their team and opponents as a general rule.

> JOHN A. TROIA OF GAITHERSBURG, MARYLAND: I couldn't believe how much pro fans (Washington Redskins) bad mouth their team. You don't get as much of that out of Husker fans.

> TRACEY MUSINSKY OF MARIETTA, GEORGIA: I live in a part of the country that has many college and pro teams—however these fans are only fans when the team is winning. That's not loyalty!

> Pafh@geocities.com (posted on the Husker List Internet discussion board): As a lifelong resident of [Pennsylvania], I have taken many a barb about being a Husker fan. I have defended my team (with facts in hand) like no other fan I've seen. On my first trip to a Nebraska game, I discovered something that separates a Husker fan from a Penn State fan, at least the fans that I've had the pleasure to be around. Nebraska fans tend to stick by their team whether behind or winning. After many visits to Lincoln, I still find this to be true.... Go to a PSU game, and you will find that their beloved Jo Pa [coach Joe Paterno] isn't so beloved the second that an opponent pulls close or God forbid, takes the lead. Jeff Kinney and Johnny Rodgers are the ones that got me hooked on Nebraska, and the Penn State fans are why I despise the Nittany Lions. Win or lose, I'm a Husker fan!

In short, says Ashley Smith, "we are all weather fans. We are always here."

But what are we to do when we disagree with fundamental decisions about the direction of the football team? If we complain and second-guess, are we not loyal? If we loyally support those decisions, are we still loyal to other bedrock beliefs, such as working hard?

This dilemma is reflected in the January 2004 (the month when coach Callahan was hired) HuskerPedia posting of BlueCreek. While lamenting changes in the football program, he also claims, "I should say now that I do support Callahan and whomever he brings in for that is part of loyalty as well. Husker loyalty needs to be extended by all fans through the good and the bad beyond the coaches we love to the program itself."[32]

Being loyal, of course, doesn't mean that we Husker fans wear rose-colored glasses to match our clothing. "Yeah, we will gripe and complain and speak our opinion," notes Pam Hanson. And, on occasion, Husker fans will boo. The odd thing about the booing, though, is how remarkable its appearance is. That is, Husker fans and players will find booing to be an extraordinary exception to the rule. Former Husker player and coach Turner Gill, for instance, recalls a 1981 game against Auburn, in which "as we ran to the locker room [at halftime], Nebraska fans booed us. (It was the first and last time I ever heard booing at Memorial Stadium.)"[33]

The general lack of booing at Memorial Stadium even extends to visiting teams, for Huskervillers try to treat our visiting neighbors with respect.

Being Respectful

Perhaps the best, and most frequently acknowledged, demonstration of Huskerville neighborliness occurs within the walls of Memorial Stadium. There, whether the Huskers win or lose, the home fans—especially those seated in the northwest corner of the stadium above the visiting team's entrance-exit ramp on to the field—will applaud the effort of the visiting team at the game's conclusion.

Being a good neighbor, Huskervillers emphasize in talk and deed, means welcoming, helping, and respecting those who visit your home—even if they are different from you. In short, says a Huskerviller living in Omaha, "We treat the fans from other schools the same as we would want to be treated." Not surprisingly, then, 88 percent of the Husker fans contacted in the phone poll for this project agreed with the statement that "others respect Husker fans."[34]

This "golden rule of neighborliness" is recalled with pride by other Huskervillers as they remember its enactments through the years. Don Taylor of Englewood, Colorado, recalls a Kansas-Nebraska game from the 1960s in which Omaha native Gale Sayers starred for Kansas: "I'll never forget I went to the game when Gale Sayers played for KU and they won and boy did he get a hand as he left, because he had set this record for the longest run from scrimmage and it broke the other record."

Years later, in 1998, Texas running back Ricky Williams had a big day against the Huskers, leading his Longhorn team to a win in Memorial Sta-

**An entrance to Memorial Stadium displays evidence of Huskervillers'
neighborliness (photograph by Gloria Strope).**

dium. Dan Koleski of Louisville, Kentucky, remembers the day: "When
Texas beat Nebraska last year up in Lincoln, they cheered Ricky Williams
off the field. And he even came back and said how impressed he was by that."
Adds Beth Townsend of Colorado Springs, "I think that act was characteristic of the class of Husker fans."

Entire teams are applauded, not just individual players. When Ricky
Williams had his big day in Lincoln, for example, the Texas victory snapped
a 47-game home winning streak. Rather than pout, complain, or holler,
Husker fans applauded the effort of the entire Texas team. Notes Doug Johnson of San Antonio, Texas: "When Texas beat us in Lincoln, there was an
appreciation of the effort by many Nebraska fans." Remembers James
Uphoff, who attended Hastings College during the same time as Tom
Osborne, and then once lived in the same Lincoln cul-de-sac as Osborne,
"I was there when Texas snapped our home win streak of many years in
1998. The fans STILL stood and applauded them as they left after the
game!"

In my first year as a Nebraska college student, 1980, I remember being shocked when a then-not-yet-national-power Florida State came to Lincoln and upset the Huskers. Strat Warden of Elizabethtown, Kentucky, also remembers the game: "I remember way back before Florida State was Florida State, Osborne gave them a chance to come up and play Nebraska and get on the map, and when they upset the Huskers early on, the people in the stadium gave them a standing ovation when they left the field."

The Huskerville neighborliness also made an impression upon the Florida State players and coaches. Recalled Florida State quarterback Rick Stockstill, "That was my first experience of going on the road and being treated well by first-class fans."[35]

His words were echoed by his head coach, Bobby Bowden: "As Bowden jogged off the field he saw something he'd never seen before: thousands of fans standing on their feet, clapping and saluting the victorious opponent. Bowden was so moved he wrote an open letter to the fans in the *Lincoln Journal Star*. 'I have never seen people with more class than I saw at Nebraska,' wrote Bowden. 'The Nebraska fans, players, cheerleaders, band, officials, coaches, etc., gave me living testimony of what college football should be all about.'"[36] And that, according to Huskervillers, is respecting others.

"We respect the efforts of the other team," proclaims Doug Johnson. We "appreciate the effort and talent of all athletes, even when we get beat," adds Beth Townsend. So, when Baylor nearly pulled off an upset of the Huskers in Lincoln, "the Baylor team got a standing ovation as they left the field," observes Doug, "and a few hundred Husker fans stayed around until after the Baylor team came out of the locker room to get on their bus, and cheered them again." Similarly, when the Wake Forest Demon Deacons visited Lincoln in 1970, Wake Forest fan Tom Preston recalls that "it did not go un-noticed in Deaconville that the Deacons received a standing ovation when leaving the field."[37]

Huskerviller Robert Davis, who had been attending Husker games for over 50 years when I visited with him in Lincoln prior to the 1999 homecoming game, connects this practice to Nebraska's agricultural orientation. "I think it is just farm community type living. They are nice with their neighbors.... I think they are more respectful of the other teams, they seem to respect the other teams more.... You have got a lot of places I have been to [where they] don't do that."

No kidding! We Huskervillers note with disdain that fans in other places tend not to practice the golden rule of neighborliness, as they berate other players, other teams, and other fans.

One of my college roommates, Jeff Baier, lived for several years in Denver and noted, "Husker fans appear to realize the difference between being at home watching a game on TV and being there in real life. I have been to games of all four professional sports in Denver. The fans yell at the players as if they are still separated by that glass on the front of their television screens. They seem to feel that because the player is paid millions of dollars to perform, every play should be worthy of a highlight on [ESPN's] *Sports Center*. A good, but unspectacular performance is no longer appreciated. Husker fans appreciate a good performance by the other team."

A Husker fan in the St. Paul, Minnesota, area concurs. He says, "I've been lucky enough to travel to a lot of other big stadiums and I think the biggest difference is that I think we're true fans. I think we're good fans, we're good sports, [but] when I've traveled to other stadiums that they you know wrote stuff on cars, they wouldn't let you get gas. I've been to places where they threw things at you and I've been to a bunch of Nebraska games and I just don't hear those stories."

Neither has Janet Haney of San Francisco. She says, "I have been to a zillion games ... and I've never seen NU fans act rudely or inappropriately toward the other team's fans. That can't be said for other college teams' fans." Or, as Mike Henningsen of Phoenix, Arizona, wryly notes, "I hang around in the stadium after the game just to see the North Stadium give the opposing team a round of applause, whether we win or lose. Boy that doesn't happen in Tempe [home of Arizona State University]!"

Nor does it happen in other places. When Alabama wins a football game, its fans ritualistically sing, "We just beat the hell out of you! Rammer Jammer Yellow Hammer! Give 'em hell Alabama!"[38] In Florida, conversely, Alabama fan Warren St. John reports that two Gainesville, Florida, reporters dressed as Alabama fans to see how their fellow Gator fans would treat them. "The experience [was] so unpleasant and the response so hostile that the reporters abandon[ed] the project midway."[39]

Huskervillers, too, have plenty of stories to share about fans in other places who fail to enact the golden rule of neighborliness. Mark LaMalfa, of the Portland, Oregon, area, points to Colorado fans as one example. "My mother, she is 60-years-old, we went to a game together ... and a group of Colorado fans was swearing at the 60-year-old lady because she was wearing red. It made no sense to me."

Other Husker fans report similar experiences from Colorado. Isabelle Lampshire, age 91, remembers attending a game in Boulder when "three seats in front of me, I saw a Colorado fan pour a can of beer over some Nebraska people, and I thought that was terrible. Another time, we were [driving] along the street and [son] Earl had one of those nice red hats on. We had the window down and a guy reached in and stole his hat."[40]

T.B., a participant on the Husker List discussion group, recalls a similarly horrible experience at a Colorado game:

> I have only been to one game in Boulder, and I was only 11-years-old, and it was my first away game ever. My mom, dad and I went out to Boulder from Lincoln and it turned out to be a terrible trip. We ended up losing, 20–10 and got treated terribly by the fans/people in Boulder. At the game, we consistently got beer thrown on us and my father was spit on. We ended up having to move to another section once we fell behind. After the game, two of my dad's friends (both men aged 35–40 who weren't the aggressive type) got into a fight at the Flakey Jakes there. It was a terrible experience for this 11-year-old kid and I never wanted so badly to go back to Lincoln.[41]

John Wilke, of Greeley, Colorado, notes that this kind of hostility extends beyond the football stadium. "From the time I showed up here [in Colorado]," he says, "I have been taunted when I wear a Nebraska sweatshirt to the supermarket, I've had disparaging comments made about my bumper stickers, etc."

While Colorado fans are often invoked as a measure of comparison, the fans of other Big 12 conference opponents are also sometimes identified as not being neighborly to visiting Nebraska fans.

Darin Ellis notes on the Husker List, "I had the 'privilege' of sitting next to the K-State section Saturday night, and I have to say that the fans I encountered were some of the worst this side of the Colorado border. Rude, cocky, and arrogant, they were some of the biggest jerks that I've seen. My entire section (including numerous young children) had to listen to their smack and view 'foreign relations' hand gestures for most of the first half. I found great satisfaction in seeing them sneak out of the stadium early in the fourth-quarter. No class whatsoever!"

In a response on the Husker List, Christopher Boilesen says, "I would have to agree that K-State fans have no class. I am a member of the UN-L Marching band and when we went down to Manhattan last year we were treated to the chants of 'in-bred red' from the student section. One of our tuba players had a football thrown at his face by some tailgaters and one girl had chewing tobacco spit on her. I am glad that Nebraska fans have much more class than that."[42]

Perhaps this is why the following joke circulated through the Internet a few years back:

> Four alumni were climbing a mountain one day. Each was from a different Big 12 school and each proclaimed to be the most loyal of all fans at their alma

mater. As they climbed higher, they argued as to which one of them was the most loyal of all.

They continued to argue all the way up the mountain, and finally as they reached the top, the Sooner hurled himself off the mountain, shouting, "This is for U of O!" as he fell to his doom. Not wanting to be outdone, the Tiger threw himself off the mountain, proclaiming, "This is for U of M!"

Seeing this, the Husker walked over and shouted, "This is for everyone!" and pushed the K-State Wildcat off the side of the mountain.

Missouri fans have also been identified as being less than neighborly to their Huskerville guests. In 1999, Steve Spitsnogle claimed on the Husker List that "Mizzou fans are the worst. I live in suburban Kansas City, and have first hand experience with this fact. Remember the ending of the last game in Columbia, and one can figure out that the fans here are super-charged to insult Nebraska in any way. Just think about the recent ticket fiasco. What low life tricks will go on on the field is anyone's guess. I've been going to Mizzou games in Columbia since the early '70s, and have met a lot of great folks. But this year they are out for blood, and it will translate to the treatment of visiting Nebraska fans."

And in Texas, a student columnist for the Texas Tech University newspaper noted that when the Huskers played the University of Texas twice in 1999, "wearing Cornhusker paraphernalia was taboo and, in isolated instances, greeted with violence."[43]

Bruce Jensen, a Huskerviller living in Connecticut, reports with disappointment how fans at the University of Connecticut treat visitors to their stadium:

> Every time the opposing team would come on the field, in warm ups and before the game, the entire crowd stood up and started to boo the opponents. The guys that I went to the game with told me that that is just the way it is here. I reminded them that it was a classless act and if they were truly fans of football, they would care more to see a good game than worry about if they were to simply win the game.
>
> After asking if they ever experienced a crowd boo at them they all agreed that they felt bad hearing it and couldn't understand why they were being booed because they were there to play their best and try to win the game too. They quickly sat down and stopped their jeering once they realized that their booing was not very sportsman-like. I also told them that you would never find that kind of atmosphere in Nebraska and you certainly wouldn't find a crowd booing the opposing team no matter who it was.

Summarizes Stew Price of Louisville, Kentucky: "Husker fans are different from other college fans because they pride themselves on displaying good sportsmanship.... Visiting fans have been so impressed by this that they write letters to the papers, etc." In fact, says Cindy Koziol of Blacksburg, Virginia, "there is rarely a week when there isn't an editorial in the paper following a home game from someone on the visitor's side praising Nebraskans for how well treated they were when they were in Lincoln for the game."

Listen, for example, to what these visiting fans have to say:

LT. COL. MIKE CAUDLE (RETIRED), A TEXAS A & M UNIVERSITY FACULTY MEMBER, WROTE IN 1999: Everything I had heard about your fans was true. You really are the class of college football fans. The only other school that I have witnessed that ranks close to you is Penn State. But you are better. Thanks for making our visit to your state and university a pleasurable and memorable one.[44]

STAN COTTEN, WAKE FOREST UNIVERSITY FAN AND ONLINE WRITER: Never in my life, well 26 years of it anyway, have I ventured into enemy territory and been treated anywhere close to as well as I was in Lincoln, Nebraska.[45]

GORDON A. TAYLOR, ASSOCIATE VICE PRESIDENT FOR ALUMNI PROGRAMS, WESTERN ILLINOIS UNIVERSITY: The people of Nebraska are simply extraordinary. From the time I crossed the state line Friday morning until I left Sunday, I was profoundly impressed by the citizens of your state. Gas station attendants, waiters, waitresses, hostesses, police officers, game day personnel of every type, and the staff at the alumni association made my visit one I will never forget.... Heck, your marching band even stopped by our pre-game social and performed a couple of numbers for us.[46]

TIM PRISTER (BLUE & GOLD ILLUSTRATED, A NOTRE DAME SPORTS PUBLICATION): Here's what I witnessed after the game Saturday night. As the Irish players exited the field through a tunnel, every Nebraska fan in that area—and that was everyone since there was only a tiny pocket of Irish fans, and they were on the other side of the stadium—stood and cheered, no honored, the Notre Dame team. That was incredible in itself. But the fans formed a tunnel all the way up to the Notre Dame locker room entrance. I would guess it was 40 yards long. Nebraska fans, lined up on each side, cheered, clapped, slapped the Notre Dame players on the back, tried to make them feel good even though they had just been embarrassed.

I didn't know which Nebraska fan to say it to, so I finally just stopped and said to the nearest red-clad fan: "I've been covering Notre Dame football for 20 years, and I've never seen anything like this. You are the most incredible fans I've ever seen."[47]

NEIL RUDEL (SPORTSWRITER FOR PENNSYLVANIA'S BEAVER COUNTY TIMES & ALLEGHENY TIMES): I have covered college football for the past 25 years, and never have I experienced the kind of atmosphere and sportsmanship created and displayed by the University of Nebraska.... Nebraska fans, hundreds if not thousands of them, packed both sides of the roped-off path to the Nittany Lion locker room underneath the stadium, and every one of them continuously cheered and reached out and patted players on the back, from the very first to the last of the Lions who split the sea of red.... The reception captured the epitome of respect for your opponent.[48]

In short, says Texas Tech University student newspaper columnist Sandeep Rao, "Fans across the nation have something to learn during every Cornhusker home game."[49]

In response to Rao's words, one reader responded online from Tempe, Arizona, "I have never understood why it is that Nebraskans are like that. It seems like they know something that the rest of us don't."[50] Adds Wake Forest fan Stan Cotten, "It seemed as if this [courteousness] was inside of them. And had been. It was their way of life."[51]

It was. And is. The elusive "something" that Huskervillers attempt to enact isn't always easy to see because we often try not to be noticeable.

8

Remaining Down-to-Earth

When fall arrives in southeastern Ohio, I'm accustomed to looking up to take in the colors of the changing leaves.

So I was feeling a bit out of sorts as I headed south on US Highway 77 one early October morning in 1999; my eyes were continually drifting off the road to take in the fall colors that covered the ground.

Yes, the ground.

Unlike the autumnal explosion of maples, oaks, and elms in southeastern Ohio, the colors here south of Lincoln were found closer to the ground. I don't remember grasses changing colors with the season. Maybe fall wasn't like this in the panhandle where I grew up. Maybe, in my youthful oblivion, I just didn't notice these more subtle colors before, what my mom calls "the simple beauty of the countryside."

As I continued my drive south on US 77, I noticed an occasional cluster of cottonwoods jumping out from the grassy sea. In fact, amidst the grasses hugging the earth, you couldn't help *but* notice the cottonwoods standing out. Their leaves were still green and their reach was magnified amidst the low-lying grasses that surrounded them. They stood out.

And standing out in Huskerville is something an individual just doesn't do. "There is definite social pressure not to put on airs," writes Steve Smith in his Husker fan autobiography. "If a resident of a small town drove down Main Street in a brand-new Mercedes, for example, he'd be greeted with scowls of disapproval."[1]

Thus, the contrast between the grasses and the cottonwoods reflects an underlying contrast in Huskerville: individuals should not stand out, but the group as a whole can. Just as we notice, and appreciate, the presence of the cottonwoods—their prevalence in Nebraska has much to do with a law designed to encourage homesteading and tree-planting in the state, the Timber Culture Act[2]—Huskervillers take pride in the stand out presence generated by Husker football *and* our devoted support of the team (more on this idea in the following section). Yet, we also appreciate the more sublime beauty of the different grasses that hug the earth, just as Huskervillers take pride in our recognition that we, as individuals, are down-to-earth.

But, what exactly, does down-to-earth mean?

Dictionaries describe the phrase as an adjective meaning practical or realistic. Thesauruses equate it with being sensible, matter-of-fact, balanced, sober, commonsensical, level-headed, and reasonable.

Huskervillers use words such as straightforward, genuine, well-rounded, honest, trustworthy, fundamental, and plain in association with down-to-earth. Says Eric Baer of Oklahoma City, "There is also probably simplicity. Lots of people that I know, they are not complex, goofy, oh that's not right. But it is more of basic simplicity, nothing fancy, nothing, just straight ahead, kind of."

Shane Bradford offered this definition to Innes Mitchell, a native of Scotland who helped me by interviewing Husker fans in Austin, Texas: "I think Nebraskans are generally down-to-earth people. I think they have strong values. They are conservative ... but I think they are very well-rounded. They come from strong family typically, just good background, well-established people. People you can approach any time, if you come from Scotland or wherever, and have a general conversation with and get a good response."

One of the more interesting definitions comes from Kurt Olsen of Colorado, whose words suggest that being down-to-earth means enacting a quality of life that is not based on material possessions: "A Nebraskan, I would say, is probably someone who's fairly down-to-earth, who likes good things but doesn't let that get in the way of the quality of their life."

As these elliptical definitions suggest, we know down-to-earth better than we can describe it. We do know that rooted people are down-to-earth, and we know that our fellow Huskervillers possess the characteristic. In fact, a 1997 survey by the University of Nebraska–Lincoln's Bureau of Sociological Research discovered that, when asked for "positive thoughts that come to mind when you think about Nebraska," the overwhelming top response was "good people." Husker football was the third most popular response.

I discovered much the same thing when I asked Husker fans to explain "why there is no place like Nebraska." "The people" was the most popular response, followed by "friendly," and "football."[3]

Being down-to-earth is, appropriately, rooted in the history of the state. From the Oto, Omaha, and Pawnee earth lodges to the homesteaders' dugouts and soddies, Nebraska's residents have quite literally made their homes of the earth. As Mari Sandoz explains in her history of Nebraska, *Love Song to the Plains*, some homesteaders built dugouts under banks while others carved blocks of earth and prairie grasses, stacked them on top of one another, and built sod houses. Even early schoolhouses in homesteaded areas were built of sod.[4]

This rooting of home to land and vice versa becomes even more profound when the homes are considered within the vastness that surrounded them. As miniatures within an immense horizon, these early homes—as well as the homes of farmers and ranchers today—seem to be the only thing that keeps people from being swallowed by the immense horizon, or perhaps blown away by a sweeping prairie gale.

Willa Cather's description of the early homesteads in Nebraska in *O Pioneers!* illustrates this relationship between home and land: "The houses on the Divide were small and were usually tucked away in low places; you did not see them until you came directly upon them. Most of them were built of the sod itself, and were only the unescapable ground in another form."[5]

Perhaps this particular type of rootedness is what leads Cindy Lenz to describe Nebraskans as "down-home, earthy people; there's a lot of farming community, their roots are in the earth. They are just down-to-earth, friendly people I think." The connections among earth, home, and the people who make their homes from and of the earth are, of course, manifest in the agricultural heritage of the state, as Cindy points out. Matt Ridder, who describes Nebraskans as "very down-to-earth people," notes, "Both my dad and my grandfather were farmers, and I just really don't know that many other states that are like that."

Being down-to-earth, then, takes on additional meaning in Huskerville; enacting your down-to-earth-ness sinks your roots into some powerful symbolic terrain. Being down-to-earth means being connected to the land in which you grew up, to a history in which homes were built from the land, and to families who made (and continue to make) lives from the land.

As a result, being down-to-earth also provides Huskervillers with the symbolic material to distinguish ourselves from others who are not rooted in the land. As Stew Price of Louisville explains, "While the rest of the country has shifted toward 'moral relativism' (whatever feels good or is effective, do it), the family system in Nebraska remains rooted in belief in God, country, and family. Chock this up to the agrarian nature of its people."

Perhaps the best way to describe down-to-earth Huskervillers is to explain two characteristics that we do not possess: (1) pretense and (2) a "winning is everything" attitude. Often, as Huskervillers describe these characteristics, we point to the person who we believe best exemplifies them: former Husker football coach and U.S. representative Tom Osborne, "the face of our state to the rest of the country."[6]

No Pretense

"Nebraskans seem often to cling to the notion that all people are and should be on a level with each other, that privilege, exceptionalism and elitism are undemocratic traits that solid citizens of the Plains should scorn."[7]

These words, written by University of Nebraska professor Charlyne Berens, might also be labeled "the cottonwood principle" because they highlight the idea that Huskervillers do not embrace those who try to arrogantly stand out above the crowd. Like the felling of a cottonwood, in fact, those who think of themselves as high and mighty are asking to be cut down to size.

Consider, for example, this joke contrasting the down-to-earth Husker student and more prideful students from other Big 12 schools:

> Three students, a student from Missouri, a student from Texas, and a student from Nebraska, are walking together one day. They come across a lantern and out pops a genie. "I will give you each one wish. That's three wishes total," says the genie.
>
> The Missouri student says, "I am a farmer, my dad was a farmer, and my son will also farm. I want a wall built around Missouri so that no one can come in and disrupt our fertile ground." With a blink of the genie's eye, "Poof," and Missouri's fertile grounds were forever sealed off from the rest of the world.
>
> The Texas student was amazed, so he said, "I want a wall around Texas so that nobody from out of state can come into our precious school and none of our Athletic Department can leave. We will forever have a great team." Again, with the blink of the genie's eye, "Poof," there was a huge wall around Texas.
>
> The Nebraska student says, "I'm very curious. Please tell me more about these walls."
>
> The genie explains, "Well, it is about 150 feet high, 50 feet thick and completely surrounds the areas they requested. No one can get in or out."
>
> The Nebraska student says, "Fill 'em with water."[8]

Perhaps Janet Haney of San Francisco had this joke in mind when she noted, "Nebraska is a place where the people are genuine and down-to-earth. Nobody puts on airs (unless they're someone from a competing team!)."

Thus, rather than constantly bragging about the state or the university's football team, we Huskervillers like to think that we simply go about our business, much as the student in the joke concisely and matter-of-factly said, "Fill 'em with water," while the other students trumpeted the virtues of their states.

Nebraskans, observes E. Steve Cassells, are "'just plain folks'—no airs."[9] University of Nebraska–Lincoln student Bart Deterding concurs: "down-to-earth, I'd say. Really if I had to use a small phrase that's what I'd say, down-to-earth, honest, trustworthy, you know. They don't go around and flaunt their stuff."

Before visiting with Bart, I had talked briefly with Chip Hall, then a first-year student from California who had been at the University of Nebraska–Lincoln for about two months. Chip said, "It is different from California and everyone is nice here. Everything is laid back. People here just have a different demeanor about them."

Remaining down-to-earth, then, has long been an integral part of being a resident of Huskerville. Historian Everett Dick notes that the state's early homesteaders would visit with one another without passing judgment about the other person's status: "Neither age, wealth, nor position made the least difference."[10]

The idea that we should not attempt to act superior to our fellow humans is codified in the Nebraska state motto, "Equality Before the Law." This creed was the result of the famous trial of the Ponca chief Standing Bear, and is enacted in the unique non-partisan, one-house legislative assembly known as the Unicameral.

Standing Bear's trial, held in Omaha, resulted in a landmark legal decision that gave citizen status to the members of Native American tribes who originally lived in the land now known as Nebraska.[11] The unicameral legislature—initially proposed in 1914 by homesteader-become-historian Addison E. Sheldon, then tirelessly promoted by maverick Nebraska legislator George Norris until its enactment in 1934[12]—is designed for openness and accountability. Ideally, legislators do not accumulate power over one another or their constituents; political parties do not assert their power over minority parties.

Of course, what's ideal in theory rarely works that way in practice.[13] Football teams are supposed to stand out, to win. Fans are supposed to bellow and scream. How is such behavior down-to-earth?

Well, it's not—if we think about this behavior as individual rather than collective. If the group stands out, however, individuals don't have to clamor for attention; it's a feeling of security that comes from the collective's success. That security, in fact, allows individuals to see one another as equal contributors to the group's success.

In the stands, then, Huskervillers tend to ignore what others might see—in different places and at different times—as status differences. In 1967, for example, *Omaha World-Herald* writers James Denney, Hollis Limprecht, and Howard Silber observed in their book, *Go Big Red: The All-time Story of the Cornhuskers*, that people from all walks of life merge within the confines of Memorial Stadium:

> There are as many different kinds of Cornhusker football fans as there are people in the State of Nebraska. Some were born and raised in Nebraska; some moved into the state recently, and the native who moves away and loses his interest in Husker football is as rare as the newcomer who fails to become a fan.
>
> Their backgrounds are as diverse as the number of seats in the Stadium. A typical knot of season ticket holders, who become fast friends over the years during their autumn meetings, may include a farmer from Stromsburg who leaves his tractor at mid-morning in order to see the kickoff; a businessman from Omaha who motors on down the Interstate; a rancher from Broken Bow who leaves at dawn and returns well after dark; a taxi-driver from Lincoln who parks his hack a few minutes before kickoff and hurries to the stands.
>
> They'll come out in all kinds of weather, and they'll follow their Cornhuskers to Columbia, Mo., or Norman, Okla., or Miami, Fla., in lemming-like hordes.[14]

Nearly 30 years later, the fans at Memorial Stadium were described in remarkably similar terms by Joe Starita and Tom Tidball: "Ranchers from Kimball and Chappell. Stockbrokers from Papillion and Millard. Teachers from Columbus and Clatonia. Farmers from Gothenburg and Indianola. Realtors from Chadron and Alliance. Fans from Bancroft, Valentine, Fairbury, Red Cloud, Anselmo, Bellwood, Broken Bow, Norfolk, Oshkosh, Verdigre, Cozad, Cody, Bassett and Burwell. Families from three-generation, season-ticket holders. Couples who plan all year for six weekends. Retirees who are taking the grandkids."[15]

As we cheer together, partners in the enacting of Huskerville, our differences melt away and our similarities are highlighted as we celebrate the uniqueness of our *group*. Individuals are no longer, say, Dick and Jane Smith from Valentine; they are Huskers.

"The camaraderie of Husker football brings together such an interesting melting pot of humanity," explains Holli Beadell Van Valkenburg. "We're like great friends that can come together once a year or 12 times a year and it feels like yesterday. Surgeons and chefs or teachers and landscapers—we all have this Husker football mania in common and for 3–4 hours nothing else matters."

That's why Husker fans can talk about an array of unique people in the singular, as a collection of people who share the same praiseworthy characteristics. Listen to Beth Townsend, for example: "In the past 10 years, since I joined the Air Force, I've lived all over the world and traveled extensively within the United States. In all my travels, I've never come across people like Nebraskans. I have met some wonderful people, but just not quite the same."

When we meet on the common ground of Huskerville as equals, we anchor ourselves to that ground—and to a way of life.

Thus, Kevin Popp, a Huskerviller who has never lived in Nebraska, can identify the presence of a "what you see is what you get" way of life in both the behavior of other Huskervillers *and* the play of the team (though he offered this insight while Frank Solich was still coaching the Huskers).

"When I think of Nebraska," Kevin says, "the people I've met in this club [Kevin was at a Kentuckiana Huskers watch party when he offered this observation] and everything, hard-working, nothing flashy, straight ahead, very honest, and that's what the offense is. It's a pound at you, pound at you.... It seems like that of everybody that I've met from Nebraska, they're so down-to-earth, they're very honest people, they're for real, they're salt-of-the-earth type. And yeah, it's very similar to their offense."[16]

As if to embody their lack of pretense, the players on the Husker football team adorn themselves in simple red-and-white uniforms that have changed only modestly over the past few decades. The players' helmets, as Stew Price reminded me, "sport a plain-jane, down-to-earth letter 'N' that hasn't changed in eons."

Husker football, as Kevin and Stew note, provides Huskervillers with a way of enacting a down-to-earth attitude. "If you do things the right way, you don't need to tell everybody about it; they will see it for themselves," seems to be the attitude. Said one Huskerviller on the telephone survey completed for this book, the Huskers are "one of the few teams in the country that don't pamper. If you don't make the grade, you don't play. If you do something wrong, you don't play."

Similarly, the fans watching the game—while we enjoy a victory—do not feel compelled to make a big deal out of the result of the game. As Todd Wolverton, a high school principal in Creston, Iowa, explains, "Heck, thousands [of fans] get in their cars and drive home after the game, some as far as Scottsbluff! Game's over, let's go home. Nebraskans are not caught up in pomp or glitz in anything, which I think best explains this attitude."

For Huskervillers, then, the second primary means of being down-to-earth is to remember that—contrary to legendary professional football coach Vince Lombardi's famous dictum—winning really isn't everything. Instead, the game is, well, just a game.

Just a Game

Carved on the outside of the University of Nebraska's Memorial Stadium are a number of short sayings designed to inspire those who enter its gates. One of those sayings, above all, succeeds in inspiring fans, players, and coaches: "Not the victory but the action; Not the goal but the game; In the deed the glory." This dictum is embraced so deeply in Huskerville that it also was added above the west entrance to the stadium.

Written by Syracuse, Nebraska, native and former University of Nebraska philosophy professor Hartley Burr Alexander,[17] these revered words embody a fundamental part of the moral code of Huskerville: doing things the right way is more important than the result.

The words of Hartley Burr Alexander remind Huskervillers of the community creed as they enter Memorial Stadium (photograph by Gloria Strope).

That's why Husker fans will applaud the opposing team, no matter what the outcome of the game. That's why other teams' fans and sportswriters will feel compelled to write glowing praise about Husker fans, such as this account of Husker fans at the 1998 Holiday Bowl from a San Diego reporter named J. Harry Jones:

> Never have I had a better time than Wednesday before the Holiday Bowl. Most of the ingredients were the same: Italian sausages on the grill, a bit of beer (perhaps more than a bit), a packed parking lot. But there was one thing different on the north side of the stadium in section B-2, one thing that made Wednesday's tailgate party the best ever.
>
> Nebraska. Nebraskans. It was the nicest group of people I've ever been around. It was a completely enjoyable experience in every way....
>
> [They] were smiling all the time. Smiling in a sort of contented way that I'm not used to seeing.
>
> Even after the game was over, after Nebraska had lost by three, their fans were in a good mood.[18]

Antone Oseka of North Platte, Nebraska, points out the uniqueness of this approach to college football. "It's rare," he says, "to enter a stadium where the game is more important than the outcome."

While recent seasons have tested this faith, Huskervillers who are disgruntled with the direction of the football program express our frustration more with the *way* in which things are done; following the wrong path leads to failure rather than success.

At the end of a lengthy and elegant post on the HuskerPedia Web site, a Huskerviller using the name BlueCreek summarized his concerns with the direction of the Nebraska football program in words similar to Hartley Burr Alexander's: "My father taught me one of life's most valuable lessons: the path you choose to victory is infinitely more important than winning itself."[19] Accordingly, as Steve Glenn told me in our phone conversation, winning will not necessarily ease the discomfort generated by the uprooting of traditions.

A few years before my conversation with Steve, Huskerviller Matt Johns of Aurora, Colorado, emphasized that doing things the right way is of vital importance in Huskerville. When he moved from Seattle to go to college in Nebraska, Matt said, he learned that Nebraskans are "hard workers that try and reach their goals and they don't really, I mean they pay close attention to how they're achieving those goals and it's not kind of a win at all costs.... It's not so much the final outcome, it's how you get to that point."

Thus, Husker football players display, as Ryan Gray of Boulder, Colorado, notes, "a sense of humility WITH victory. This is important as well.

We Nebraskans have always taken victory with a sense of humility and a sense of pride." In addition, as we saw in the Working Hard chapter, Huskervillers seem to take as much pride in the accomplishments of the football players *as students and people* as what they do on the field.

Listen to Loren Wagner, for example, talk about how the Husker players and coaches do things the right way:

> No one has more Academic All-Americans than the University of Nebraska. No university does a better job of making sure that their athletes put their education first.
>
> No one has ever had the amount of success that NU has had and never had a serious NCAA violation. They do it over and over every year and they accomplish tremendous things that people outside of the state claim can not be done without breaking NCAA rules. Yet when the NCAA investigates they find absolutely nothing. They do it and they do it the right way.

When football is just a game, as these Huskervillers emphasize, the lessons learned by fans and players are more important than the outcome of the game. Not every game can be won, and not every season can result in a national championship. Not every relationship works, and not every harvest is bountiful. Even when we work our hardest, we may not experience success. Explains Doug Bottger of the Seattle area, "I think in Nebraska we can accept losing. We don't like it, but it happens." Echoes Pat Ferguson of Lakeland, Minnesota, "Despite what anyone else in the country thinks, we know that a loss is not the end of the world."

Losing happens. In football. In life. So, notes Huskerviller Paul Davie, the football players "have instilled it upon them that you are out there playing a game and that is it. You know the game is part of your life but it is not all of your life." Perhaps the best representative of this ethos is former Husker head coach Tom Osborne, whose 1985 autobiography is entitled, appropriately, *More Than Winning*.[20]

Tom Osborne: Epitome of Down-to-Earth

On January 16, 2004, a Minnesota-based member of the HuskerPedia Web site discussion group going by the name of Calla observed in the wake of Frank Solich's firing, "It is not just the number of wins and losses that matter here in Nebraska. And that is why we fired a coach with a 9–3 record. It is about the process. That is what TO [Tom Osborne] taught us. If you do the right things, the right way, for the right reasons, the outcome takes care of itself."

Two young Huskervillers look up to a statue of the down-to-earth Tom Osborne guiding the late Husker quarterback Brook Berringer (photograph by Gloria Strope).

When the outcome takes care of itself, you don't need to get carried away with the results, because you have more games or days or harvests ahead of you. Tom Osborne epitomizes this belief in Huskerville.

"I couldn't venture at who might be more 'Nebraskan' than Tom Osborne," my college roommate Jon Johnston noted on the Husker List discussion group. Adds Loren Wagner, a teacher and football coach in Culbertson, Nebraska, "He epitomized the average Nebraskan.... Much like the Nebraska farmer ... Dr. Tom was willing to put in 16-hour days to win big and do it legally without compromising his ethics and sense of morality."[21]

In fact, as I look up on my office wall to a framed newspaper insert with a photograph of Osborne being carried off the field by his players following the winning of his first national championship, I am struck by two things. First, Osborne is looking down, not up—as if he is uncomfortable being elevated by his players and thus disconnected from the earth. Second, he is not waving or acknowledging the cheers that must have been cascading down upon him; he is, if anything, looking like he wants to be out of the spotlight, almost as if he is trying to slide off the shoulders of the players carrying him.

Ten years prior to that photograph, Osborne had written, "It must be discouraging at times for the assistant coaches to read or hear of the things that 'I' have accomplished in terms of won-lost records, championships, and honors. In reality, all of us know that it truly is 'we' who have done those things."[22] Osborne's acknowledgement of the hard work of his neighbors embraces much of what Huskervillers have praised in the preceding two chapters.

That Huskervillers see Osborne as an embodiment of our down-to-earth attitude is evident in many ways.[23] First, his players over the years have remarked upon his enactment of this attitude. "My first impression of him," says Bobby Newcombe, "was that he was very down-to-earth."[24] Confirms Ahman Green, "He told me everything straight up and was real honest with me. Out of all the college coaches who recruited me, he was the most down-to-earth coach."[25]

Even when the Huskers lost to Miami in the heartbreaking 1984 Orange Bowl, the game where Osborne elected to try to win the game outright with a two-point conversion rather than kick an extra point to ensure a back-door national championship, defensive player Mike McCashland noted that—following the incomplete pass for the two-point conversion attempt—"His expression didn't change—none whatsoever.... He had the same attitude going into every situation. If you play the best you can play, that's all he ever asked for."[26]

Second, Osborne's popularity is evident in the tremendous support he has received in his campaigns for public office. In his first campaign for the U.S. House of Representatives, Osborne received 82 percent of the vote. Two years later, in 2002, no Democrat would run against him and he earned 93 percent of the vote against a Libertarian candidate. In 2004, facing Democratic and Libertarian opposition, he still garnered 87 percent of the vote.

Although he lost the 2006 Republican gubernatorial primary to the incumbent,[27] Osborne embodied the words on Memorial Stadium in his concession: what's important, he said, "is not the final score, the final result. It's how you go about it."[28] No wonder that sportswriter Tom Shatel's postmortem on the campaign concluded, "He will always be our football legend, our John Wayne and Jimmy Stewart, our No. 1 citizen, the guy we would most want to send to the podium when he world asks, 'Who represents Nebraska?'"[29]

Finally, Husker fans share stories about our encounters with the down-to-earth Osborne, who is known both by the guy-next-door nickname of "TO" and the respectful "Dr. Tom."[30]

My own story is relatively short and simple, but telling. I was in graduate school, running laps on the short dirt track in the bowels of Memorial Stadium. Osborne was finishing up his running as well. Notably, he was not working out in the Athletic Department facilities or at some fancy sports club. I was a bit abashed as he walked by and was torn by my instinct to be friendly and my desire to respect his privacy. I half looked up and was greeted with a simple "hi" from the down-to-earth guy. In retrospect, and after hearing the stories of others, I guess I shouldn't have been quite so surprised.

Listen to Jack Kovacs, for example, in an e-mail message he sent me about meeting Osborne:

> I obtained tickets for a Chamber of Commerce luncheon at which he was the speaker. Frustratingly, I tried to position myself "near" him while he was talking to others, so that my son could take a picture of me near him. It didn't work.
>
> After lunch and his talk, he was walking to the back of the large room to sit at the table to autograph his books. Remembering [what] others who had mentioned meeting him on campus and talking to him had said about his being so cordial, I made a decision which goes against my "grain." I walked up to him and asked if I could have my picture taken with him. He responded that "they" wanted him to get back to the table, then he said "Oh heck, come on." We stood off to the side and he put his arm around me and.... well, the attached photo is the result. (That's why I have that silly grin on my face).[31]

Another fan, Joe Winkler, remembers this Osborne anecdote: "I also remember when we were playing Oklahoma State one year, the coach had hyped the game up to the highest level (it was there) and was saying things such as, 'They are going to have to keep the women and children off the streets,' and TO just kept to the basics, said that it was an important game, but just a game, and that all games are important, but they are just football games, not wars or once in a lifetime opportunities, but just games."[32]

Summarizes Barbara Gottschalk: "For the past 25 years, I've thought the football team strongly reflected the character of Coach Osborne, and Nebraskans view him the way they'd like to view themselves—honest, hard-working, fair, decent, etc."

So, what happens when we do *not* see a relationship between the head coach, the team, and ourselves? What happens when the coach stands out from the crowd by calling opponents' fans "f****** hillbillies" or by appearing to make a throat-slash gesture to a referee during a game?[33] If the team doesn't meet our expectations, and we do not see a team commitment to the bedrock beliefs of Huskerville, how do we make sense of "in the deed, the glory"? Do we remain down-to-earth or do we jump up to shout, "This isn't right!" If we do jump up to shout, are we failing to adhere to our own beliefs?

As these questions suggest, I don't mean to suggest that being down-to-earth is the same thing as being without pride. Certainly, we individually take pride *in being* down-to-earth. We also take pride in the collective accomplishments of our team and of those, like Tom Osborne, who embody what we value. As I've tried to emphasize, we have no problems with collectively standing out; in fact, the next section examines the many ways in which we are proud that Huskerville receives attention—and how each of those ways says something in particular about how we experience life in Huskerville.

III

Cornhusking

9

Cornhusking:
Productive Parties

Every spring, just about the time Nebraska's farmers prepare for planting and its football team prepares for spring practice, the state is invaded by roughly half a million uninvited—but welcomed—guests.

They arrive in droves for their ritual gathering. They begin their journey in the southwestern United States, usually traveling in groups, and typically take the entire day to make the trip. Once they reach Nebraska, they settle in at the same place they do every year. When settled, they begin to make friends, dance, and eat—often corn products. When something exciting happens, large numbers of them will jump up into the air while others will shout out. They are "large, loud, and fun to watch," notes one longtime observer.[1]

The sandhill cranes who stop to visit the banks of Nebraska's Platte River for a few weeks each spring as they migrate northward are not unlike a gathering of Husker football fans who have congregated to watch a Nebraska football game. This "largest group of cranes in the world"[2] clusters in groups of 10,000–15,000 in roosting spots along a 60-mile stretch of the Platte in central Nebraska. "The sunrise and sunset flights of tens of thousands of cranes," writes Nebraska biologist Paul Johnsgard, "provide a sight that overwhelms the senses, the din of the birds almost making one dizzy."[3] Adds reporter Laura Bly, "Their horn-like voices, when raised raised in unison ... sound like the aftermath of a home team touchdown at a Cornhuskers football game."[4] With a bit of imagination, then, the red crowns of the cranes might well suggest a group of Husker fans wearing red hats.

The pilgrimage of the sandhill cranes to the Platte River in central Nebraska is reminiscent of the pilgrimages of Husker fans traveling to support the Nebraska football team.

In 1988, *New York Times* reporter Malcolm Moran, sounding a bit like
an ornithologist observing humans, described the migration of four travelers heading toward Memorial Stadium:

> Right about 2 o'clock in the morning on those special Saturdays, when
> the automobile turns southeast onto State Highway 92, Harold and Polly Gen-
> try and Darrel and De Willet, two retired couples who live in nearby Gering,
> begin another autumn adventure.
>
> For miles and miles, theirs is almost always the only car on the two-lane
> highway through the middle of the night. They watch out for deer as they pass
> ranches and leave the darkened sand hills in the Nebraska panhandle.
>
> They turn south onto 385 at Bridgeport, and finally reach Interstate 80 at
> Sidney. An hour disappears as the car passes from mountain to central time,
> and soon, about a half-hour before their 8 A.M. breakfast stop in Kearney, a
> large orange sun appears on the horizon to signal the start of football Saturday.
> By then they have joined the others on the interstate, almost all in red, as they
> point east toward Lincoln, the state capital and emotional focal point.[5]

Eight years later, Joe Starita and Tom Tidball offered this version of
the ritual pilgrimages to Lincoln:

> Some will come from Kansas and Colorado. Others from Iowa, Missouri
> and Wyoming. From California, New Mexico, Arizona and the Dakotas. But,
> mostly, they will come from Nebraska. Laden with sandwiches and soda, kids
> and pets, pennants, flags and banners, portable grills and portable radios, blan-
> kets, coolers, a thermos of coffee and tickets, they will pile into station wagons,
> sedans, campers, trucks, pickups, buses, jeeps, four-wheel drives and RVs,
> flowing from all corners of the state, tributaries of red meandering across the
> fall countryside, past downtown office buildings and suburban shopping malls,
> past fields of corn and wheat, past feed lots and the Pony Express route, cutting
> through the heart of old buffalo country, coming down through the shortgrass
> prairie, heading for the huge concrete shell embedded on the western bank of
> the University of Nebraska campus.
>
> They will all come to Memorial Stadium, like they always have, filling
> every seat for every home game in every autumn for more than a generation.[6]

This sense of tradition, a feeling of "this is the way it has always been,"
permeates the migrations of both the cranes and Husker fans.

When writer Paul Gruchow speaks of the cranes' congregation as a
reminder of "the way in which a community endures and accumulates a history despite the frailties of the creatures who inhabit it,"[7] I think of how
generations of individual Huskervillers have continued to gather in ways
which make us believe that we have always all stuck together in all kinds of
weather. In fact, sandhill cranes, like Husker fans, are exceptionally loyal
creatures; unlike many other animals, their mates become lifelong partners.[8]

Both of these traditional rituals—the migration of cranes and the migration of Husker fans—share much in common with another kind of traditional gathering: the cornhusking. At the conclusion of each fall harvest, those farmers who grew corn invited their neighbors over for a gathering that was a something of a communal work party. While they helped husk their neighbor's corn, the neighbors would share in food, drink, song, dance, and games.[9]

I have to admit that I don't recall hearing much of anything about these get-togethers when I was growing up, but I happened to stumble across the word in my home dictionary a couple of years back when I was looking up another word. The entry reads: "a social gathering for husking corn, usu. followed by refreshments, dancing, etc.: also called *husking bee*."[10]

One of the reasons I hadn't heard much about cornhuskings is that, ironically, they were apparently not all that common in a state now officially known at "The Cornhusker State."[11] Mari Sandoz's *Old Jules* refers to "husking bees" within a list of other social gatherings held among the northwest Nebraska homesteaders.[12] University of Nebraska professor Mamie J. Meredith, writing in 1938, found other evidence that cornhuskings were held in other parts of the state. She quotes one Nebraskan's memories as they were reported in an October 13, 1875, *Nebraska Journal* newspaper article: "Oh those old husking bees in the wide roadways of the old red barn on the hillside! How memory goes back to them and the years of time are rolled backward, and the heart warms again with the fire of youth."[13] In addition, writes Meredith, many different kinds of bees were held throughout Nebraska; each kind, she notes, was "an important part of the social life."[14]

Meredith's statement points to the fact that these gatherings, when held in Nebraska or elsewhere, combined both work and play. In fact, historian Bruce Daniels refers to such a gathering as "the productive party."[15] Nebraska historian Everett Dick explains what happened at these productive parties: "The neighbors went to a home, sat in the barn, husked the corn, and shelled it by rubbing a cob on the ear. After two or three hours of this activity, the group went to the house for a good supper. Men, women, and young people, then played all sorts of games."[16]

So, the more I learned about cornhuskings the more I was struck by the appropriateness of the nickname Cornhuskers. Cornhuskings—whether communal productive parties or contemporary contests—seem to connect the state's agricultural heritage with football, and provide a means both for coming together and showing others what you're made of.

I think "playful work" or "productive party" is a good way to describe both the activities of those early cornhuskers and today's Huskervillers.

Husking corn was tedious and time-consuming work, so cornhuskings were used both to get the work done more quickly and to have a good time doing it. Being a sports fan is also a kind of playful work.[17] Fans play while watching others play, yet their playful performances—as we have seen in prior chapters—are vitally important efforts regarding their collective identity. Observes communication scholar Donal Carbaugh, "Fans gather, then, as fans, not only to celebrate their favored team, and not only for some degree of release through competition and intense social activity, but moreover for some degree of communal integration through the celebration."[18]

Nonetheless, many people tend to dismiss the seriousness of fan play. They define fan performances as excessive, perhaps even juvenile, and most definitely unimportant in light of more serious issues. Perhaps this is why, from the Puritans onward, we have valued the productive party as an appropriate means of integrating work and play. In many ways, these productive parties are cultural rituals, or repeated activities in which the participants affirm what the group stands for.[19] "Rituals," notes respected theology professor Tom Driver, "are a kind of playful work."[20]

Cultural rituals not only do the serious work of playfully affirming a group's values, they do so in a way that "transports the participants to another world."[21] The other world of Huskerville is, in fact, created through the actions of those of us who "live" there. "Human beings are not placed," observes ritual scholar Jonathan Smith, "they bring place into being."[22]

These places, as I've noted earlier, are treated as real by those of us who take up residence there. That we continue to treat them as real long after the football game is over is due to the exceptional experience of the productive party. "The feeling of being 'apart together' in an exceptional situation," play scholar Johan Huizinga explains, "of sharing something important, of mutually withdrawing from the rest of the world and rejecting the usual norms, *retains its magic beyond the duration of the individual game*."[23]

Sociologists Mary Jo Deegan and Michael Stein identified the ritualistic nature of Husker football back in 1978 when they published an article in the *International Review of Sport Sociology* entitled, "American Drama and Ritual: Nebraska Football." As the title of their article suggests, though, their focus is on game day as "a major ritual event enacting *American* values and themes,"[24] rather than on the uniquely Nebraskan characteristics of Husker football rituals.[25]

As I hope the preceding chapters have illustrated, engaging in the serious play of being a Husker fan is rooted in Nebraska's history, social relations, and the ways in which the football team approaches its own serious play. The rituals surrounding Husker football provide Huskervillers with sufficient symbolic material to carry forward the historical and social dimensions of our collective identity.[26] Or, in other words, enacting the principles of hard work, being neighborly, and remaining down-to-earth as a Husker fan reinforces their enactment in everyday living.

Are the rituals of Husker fans *necessary* to the enactment of these ideals in everyday life? Perhaps not.

But I think, for those of us who live in Huskerville, engaging in these ritual experiences energizes and reaffirms our commitment to these ideals— and perpetuates the very idea of Huskerville. This happens in three ways: (1) our Husker rituals move us from a mundane, isolated place into a transcendent, collective place; (2) they position that place in relation to other places through comparative performances; and, (3) the rituals provide a sense of order, or give shape, to that place.[27]

This is a story of Cornhusking. Here, people from different walks of life, in different places around the world, gather in a transcendent place called Huskerville. This place puts Nebraska on the map while also providing us with a small, secure world where everyone seems like family. We know that there is no place like Nebraska, we want others to know that, too, and we're confident that our neighbors in Huskerville believe the same thing.

10

The Spirit of Huskerville: "There is No Place Like Nebraska"

A number of years ago, my wife, Christie, our daughters, and I were seated inside a Mexican restaurant called Don Pablo's. Going to Don Pablo's was a bit risky. Although I had converted Christie to the joys of the Mexican food that I grew up with in Scottsbluff, the girls were a harder sell. Chelsea, then six, would eat her fill of chips and mild salsa, but then 13-year-old Brittany had her heart set on an Italian feast at her favorite "eat out" place: Olive Garden. Moreover, she had resisted any forays into Mexican restaurants not named Taco Bell. To our surprise—and hers—Britti loved Don Pablo's.

Almost as a big a surprise to me was the big screen TV facing me ... the Nebraska-Missouri game was on. Shamelessly, I kept one-and-a-half eyes on the football game; I was slipping into Huskerville.

Fortunately, for the sake of family harmony, a nefarious non–Husker employee of Don Pablo's switched the television shortly before our food arrived. After I apologized for getting sucked into the game, Christie assured me that they all found my little trip to Huskerville amusing. In fact, Christie told me, Britti had offered one of her patented, yet good-natured, eye rolls to Christie at one point.

I, being "in" Nebraska, had not noticed.

I was the only person around vaguely interested in the game, yet that didn't stop me from leaving the physical environment around me to join my friends in Huskerville. This experience was significantly different than the last time I had watched a Husker game in a public setting. I was in McGee's in Chicago, surrounded by 22 televisions and about 200 other red-clad Husker fans. I was yelling, moaning, and shouting. I was exchanging high fives with fellow Husker fans Tim Borchers and Ron Whitt after big plays, enthusiastically "waving the wheat" following Husker touchdowns, and bellowing "Go Big Red" with the multitudes each time the McGee's staff finished playing the Nebraska fight song.

How, exactly, could I be "in" Nebraska—oblivious to what was occurring around me—while physically located hundreds of miles away? The answer is what ritual scholars call "leaping" or "separation."[1] Rituals, even (or perhaps especially) those involving college football, are transportation devices that move us from the ordinary and mundane to the transcendent and special.[2]

Communication scholar H.L. Goodall, who earned his doctorate at the football powerhouse of Penn State and taught for a few years at Clemson, observes, "football ... can be played, watched, and understood as a simple game of balls, bodies, and contexts; or it can be played, watched, and understood as an opportunity for a deeply mystical enterprise, a chance to align, to coordinate, to harmonize, to dignify, and to experience transcendence."[3]

What Goodall is talking about, and what every devoted sports fan has experienced, is a phenomenon that anthropologist Victor Turner calls "communitas." Communitas, as its etymology suggests, refers to the experience of being in a community—but not just any community. No, communitas is a special, ineffable feeling of community, an experience in which you feel communal bonds with others, not mere shared affiliations. This is an involvement so intense that you lose track of what is occurring around you (such as daughters rolling their eyes). Communitas, says Turner, "is almost always thought of or portrayed by actors as a timeless condition, an eternal now, as 'a moment in and out of time,' or as a state to which the structural view of time is not applicable."[4]

Husker fans know communitas. The intensity, the devotion, the notions of Huskerville being "in the blood" and "always home"—all of this points to the existence of communitas. Husker football is Nebraska's version of a giant, ongoing cornhusking. So, when Huskervillers converge, we recognize that we are in a unique place—one that transcends the ordinary and provides an electrifying experience unlike what any other place affords.

"Nothing in the world can compare to the sights and sounds of a Saturday game day in Lincoln, Nebraska," writes Jack McHenry of New York. Adds Elizabeth Cooley of Washington, D.C., "I was on faculty at Washington University, University of Virginia, Iowa State University, and went to grad school at University of Michigan. None compare."

Truly, Huskervillers believe, "there is no place like Nebraska." Explains one Husker fan from the suburbs of Kansas City:

> I think that there truly is no where else in the college ranks or even more precisely college football ranks like Nebraska. The fans, the tradition, the players, the intensity, the fervor on game day. I've been to many other universities and colleges around the nation and that "feel" just isn't there. When I moved to the greater KC area everyone told me that going to a Chiefs game and being in the stadium was electric and one of the most exciting things ever. While it was exciting I was a bit let down and all I could think about was the electricity and excitement in the air on a Nebraska Football Game day. I have found nothing to compare to it or rival it.

I have tried to explain this belief to my wife, as I noted before, but darned if I could explain what made Husker football unique. The numbers I've quoted throughout the book—the sellout streak, the third largest city in the state thing, the number of watch parties, etc.—tell part of the story, but not all of it.

Huskerville simply feels different to us. The feel is something that almost defies description. Matt Hinkle of Wichita, Kansas, explains, "It's more something you 'feel' than can be explained with words."

That's what Huskerviller Norm Smith realized as he talked to a Miami fan at the Orange Bowl one year: "[The Miami fan] said he couldn't begin to understand Nebraska fans. He said Miami fans would go to the Orange Bowl to see their team, but that's about it. He saw the thousands of us in the stands and he just shook his head. I guess it's kind of hard to explain to outsiders. They don't really understand."[5]

Maybe our difficulty in explaining this feeling is why Dietrich Dirks and Harry Pecha offered the ambitious yet ambiguous claim that "there is no place like Nebraska" when they penned the song of the same name. The experience of communitas, after all, is hard to put into words. As New Jersey resident Annette Frain points out, she simply tells people, "Because there is no place like Nebraska, and for some reason that is the only way I can explain it."[6]

As I noted in the introduction to this book, I also have had trouble answering the question. So, as I communicated with other Huskervillers, I asked them what they would tell someone if asked, "*Why* is there no place like Nebraska?"

As a whole, their answers have helped me sort through my initial inability to answer the question. They have also given me reassurance that the question is not an easy one to answer. Scott Campbell points out, "Even though we all share this, it is entirely subjective and indescribable in discursive terms."

Scott's words are echoed by John Craig of Denver, who also importantly emphasizes that the *experience* of Huskerville is absorbed in ways that defy description. He says, "I always politely change the subject whenever it becomes necessary to explain what a 'Nebraskan' is, because I learned many years ago that there are no words that adequately convey what it is to be one. It's something that can't adequately be verbally described, only experienced."

Lee Moe of Washington, DC, concurs. "You would have to live in Nebraska to understand," he explains. "It is hard to put in words."

"That is hard to explain," agrees Jill Hayhurst of Topeka, Kansas. "I have heard, 'you do not live in Nebraska anymore,' many, many times. I think it is about culture and family. It is a sense of belonging and support. This is difficult to answer; explaining why you are a devoted fan is hard. A person must experience Memorial Stadium to even come close to understanding."[7]

Perhaps, then, strange as this might sound to some, what happens in Huskerville is a type of spiritual experience akin to the idea of reciprocal appropriation mentioned in the Rooting section. When you enter Huskerville, in other words, it enters you. When you experience the ineffable, it becomes part of you. The experience is so profound that it etches itself upon your soul.

"The spirit they [the players] exhibit is transmitted to the entire state, absorbed and becomes part of us," explains Ann-Marie Duffy, who still calls Huskerville home while living in Ireland. Adds Dick Beverage of California, "I'm still proud of my state and my team, even though I haven't lived in Nebraska for 45 years. They have a hold on me that defies reason and explanation."[8]

Maybe I'm waxing a bit poetic here, but cultural rituals have that kind of effect. If they really are meaningful, if they're anything other than formulaic, they have to transcend the here and now and leave you with something extra, something special, something so intoxicatingly powerful that it never leaves you. Mike Johnson of Atlanta concurs, "This excitement is so gratifying and intense that it stays with you forever."

You also want to share it with others. I am convinced, for instance, that if my wife and daughters were to join me for a Husker home game, they would better understand why I felt compelled to write a book about being a fan of a football team. Part of the problem, I suppose, is that "being a fan of a football team" is a mundane phrase that does not begin to capture the experience of being in Huskerville.

Tom O'Grady of Goshen, Kentucky, feels my pain.

> I've lived a lot of places ... [and] I routinely try to get people to try to go back for a game or something, to watch the games. And you know I just tell them, I said, you know, it's one of those experiences when the team comes out of the tunnel, and you hear the roar of the crowd get started, it gives you goosebumps. You know and I said I still get goosebumps. You know even when I say it, it gives me goosebumps. And like now. It's just that electricity. There is no place that's quite like Nebraska all in its own.

Not so secretly, then, Huskervillers like Tom and I believe that once people visit our home, they will want to stay.

Huskerviller Jack McHenry, who now lives in New York City, went to college at the University of Michigan, home of the largest college football stadium in the country. Yet, he says, the atmospheres in Lincoln and Ann Arbor cannot be compared. So, he says, "I make it a mission of mine to take one of my undergraduate friends from Michigan back to Lincoln for a game each year."

Jack's mission reflects what Mike Eaton of Arlington, Virginia, believes: "Husker pride, if displayed properly, is also infectious to those around us."

Other Huskervillers offer testimony in support of this belief. Keith Petrie of Des Moines, Iowa, for example, says, "You'll never understand until or unless you experienced it. When I've told friends this and some have moved to Nebraska, when I see them again, they say I was right!"

John Wilke of Greeley, Colorado, claims, "I'd say if I have to explain it to you, that you haven't experienced it. Once you experience it, I won't have to explain it to you." He goes on to tell a story about people he has worked with becoming Huskervillers. These people, mind you, never lived in Nebraska. John explains, "My boss is a native of Illinois. He went to a game in Lincoln, and he immediately adopted the team. He's perhaps a bigger fan than me. I have a co-worker from Iowa, same thing."

John's colleagues illustrate the wisdom shared with me, respectively, by an anonymous respondent to the telephone survey and by a HuskerPedia member using the name Calla: "Husker fans aren't necessarily born in Nebraska" because "being a Nebraskan is something in your heart, in your soul. It is not about where you were born."[9] In other words, no matter what your beliefs about sports, football, or Nebraska, you can convert to being a Husker fan.

I ran into such converts in many places. Some had family ties, such as one of the Huskers for Ohio founders, Chris Eaton, a native of Kentucky who married a Nebraskan. "His wife's Nebraska fanaticism converted him to a Cornhusker almost immediately."[10] Marty and Barb Martinson's Arlington, Virginia-based son-in-law "had never been to a Nebraska game [and] was not a Nebraska fan until three years ago." As Barb and Marty explain in tandem:

BARB: "He became an instant fan."

MARTY: "They flew in here, went for a game, they bought out the bookstore."

BARB: "But you know he wasn't even much of a really big football fan. I guess he liked football. He said that he had never had an experience like being in the Nebraska stadium."

Other converts visit Huskerville with friends, then decide to take up residence, such as Matt Ridder's watch party friends in the Denver area (one is from Illinois, one from Colorado, and one from Texas; "I'm the only one actually from Nebraska," Matt says).

Some, like Monty Seidler of the Washington, DC, area, simply stumble into Huskerville, become smitten, and then proclaim, like Monty, "I'm a born-again Nebraskan."

Once they're in, these converts become as steadfast in their loyalty as any born-in Nebraska Huskerviller.

Rocky White, for example, came to Lincoln to attend the university, then moved out of Nebraska after he was finished with school. "I was never a member of the state," he says, "I was just a, I mean, I didn't become a resident, all I did was to go to school here and leave, but you know, I am a Nebraskan at heart." Notably, Rocky, now living in Reno, shared this with me in front of the Nebraska bookstore in Lincoln as he returned for the 1999 homecoming game. His children, too, attended the University of Nebraska.

No doubt other fans and other teams and other places have their share of converts, too. And, I suspect, they also might have a difficult time explaining their devotion. I think that's because the experience of being with others in places like Huskerville is more than simply being with them. This type of being with—as Victor Turner asserted in his discussion of communitas—is more like communion, a mutual sharing, a type of spiritual fellowship.

Not surprisingly, as my language about ineffable experiences, congregating, and converts has not-so-subtly hinted, the ambiguous—and thus useful—notion of "spirit" is often invoked to explain the feeling that is in Huskerville.[11] But spirit, in a more secular sense, is also the foundation of sports. In his immensely enjoyable book *The Joy of Sports: End Zones, Bases, Baskets, Balls, and the Consecration of the American Spirit,* Michael Novak argues that sports "are pledges of our ultimate liberty of spirit."[12] To succeed in sports, we must unleash that ineffable source of energy known as our spirit, knowing that "other elements being equal, the more spirited team will win."[13]

As fans, we do all we can to help our teams win. We don't just watch; we participate. We scream, holler, and bellow without a whit of self-consciousness, desperately seeking to infuse our team with some of our spirit. And, in the process, we leave the here-and-now to find ourselves in a different place. Rooting is an exercising of the spirit. Being a fan, writes inspirational author Bob Welch, "connects you to something bigger than yourself."[14] Huskerviller Gary McGirr agrees. "There is a force of energy that binds us all together; a spirit of oneness," he says.

Because the spirit of Huskerville is absorbed by its residents, that spirit energizes our lives in ways that reach beyond football. Being a football fan is fused with how we live our daily lives. "The Huskers are an indelible part of the state's spirit," notes Jim Burkhard of Cambridge, Massachusetts. "The team is not flashy, but consistent, stable, and very hard working—just like the state."

Mike Eaton of Arlington, Virginia, illustrates this idea when he says, "Nebraska is my life. I was born there and graduated from UNL in 1983. I am a career officer in the world's greatest Navy and my connection to Nebraska has been a constant in my life in my travels throughout the world to include service in the Persian Gulf and living in Japan. The Go Big Red–Husker spirit is a unique characteristic that is refined over a number of years—including years away from the state, but the spirit of Nebraska always travels with me."

Philadelphia residents Bill and Barbara Lombardo concur. As part of a longer tribute to Nebraska on their Web site, they write: "Although we left that wonderful place called NEBRASKA in 1972 (yes, right after the 1970 and 1971 NATIONAL CHAMPIONSHIPS, we've NEVER lost that Nebraska Spirit.... THEY ARE US and WE ARE THEM in Spirit. BIG RED SPIRIT."[15]

Not surprisingly, many Huskervillers reach for the parallel of religion to describe the depths of our devotion. When she's asked to explain the "no place" issue to folks in Kansas, Candy Hodge says, "The best analogy I can make is to religion. Husker sports, especially football, is almost religious in its hold. Go anywhere in Nebraska on game day and fans are attending a ritualistic worship service—NU football."

Curt Eurich of Whitesboro, Texas, writes, "I learned to 'worship' the

Huskers when I was 3 years old," and Strat Warden of Elizabethtown, Kentucky, admits, "I guess it's kind of like a religion. When you grow up in it, it just becomes a part of you." Adds Paul Davie of Seattle, "It is like going to church—going to the Nebraska stadium on Saturday."

Even outside of those Saturday services, Brandt Mackey of Arlington, Virginia, notes that "like many religious zealots dissect and debate the Bible, Husker fans sit in the coffee shops and cafes dissecting and debating all aspects of the Cornhusker football team."[16]

The religion parallel is also useful, if potentially off-putting, when Huskervillers who don't live in Nebraska are asked to explain their continuing allegiance. David Bowman, a dentist practicing in Seneca, Kansas, illustrates:

> I was born and raised in Pawnee City, Nebraska. I have been in Seneca since 1986. I am often asked when I am going to take down my Husker posters and become a K-State or KU fan. My response is simple. I ask the patient what religion they are, and in Seneca over 90% of the population is German Catholic. When they respond "Catholic," I ask them if their job transferred them to Salt Lake City would they become Mormon. Of course, they say no. I say "you've answered your question." When you are born in Nebraska you are either a Husker fan or an atheist, because "being a Husker" is the state religion that bonds everyone in the state from Falls City to Chadron.

No wonder that people argue that maybe we Husker fans take this devotion thing a bit too far! Sociologist Michael Stein argued back in the 1970s, for example, that Husker fans collectively fit the definition of a "recreational cult" practicing its own civil religion.[17]

From the outside, that may be true. Huskervillers, however, recognize that in our zeal to explain the spirit of Nebraska, we use religious parallels as an explanatory device not as a comparison of equal institutions. As Paul Davie of Seattle explains, "This is our religion, I guess ... but it would never take the place of church."

Of course, that's not to say that we Huskervillers don't sometimes find ourselves mixing football and church. Robert Lee Smith recalls such an event:

> My very first memory is heading for mass with my family one day in late December 1972. I was almost three and my father had returned from the war in time to celebrate the holidays. When we entered the chapel I saw my father, who had seen God knows what in Vietnam, physically stunned. The entire parish was wearing red. They wanted to show that the fact they were Catholic did not mean they were going to refuse to be Nebraskans. The game ended up being as impressive a showing: Nebraska 40, Notre Dame 6 in Bob Devaney's swan song.[18]

Robert's story illustrates the revered status of Nebraska football in Huskerville. But his is not the only story that good-naturedly remarks upon how Husker games rival more traditional church-based events such as weddings and funerals. Says Husker fan Carol Collinsworth, with only a slight bit of exaggeration, when the Huskers are playing football, "You don't go to weddings. You don't go to funerals."[19]

A joke shared with me by both a high school friend and a college friend illustrates this commitment:

> A guy named Bob receives a free ticket to the Nebraska Cornhuskers football game from his company. Unfortunately, when Bob arrives at the stadium he realizes the seat is in the last row in the corner of the stadium—he's closer to the Goodyear blimp than the field. About halfway through the first quarter, Bob notices an empty seat 10 rows off the field, right on the 50-yard line. He decides to take a chance and makes his way through the stadium and around the security guards to the empty seat. As he sits down, he asks the gentleman sitting next to him, "Excuse me, is anyone sitting here?" The man says no.
> Now, very excited to be in such a great seat for the game, Bob again inquires of the man next to him, "This is incredible! Who in their right mind would have a seat like this at the Husker game and not use it?"
> The man replies, "Well, actually, the seat belongs to me; I was supposed to come with my wife, but she passed away. This is the first Husker game we haven't been together at since we got married in 1967."
> "Well, that's really sad," says Bob, "but still, couldn't you find someone to take the seat? A relative or close friend?"
> "No," the man replies, "they're all at the funeral."

Bob's extreme commitment is of course the punch line of the joke, yet the humor derives from Huskers' awareness that a kernel of truth can be found within the story. Former Husker player Larry Wachholtz notes, "I have actually been to funerals where the Nebraska fight song is played."[20]

It's also played at weddings. Jessica Kennedy of the University of Nebraska Alumni Association shared this story, written by her friend Matt Waite,[21] about one wedding:

> Really, I swear. This actually happened. I went to a wedding Saturday and a Husker pep rally broke out. Went through, nice service, all the vows and all, and the preacher presents Mr. and Mrs. Married and through the applause you can hear the processional music start. It was the Nebraska fight song. And, like faithful football fans, the wedding guests start clapping in beat to the song, somehow forgetting they are in a church, not Memorial Stadium. So some of us are laughing hysterically, because it is just stupid that they are playing "There Is No Place Like Nebraska," and the song keeps playing. You know the part, near the end, where the trumpets sound and people shout "GO HUSKERS!"? Yes. They yelled "GO HUSKERS!" in the house of God and didn't bat an eye.

So from a wedding, we are presented with the philosophical construct of in Nebraska, is football God, or is God football? (And, by the way, the wedding party entered the reception to the sounds of the Tunnel Music, for those of you who have been to a Husker home game and know what I am talking about). Sick, sad world, eh? Wanna know where they are going on their honeymoon? Nebraska vs. Texas in Austin. Her idea.

Jessica added a few additional details about the event and the couple. "I might add that instead of bubbles or butterflies or rice or noise makers, we released red and white balloons.... Also, on the dance floor, there was a large wooden red "N" with red Christmas lights outlining it.... They have— or at least had—a room decorated in NU decor. I should also add that the groom was L'il Red, our inflatable mascot, for a year during college."

In some cases, however, either the bride or groom forgets to check item 30 on a "You know you're from Nebraska if ..." list circulated through the Internet a few years ago: "Football schedules are checked before wedding dates are set."[22]

My college roommate Jon Johnston recalls his wife's reaction when her brother announced that his wedding would be held on October 29, 1994: "Does he know what day that is? It's the day of the Colorado-Nebraska game!" Her brother, thanks to Jon, was officially named (at least by ESPN Radio's talk show host, the "Fabulous Sports Babe") as "The Geek of the Week."[23]

Brian Walton explains what often happens when a wedding-game conflict arises:

> About 20 years ago, a good friend and former Nebraskan decided to be married. His wife-to-be and her family were Californians, living in the desert in a small town called Lake Elsinore. To facilitate the many family and friends who would be traveling in from near and far (mostly far), they decided to hold the gala festivities on Thanksgiving weekend.
> Unfortunately, none of them, other than the groom, who was totally without voice in the entire matter, realized or cared that the biggest Nebraska game of the year, the one against hated rival Barry Switzer and Oklahoma, was scheduled to start during the wedding reception.
> As the wedding completed without a hitch and the reception began, the father of the groom (a Nebraskan, remember) grew increasingly nervous as the various lines were manned and photos were taken. As the reception began in earnest, he completely disappeared.
> After awhile, this became obvious, and I was among the tuxedo-clad individuals who were called upon to form a search party. Turns out, we disappeared, too, once we found Dad. He was holed up in the back room of the reception hall, huddled up against a 10″ black-and-white television screen watching the NU-OU game live! ... There ended up being at least a dozen of us

hooting and hollering in that little room as we jockeyed for position to see that little-bitty screen. I remember it just as if it were yesterday.

Eventually, the bride and her family grudgingly forgave us for our transgressions. And, believe it or not, the next day, the day after his wedding, who showed up to watch that game tape at our motel, but the groom himself, who was quite put out by his Dad. Not that he slipped away. Not that he ended up with most of the Nebraska guys with him. No, his son was angry that he had to miss the action himself![24]

As Brian's story illustrates, we hate to miss out on opportunities to visit the transcendent, collective place of Huskerville. The spirit of camaraderie, of being with special people while doing something special, is so compelling that it pulls us away from important life events (or prompts us to incorporate that spirit into those life events!) and leaves us grasping for words to express its allure. Although we might feel a bit awkward in employing the language of religion to do so, the profound feelings we experience often reduce us to using such words.

Perhaps we struggle so much with our words because we're trying to give voice to such a unique experience that "football game" seems incredibly insufficient. The captivating appeal of Huskerville lies beyond the game. It is a place where football, culture, history, landscape, and good-hearted people converge.

"The community spirit that's in small towns in Nebraska is the same kind of spirit that's held the team together for so long," says Kurt Olsen. While that spirit is "not something you can verbally explain," notes Brandt Mackey of Arlington, Virginia, Huskervillers know that "it's a combination of experience, including interaction with the people and lifestyle, the landscape, and sharing the common bond that ties me with my home: Husker football."

Husker football thus provides a means of integrating and ordering all that matters to Nebraskans. It does so in a way that leaves us genuinely believing that "there is no place like Nebraska."

At least it has done so.

Now, we're not so sure—and that's a problem.

The student newspaper at the University of Nebraska–Lincoln, the *Daily Nebraskan*, opined at the end of the 2004 season, "We've all heard about the streaks that were broken; first non-bowl season since 1968, worst record since 1961. Fewest rushing yards since God knows when. It all goes to show this is not the same Nebraska team we all grew up watching and loving. And it never will be again."[25]

"And it never will be again." These words underscore our fear of being uprooted. For some Huskervillers, in fact, the *Daily Nebraskan*'s words rang true. For them, the football program has severed its link to the state and its citizens. A Husker fan using the online name of FeelLikeAStranger laments: "My father's corn husking hook is on a shelf in my bedroom. I look at it whenever I go by and know that I am the son of a Cornhusker in the truest sense. The Nebraska football program was a microcosm of the identity, work ethic, and values of the state and its people. Sadly, that era has passed us by."[26]

Omaha resident Larry Sampier wrote to the *Omaha World-Herald*, "UNL had a great tradition of football.... [But now] the Big Red Machine is no more. It needed a shot in the arm. It got its heart cut out."[27]

My college friend Tim Hindman, too, bemoaned the loss of tradition. He wrote in an e-mail to me, "If [Callahan] can develop a winning team, fine, but it just won't be the same ... Nebraska is just like any other football school now."

If we're "just like any other football school," how can we possibly claim that "there is no place like Nebraska"?

I wish I knew the answer.

I do know, though, that our desire to embrace the belief that "there is no place like Nebraska" is vital. For too many years, and still today, we have suffered from outsiders' assessments of Nebraska as a "no place"—a desolate, blank spot on the cultural map. Huskerville, however, puts us on the map—as a big red presence.

11

A Big Red Presence:
Standing Out on the Map

"Are we there yet?"

I asked my parents that question more times than I care to remember as we made the 350–mile drive from Scottsbluff to visit relatives in Hastings, Nebraska. Try as we might, my brother Chuck and I simply could not manage to entertain ourselves during the entire trip. Aside from a stop at Ogallala's Front Street (a re-creation of a nineteenth century Main Street), there was—to our young eyes—simply nothing to see along the vast stretches of U.S. Highway 26 and Interstate 80.

My childhood experiences help me to understand why people passing through Nebraska today think of the place as empty or boring. Or, as Mari Sandoz once noted, Nebraska has long been thought of as "that long flat state that sets between me and any place I want to go."[1] Perhaps *this* is what non–Nebraskans think when they hear us say, "There's no place like Nebraska."

As my college roommate Jeff Baier humorously observes, however, longtime Nebraskans know that the state is much more than a long, empty stretch of highway: "The Huskers are the one good thing about Nebraska that we have let the rest of the country see. We let the rest of the country think that Nebraska is a flat, boring state by putting I-80 where we did."

Apparently, our little ruse worked.

Andrew Baggarly, a reporter for the *Oakland Tribune*, began his story on four San Francisco Giants baseball players with Nebraska roots with this witty observation: "If you drove across a stretch of the Nebraska plains on Interstate 80, you'd swear there are more grain silos than people."[2] The attitude reflected in Baggarly's comment is described by a southern California Huskerviller named Geri as "this, 'There is nothing in Nebraska. Who would want to live there?' attitude."[3]

Like other Huskervillers, Joel Sartore has run into this attitude before. In the introduction to his photographic essay on Nebraska, he writes: "'I'm from Nebraska.' I repeat this phrase several times a week. Usually it's because I've met someone, somewhere, who's curious about the twang in my voice. Most folks just shake their heads in disbelief, especially if they're from the East Coast. 'I flew over Nebraska once,' they say. 'It was brown and flat. I shut my window shade and slept.'"[4]

These folks, to their detriment, make the mistake of thinking that open space is empty space. "To this day," observes John Potter of the Nebraska State Historical Society, "[Nebraska] suffers from a blank spot mentality to the rest of the world."[5]

We blame a lot of this "blank spot mentality" on Major Stephen H. Long.

In 1820, Long returned from an expedition to the Rocky Mountains with a map labeling the part of the country that would become Nebraska, "The Great Desert." The label was found on maps for the next 50 years. "In regard to this extensive section of country," Long wrote, "I do not hesitate in giving the opinion, that it is almost wholly unfit for cultivation, and of course uninhabitable by a people depending on agriculture for their subsistence."[6]

Since then, non–Nebraskans have had a good deal of trouble figuring out where the "no place" of Nebraska exists. When Mari Sandoz first wrote of her memories growing up among the Kincaiders in the Nebraska sandhills, "she encountered editors in the East who doubted that the region she described actually existed."[7]

"Is that near an ocean?" I was once asked by a student from a college outside of Nebraska. At the time, I was a college sophomore and I wasn't quite used to this blank spot mentality. Sure, I had heard my share of jokes about Nebraska on sitcoms such as *WKRP in Cincinnati* (where radio nerd Les Nessman dreamed of going to Omaha for a pork producers convention) and *Welcome Back, Kotter* (where New York City comedian Gabe Kaplan made fun of his Nebraska born-and-raised wife). But I had been surrounded by Nebraskans growing up, and I had traveled only as far as the states bordering Nebraska. Now, live and in person, was the embodiment of sitcom humor—only the guy wasn't joking. He simply had no clue, and didn't seem to feel the slightest bit awkward about not knowing the location of a state that sits smack dab in the middle of the contiguous 48 states.

I was, in a word, stunned.

Imagine then how Nebraska Wesleyan history professor Ron Naugle, co-author of a respected Nebraska history textbook, feels today when he runs into *professors* at academic conferences who aren't quite sure where Nebraska is located. "For most of them," he says, "Nebraska is some place 'out there.'"[8]

Another historian, Donald Hickey, opens his history of Nebraska by noting that "when I moved into Nebraska in 1978, many of my friends (particularly in my native state of Illinois) had trouble remembering where I lived."[9] Similarly, an online fan with the name of Kyhusker recalls, "I grew up in Michigan, where people thought of Nebraska as a vast nothingness west of the Missouri River."

No wonder, then, that one of the items on a "You might be a Nebraskan if..." list I received was, "You can locate Nebraska on the United States map."[10]

To be fair, Nebraska *is*—technically speaking—the ninth most desolate state in the nation. On average, you can find just 22.3 Nebraskans in every square mile of the state.[11] Factor out the three-quarters of a million Nebraskans (out of 1.7 million) who live in the Lincoln and Omaha areas and, well, let's just say the population density average drops significantly.

So, when non–Nebraskans *see* Nebraska, they are not always impressed. From their vantage points—typically a highway—they see emptiness, nothingness, vast stretches of uninhabited land. Of the 535 Nebraska communities listed by the U.S. Census Bureau, only 16 of them have populations over 10,000 (and three of those are considered part of the Omaha metro area).[12] Eleven of Nebraska's 93 *counties* have populations under 1,000.[13] Forty percent of the state's towns have fewer than 250 residents, and the town with the median population is Brule, with 334 residents.[14] Gertrude Stein's famous phrase, "there is no there there," might well serve as the motto of those who see Nebraska by driving through or briefly visiting.

When these folks don't see anything, they *overlook* Nebraska and its people. Consider the case of the Poppers. In 1987, Rutgers University professors Frank and Deborah Popper noticed the dwindling population and declining socio-economic figures of much of the rural Great Plains. They proposed envisioning much of this area as an ecological reserve that they labeled the Buffalo Commons. Although they later insisted that they were writing metaphorically and as a way of prompting thinking about the best ways to manage the economic and ecological resources of the area,[15] folks in the Great Plains in general did not take kindly to a couple of New Jersey professors telling them how to best use their land.

In 1990, the Poppers visited McCook, Nebraska, to talk about their ideas.[16] As Mary Ellen Goodenberger reports, "the over-riding sentiment was that the Poppers should return to New Jersey and let southwest Nebraskans pursue their persevering ways."[17] To "honor" the Poppers' ideas, the people of McCook decided to tell their own stories, rather than let the Poppers do it for them, in an event they called the Buffalo Commons Storytelling Festival.

The response to the Poppers' Buffalo Commons idea exemplifies the disadvantage of relying upon vision as a way of knowing: vision breeds false confidence.[18] While it allows us to *pull in* much of what surrounds us, it also keeps us from *going to* what surrounds us. In other words, our use of vision to overcome distances paradoxically keeps us distant from the world around us.

The Poppers, from the perspective of those in the Great Plains, could not possibly know the area they were writing about because they worked in New Jersey; they were too far removed, too distant. Similarly, when coach Callahan refers to Huskervillers as "the people *out there*" at the end of the sentence, "I love Nebraska and what it stands for and what it means to the people out there,"[19] we recognize that he is seeing us from a distance.

When people see us from a distance or do not make the effort to understand the experiences of those they cannot see, they are bound to make some unfortunate assessments. Consider this thoughtful description of the state and its inhabitants offered by travel writer Bill Bryson:

> I was headed for Nebraska. Now there's a sentence you don't want to have to say too often if you can possibly help it. Nebraska must be the most unexciting of all the states. Compared with it, Iowa is paradise. Iowa at least is fertile and green and has a hill. Nebraska is like a 75,000-square-mile bare patch. In the middle of the state is a river called the Platte, which at some times of the year is two or three miles wide. It looks impressive until you realize that it is only about four inches deep. You could cross it in a wheelchair. On a landscape without any contours or depressions to shape it, the Platte just lies there, like a drink spilled across a tabletop. It is the most exciting thing in the state.
>
> When I was growing up, I used to wonder how Nebraska came to be lived in. I mean to say, the original settlers, creaking across America in their covered wagons, had to have passed through Iowa, which is green and fertile and has, as I say, a hill, but stopped short of Colorado, which is green and fertile and has a mountain range, and settled instead for a place that is flat and brown and full of stubble and prairie dogs. Doesn't make a lot of sense, does it? Do you know what the original settlers made their houses of? Dried mud. And do you know what happened to all those mud houses when the rainy season came every year? That's correct, they slid straight into the Platte River.
>
> For a long time I couldn't decide whether the original settlers in Nebraska were insane or just stupid, and then I saw a stadium full of University of

Nebraska football fans in action on a Saturday and realized that they must have been both.[20]

If nothing's there in the eyes of outsiders like Bryson, then the people who choose to live in Nebraska must surely be backward, misguided, foolish—or all of the above.

So people like Paul Finebaum, author of *Why I Hate Nebraska*, "humorously" describe Nebraskans in not-so-fine ways:

> Most Nebraska students really do dress like the Cornhusker.
> Nebraska's campus may not be the end of the world, but you sure can see it from there.
> Most Nebraska students think "safe sex" means closing the barn door.
> Usually the biggest bone of contention when 2 Nebraska graduates divorce is who gets to keep the trailer.
> Johnny Carson isn't the average Nebraska fan—he still has all of his teeth.
> Nebraska fans believe that the New York Stock Exchange is a bunch of Northerners getting together to trade cows.[21]

(I should note that, unlike hard-working Huskervillers, Finebaum seems a bit lazy. He has written numerous books of the same type, using primarily the same jokes while changing the target state or university. His use of "Northerners" in the last joke is revealing; his initial book was set in his home state of Alabama.)[22]

Folks like Finebaum don't display fine humor so much as they recycle *Green Acres* jokes. For example, as Nebraska prepared to play in the 2002 Rose Bowl following the 2001 season, *Los Angeles Times* columnist T.J. Simers followed Finebaum's lead by writing a "humorous" column describing the Huskervillers who were about to visit California. Referring to Nebraskans as "yokels" and "hicks" who live "back in the sticks," Simers cleverly offered to name the RV parking lot reserved for Husker fans as "Hick Haven," adding "there will be no public facilities available in Hick Haven, although I shouldn't think that'll bother these people."[23]

What does bother "these people," though, are demonstrations of ignorance and arrogance. After years of enduring cheap shots from people who simply pass through Nebraska, or—worse yet—blindly write from offices hundreds or thousands of miles away, we Huskervillers appreciate a strong defense. We learned from our homesteading ancestors that you have to roll with the punches, but to fight back when necessary. So, when we Nebraskans feel attacked by outsiders, we respond much like the football team's fabled blackshirt defense (that the defense has a nickname is a sign of how seriously Huskervillers take defense).

In addition to the response given the Poppers and their Buffalo Commons proposal, T.J. Simers' column generated a slew of replies—many of which were posted on the HuskerPedia Web site after it displayed the column and a response from Garrick Baxter, communications chair of the Oregonians for Nebraska alumni group.[24]

BETTY, FROM TEXAS: I get really p—— off when I read the garbage that comes out of these people's mouths.... If you go to this guy's newspaper office, show him what class is all about. Something he knows nothing about.

SUSAN, FROM OREGON: This hick from Nebraska lived in your "fair" city for over 6 years and could not wait to get out. Hicks from Nebraska generally choose to avoid living through riots, drive-by shootings, car jackings and other intelligent outings that you seem to enjoy there.

JANET, FROM NEBRASKA: I cannot, repeat cannot, believe the impression people on the West (Left) Coast have of we Nebraskans. I am extremely proud to be from this part of the country where values are valued and people are real, not plastic.

KIM, FROM KANSAS: As for the Nebraska hicks, while we represent less than 1% of the population, we have produced 59 Academic All-American athletes, far more than any other school in America. I don't think California schools even show up on that radar screen.

RON, FROM OKLAHOMA: As NU fans we can overlook weak-minded insults like yours. Our football team normally takes care of things on the field.

JAMES, FROM TEXAS: I always laugh at these types because they perpetuate the myth that we are all farmers and all live in Nebraska in sod huts. In fact, we are everywhere and we are everyone. Our blessing is that we carry the Nebraska "goodness" with whether we live in Nebraska or in Oregon (or Texas or Arizona or California...).

These responses most certainly reflect the attitude embodied by Kentuckiana Husker Kit Price in a response to Bill Bryson's derisive description of Nebraska: "What's your reaction to this commentary? Does it embarrass you? Insult you? Do you find yourself, like a true blackshirt, leaping to Nebraska's defense?"

Defensiveness, notes author Joel Garreau, is in abundant supply in Plains states like Nebraska. In words that could describe the allegedly sophisticated humor of folks like Paul Finebaum, Bill Bryson, and T.J. Simers, Garreau observes: "Some avant-garde sections of society, of course, don't see the Breadbasket as the ratifier of anything. They just see us as behind the times and, for that matter, not too smart.... Not surprisingly, Plains folk end up being defensive."[25]

Really?

Listen to what these Nebraskans said when I asked them, "What do you think about how the national media characterize the Huskers and/or Nebraska?"[26]

> "Commentators that are totally against Nebraska."
> "The media waits for something to happen to put them down."
> "East coast doesn't really respect Nebraska as much; TV seems to care for the other team more than Nebraska."
> "They're not very favorable, even when we had the winning teams. The announcers really put in those digs."
> "Portrayed as a bunch of hicks."
> "Make them look like dumb people, look like stupid backwards farmers."
> "Hicks from the cornfields."
> "Think we're hicks."
> "They think we're hicks."

Huskervillers have not cornered the market on snubs, I know. Find a place, and you can no doubt find a group of people who feel dismissed by some other group who thinks itself superior. Kansan sports writer Grant Wahl, for example, sniffs, "We don't like fancy-pants East Coast writers who stuff *Wizard of Oz* jokes into every Jayhawks story."[27]

For these denigrated groups, sports provides a way of getting even, of showing those snooty, allegedly superior others exactly who has the right stuff. Author and Arkansas Razorbacks fan E. Lynn Harris writes, "To me every Razorbacks win was a victory of my small, misunderstood state. I was tired of my cousins in Michigan (where I was born) calling Arkansas a hick state."[28] Alabama fan Geoffrey Norman calls "winning in football as validation. A way of getting back at the people who have dissed you for so long as a bunch of rubes."[29] (Auburn fans feel the same way when they beat Alabama.)[30]

The outcomes of games, viewed in this respect, mean a great deal for those who are performing. Will Blythe points out in his discussion of the North Carolina–Duke rivalry in basketball: "The living and dying through one's allegiance to either Duke or Carolina is no less real for being enacted through play and fandom. One's psychic well-being hangs in the balance."[31] Author Joe Queenan recalls that not so long ago the victories of the Notre Dame football team meant more than an extra digit in the win column. "In my father's lifetime," he recalls, "Irish-Americans were still low enough on the socioeconomic ladder that Notre Dame's pigskin exploits resonated far beyond the gridiron."[32]

In essence, what we have here is an organized, state-supported version of saying "take that" to those who think they're better than us.[33]

Husker football victories, and the performances of the fans who support the team, offer an irrefutable demonstration that the so-called hicks' "right way of doing things"—working hard, being neighborly, and remaining down-to-earth—is both effective and worthy of emulation.[34] For better and worse, football is how we reveal our best stuff to the rest of the world.[35] Huskerviller Beth Townsend notes, "A knock against the Huskers is a knock against our way of life.... To see [the team] perform well, in any sport, reminds us and the rest of the world that, regardless of how old-fashioned our belief system may be, if you follow it, you will succeed in ways that you cannot imagine."

The performances surrounding football games provide undeniable evidence that those who believe their ways to be superior are sadly mistaken. These rituals, in our eyes, correct the social order. "Here," says E. Steve Cassells, "is an empirical demonstration we can stand in there with the best of them."

We take more than a little guilty pleasure in providing these empirical demonstrations, too. "It is so fun to be a fan of a team from a state with such a low population base that beats teams from more arrogant states every week!" exclaims Scott Pagel from Taipei, Taiwan. Adds Pat Ferguson of Lakeland, Minnesota, "We also use the Huskers as a means of recognition. We think that if we can have fewer than 2 million residents and still recruit players from all over, in addition to the home-grown players, and be competitive on a national level, well, we must be doing something right."

These victories—as well as the performances of fans—send the cultural message that Nebraska should be noticed, not overlooked. When people remember Nebraska, no matter what the score, Huskervillers have effectively provided a counter-statement to the blank spot, nothing there, mentality. "The Cornhusker football team," writes Tim Hindman, "is evidence that there is more to Nebraska than what can be seen from the Interstate."

"The Huskers," continues Kansas-based Husker Gary McGirr, "put Nebraska and UNL on the map." Gary's words are echoed by former Husker player Mike Beran, who played for Bob Devaney's teams in 1971 and 1972. He explains, "[Devaney] put the state on the map. I can still remember going to the Washington, DC, area in 1963 to see some of my cousins back there, and they seriously still thought that we fought the Indians and still rode around in covered wagons. That was the East Coast's view of Nebraska."[36] Now, however, Nebraskans believe that the Huskers have generated respect for the state of Nebraska; in fact, 83 percent of those polled in the Scripps Survey Research Center survey—including non-fans—said so.[37]

For a long time—at least since Long's expedition in 1820—Nebraskans and our land have seemingly been, respectively, backward and invisible to others. Now, however, notes a globetrotting Huskerviller, "I'll tell people in other countries that I'm from Nebraska and they immediately connect with the Cornhuskers."[38] Non-Nebraskans "may have never been to Nebraska but they know Nebraska football," says Robin Baer of Oklahoma City. Affirms Ireland's Ann-Marie Duffy, "Whenever I tell other Americans where I am from, they usually say, 'Go Huskers, Go Big Red.' That is the one thing that Nebraska is really known for: the Huskers."

When those outside of Huskerville dismiss or overlook Nebraska, Husker football generates a presence that cannot be ignored. When non–Nebraskans can't find Nebraska on the map, Husker football elevates the state's profile. While the sower statue rises up above the plains for all Nebraskans to see, we believe the Husker football team rises up to show the rest of the country what Nebraska is all about.

Husker football lifts the bedrock values of Homesteading and gives them what communication philosopher Ramsey Eric Ramsey calls "relief": "We attempt to bring relief and call for relief for those of us who suffer, and we bring the world into relief by raising it out of its flattened character.... Out of the flatness it raises possibilities."[39] Ramsey's first sense of relief might be a bit overstated for Huskervillers, but it does speak to the feelings of being slighted that we have experienced over the years. Our suffering is of the psychic variety, a feeling that others look *down* upon us. We experience relief when these others look *up* to us, whether the admiration derives from the performance of the team, the fans, or a combination of the two.

The second sense of relief is perhaps more pertinent in this case. Just as a relief map of Nebraska would show that the elevation increases by nearly a mile from the southeast corner to the southwest corner,[40] Husker football serves to lift the state's cultural reputation out of its geographical moorings; out of the flatness it raises possibilities for seeing Nebraska differently. In particular, Husker football demonstrates for others that the so-called hicks have historically triumphed over adversity, and will continue to do so as long as we remain rooted by working hard, being neighborly, and remaining down-to-earth.

The Big Red Presence generated through football is a way of saying to those who denigrate Nebraska, "See what you're missing!" We can then suggest that people like Bill Bryson, Paul Finebaum, and T.J. Simers enact the "Advice from a Provincial" outlined by Nebraska poet Don Welch:

When you drive down our river-road,
Spare us your talk about our backwardness,
Of how mile after unrelieved mile dispirits you,
Of how there is nothing, simply nothing to see.
Go back to your home and work on your eyes.[41]

What they'll see, at first, is a lot of red things (clothing, hats, mailboxes, flags, etc.)—and not just on game days. Every day, Huskervillers signal our commitment to our helmeted ambassadors, and provide non-Nebraskans with things to notice, by displaying red Husker items. Strangely enough, such displays are awfully similar to what street gangs call "representing," or the demonstration of one's allegiance through nonverbal performances designed for others.

This idea comes from the late Northwestern University communication professor Dwight Conquergood, who spent a good deal of time hanging out with a Chicago street gang called the Latin Kings. He learned that "the key term in gang communication is *reppin'*, short for *representing*. It refers to a repertoire of communication practices whereby gang members enact, and thereby constitute their gang identity. Reppin' encompasses everything from wearing the signifying gang colors, throwing up hand signs, and calling out code words to inscribing elaborate graffiti murals."[42]

In Huskerville, representing occurs in much the same way. First, we represent through our behavior—by working hard, being neighborly, and remaining down-to-earth. We are all representatives of Nebraska and thus attempt to represent Nebraska well in what we do. Monty Seidler, the Huskerviller who has never lived in Nebraska, points out, "As far as [others] are concerned I'm a Nebraskan and I represent Nebraska and if I really choose to believe what I am saying, then I should be representing properly.... I learned that from people like Tom Osborne, from my wife, from other Nebraskans."

We also represent Nebraska through visual displays and signs. For example, my grandmother Varla, who resides in an assisted living facility in Scottsbluff, devoutly represents Huskerville with her red clothing every football Saturday.

"You can tell a Nebraskan," claims Marshall Widman of Leawood, Kansas, "Somewhere on him or her is a Nebraska logo." Being a Husker fan who represents is the equivalent of saying, "'There aren't that many of us around, but they'll know we're here!'" according to Matthew Grosz of New Bern, North Carolina.

It's been this way for quite some time. In 1892, when Nebraska played

Illinois and revealed its then-new school colors of scarlet and cream, "'Everybody in the remotest degree of sympathy with the Nebraska team' wore [the new colors]," according to a newspaper account of the time. "Spectators arrived in carriages decked out in red and white ... university professors wore the colors, carried flags and got as excited as anyone. Flags with every combination of scarlet and white were swung to the breeze on canes. Red neckties were common, and one fellow even wore a vest half red and half white."[43]

A couple of decades later, the team name of Cornhuskers had become well-established and football began working its way into everyday life around Lincoln. In 1938, University of Nebraska professor Mamie Meredith observed, "One of Lincoln's leading hotels is the Cornhusker. A campus restaurant is the Husker Inn and Highway 77, which extends across the continent, is the Cornhusker."[44]

Today, the color red and the names Husker and Cornhusker permeate the state of Nebraska. Terri Frei, a writer for *The Sporting News*, only slightly exaggerates when he writes, "Half of everything in Lincoln is named Cornhusker something, I believe, and I can't understand why they haven't painted

Coming or going, Huskervillers represent their loyalty to others (photograph by Gloria Strope).

the Capitol dome, the tallest structure in town, red as well."[45] Akron *Beacon Journal* sportswriter Terry Pluto agrees. "I am convinced that you aren't allowed in [Memorial Stadium] without a red jacket," he writes.[46] ESPN.com writer Jim Caple was similarly stunned when he visited Lincoln.

The amazing thing is not that the six checkout lines at Nebraska's Memorial Stadium gift store were a dozen customers deep an hour before last Saturday's game against Utah State. The amazing thing is that anyone in Nebraska still feels the need to buy more red T-shirts.

Have you ever shown up at a formal dinner wearing jeans and a T-shirt? That's how I felt wearing—gasp!—a blue plaid shirt to a Nebraska game. I've been to St. Louis Cardinals games in the postseason but I've never seen this many people dressed in red. As far as I could tell, I was the only one not wearing Big Red aside from the visiting Utah State players.[47]

We quite literally "wear our hearts on our sleeves," claims E. Steve Cassells. "Part of being a Nebraskan," explains Steve Smith, "means dressing in team colors and visibly proclaiming your devotion to all things Cornhusker."[48]

Ken Maddox, who lived in Nebraska only during his college years, remembers his first exposure to this bedrock principle of Huskerville: "We were in for Thanksgiving weekend, and it was the day the Huskers played Oklahoma, and I went to the mall that day, not knowing what Nebraska was like. I went to the mall and every single person I saw was wearing red. Driving down the street, everybody I saw was wearing red."

This red-wearing, Husker-signifying stuff extends well beyond the borders of Nebraska, too. You may well find the equivalent of "Welcome to Huskerville" signs outside of Husker fans' homes, no matter where we live. Microsoft executive Jeff Raikes, a Nebraska farm boy in his youth, and his three children raise a red Husker flag outside their Seattle-area home every Nebraska game day.[49] My friends Scott Titsworth and Lynn Harter also proudly fly their Husker flag in another Athens, Ohio neighborhood on game days. They used to live in the Fargo, North Dakota–Moorhead, Minnesota, area prior to coming to Athens. There, my former graduate instructor Ann Burnett flew her Husker flag on game days as well, though she noted that her neighbors wondered why they had a red flag with a white "Z" on it (the "N" looked at sideways).

These flags can also be found in Huskervillers' mobile homes. International teacher Arthur Hudson tells me that "somewhere in Kuwait there is a blue and white Chevy with a big "GO BIG RED—CORNHUSKER" sign in the back window. And our little white Russian-made Niva here in Yerevan,

Armenia, also has a big rear window sticker with NEBRASKA CORN-HUSKER on it. There are also lots of friends in Kuwait, Singapore, and Armenia wearing Big Red t-shirts."

Back in the U.S., a Huskerviller living in Minnesota offers this memory about representing Nebraska away from home:

> A really neat thing happened when I was growing up. My mom was very much a Husker fan as well. And my parents got divorced when I was ten. My mom is still so devoted to the Huskers; she got an opportunity to travel down in an RV with a bunch of people from channel 7 and channel 3 and so she took my brother and I and we went down to Florida for the Orange Bowl, which was really awesome.
>
> My senior year, my mom approached my little brother and I (we were the only two living with her at the time), and she asked us, "What would you want to do? Would you want to go down and see an Orange Bowl or would you want to have a Christmas?" Couldn't afford both. So we literally chose, go down to the Orange Bowl to watch the Huskers play.
>
> We didn't have a Christmas tree, we had no presents except for what my mom gave us. She did wrap one present for each of us and what they were was sun glasses. So when going down to Florida we'd have sunglasses to wear. But we did go down, I mean no other presents. Actually, we gave it all up just to be able to go down to a Husker game.
>
> And while we were down there it happened to be when they played Clemson. First of all, when we parked the RV in a lot, a camper's lot, my mom immediately got out the Husker flag that she had a friend hand make and she went knocking. She went around the RV park and she was knocking on everybody's door to come and join. We were going to go through and walk around and chant "Huskers," "Go Big Red," and things like that.
>
> And we ended up running into a little group of Clemson people as soon as we parked the RV in the RV thing. They had spray paint and they put a little, you know, the Clemson, they have a paw, they encircled our RV with their paw prints. So that's why my mom got out with the flag. And we went out and knocked around and we had a whole huge group of Nebraska fans following behind us with our flag. And we were chanting "Go Big Red" and everything.

Sounds just like a Husker watch party. There, Huskervillers—especially those who live outside the state of Nebraska—are determined to let others know "we're here." In both McGee's in Chicago and the Lucky 7 in the Seattle area, I found myself surrounded by red-clad Huskervillers, who were in turn surrounded by Nebraska signs and paraphernalia.

All this can be a little overwhelming to an outsider, but that's the point. We're representing Nebraska and its way of life. We might be down-to-earth individuals, but we want to make darn sure that we're not collectively overlooked anymore.

You see, much like early explorers felt compelled to stick a flag in the new territory they discovered or conquered, Huskervillers can't help but announce our presence to others when we're in new territory. For example, on the wall in my home office I have a small sign that proclaims, "Go Big Red," with "North Texas Nebraskans" in smaller letters below. The sign, a gift from Innes Mitchell (a friend of a friend who helped interview Husker fans in Texas), was a way of announcing our presence in the state of Texas.

Rex Lathen, the owner of the company that made the sign, is a Husker who moved to the Dallas-Fort Worth area in 1981. Rex and his wife, Judy, initially made signs simply stating "Go Big Red" to plant on the highway outside a 1996 watch party. The next year, the alumni chapter leader, Bob Van Horn, asked if they could make signs that also included "North Texas Nebraskans" to take to the Husker game against Baylor in Waco, Texas. Rex admits that he felt a bit "sheepish" carrying the signs into the stadium, but soon discovered that other Husker fans were glad to have them.

Later that year, at the Big 12 Championship game in San Antonio, Rex and Judy took about 1,000 signs to the Husker pre-game gathering. They opened the boxes, wrote, "Free—Take One," on the flaps, then left to enjoy San Antonio's beautiful Riverwalk area. Noticing other Husker fans—"Of course we all had our red sweatshirts on," Rex said, in a "goes without saying" kind of way—Rex and Judy weren't quite sure what to expect when they returned to the boxes. "There were maybe 50 left," he said, "so we grabbed a couple for ourselves before they were all gone."

Since that time, Rex's signs have traveled to places like Austin, Texas; Norman, Oklahoma; and even Lincoln, Nebraska. And, like good neighbors, Rex and Judy gladly share the signs—over 10,000 since 1997—with their Huskerville friends free of charge.

That Rex and Judy's sign remains posted in my office today is a reminder that representing doesn't stop on game days. It's a year-long, everyday activity. Not surprisingly, then, Huskerviller Ehren Mitzlaff noticed that in the news reports about then-President Clinton's long-awaited first (and only) visit to Nebraska, "in every single scene, someone was wearing either a Husker hat, shirt, or coat."

These displays of red are so pervasive they become almost mundane to those of us living in Huskerville. I recall treating as "no big deal" the statement of University of Nebraska–Lincoln student Spencer Murdock the night before the 1999 Iowa State game: "I am from 250 miles away [Bassett, Nebraska], but almost everybody in my town has a Nebraska sign or a mailbox, or a t-shirt. Kids grow up and I mean the first thing they get is a Nebraska football outfit."

Wearing Husker clothing is but one dimension of the everyday kind of representing that occurs throughout Huskerville. In Leavenworth, Kansas, for instance, a Huskerviller says, "I see an on-coming car at least once a day (usually a different vehicle) with Husker emblems or front plates (Kansas is a one-plate state, for those who don't live here) and I can think of a least a dozen houses or more, easy, that have Husker memorabilia of some kind displayed in their front yard."

In addition, Huskerviller Kurt Olsen proudly proclaims, "I have Husker emblems and things on my truck. My motorcycle helmet looks just like a Nebraska football helmet." Other Husker symbols are often displayed as well, as Los Angeles reporter Bill Plaschke discovered in his interactions with Huskerville residents.

> The cute little thing is only 7, yet in January she will be attending her sixth bowl game.
> She will come here with her family from Omaha, in a Cadillac with "Husker" on the door and "GONU" on the plates.
> She has posed on the family holiday cards with a Nebraska football and Nebraska helmet, but she's too small to lug those things to Pasadena. Instead, she will show her pride by dressing in a little red vest adorned with a white "N."
> Just another of the thousands of Nebraska fans expected to gather here for the Rose Bowl.
> With the possible exception of, she's a dog.[50]

Husker fan Geri explained on the Husker List that she, too, seeks to represent her allegiance to Huskerville in a number of ways.

> My co-workers think I am "eccentric," because I have a set of red "Huskers" scrubs, and "N" earrings that I wear on the nights of game days, and they say, "You sure wear a lot of red!" on the other days. I have a red car and a Husker car flag, Go Big Red license tag holders, and a Husker Fanatic stuck on one of the windows. (I hope I am getting one of those horns that plays "There is No Place Like Nebraska" for my car for Christmas.) We have a Husker flag hanging in front of our house on game days.[51]

I'm almost ashamed to admit that I don't have a Husker flag, too (maybe I can get one for Christmas?). But I make up for this deficiency in other ways. The north wall of my home office, for example, is a veritable (Husker) gang graffiti mural, and can sometimes stun visitors to the house. I have the following items, in addition to Rex and Judy's sign, on my wall collage and on the shelves against that wall:

> Two Husker pennants
> Two posters with the Husker season schedule
> Two photos of Memorial Stadium

Two framed issues of *Sports Illustrated* with Huskers on the cover
Two framed programs from Husker games
Two unframed programs from Husker games
Three commemorative Husker editions published by Nebraska newspapers, two of which are framed
Two Husker checks from previous checking accounts
Two ticket stubs to Husker games
Three Husker drinking cups
Two handmade Husker crafts, given to me as gifts
One Husker clock
One 32" tall Herbie Husker wood figure
One Husker wind chime
One Husker windsock
One plush Husker football
One wooden Husker football
One Husker canister
One Husker football bank
One media pass
One Pennsylvanians for Nebraska license plate holder
One plush "Bless My Huskers" red bear
One stuffed bear wearing a Husker onesie, which my youngest daughter
Emmy outgrew years ago

Even I was surprised by the time I finished taking inventory. Not that I should have been, since I was wearing my Nebraska sweatshirt, drinking my morning pop (not soda) out of a Husker coozie, staring at my computer monitor with a Husker decal attached to it, while I compiled the inventory on my Husker notepad that was sitting on the desk next to my Husker key ring. (For what it's worth, I didn't use my Husker pen to write the list. To Husker fans, I apologize. To non–Huskers, I can say, "See I'm not so bad!")

Decorating rooms in homage to the Huskers is not all that unusual. My Uncle Larry and Aunt Judy, shortly after moving from Nebraska to Colorado, reminded themselves of their Husker roots by creating a Husker bathroom decorated in red and white, with Husker insignia just about everywhere you can imagine.

They are not alone. Nebraska Red Zone catalogs routinely feature shower curtains (and Husker curtain hooks), toilet seat covers, towels, rugs, wastebaskets, soap dispensers, toothbrush holders, soap dishes, and night lights—all emblazoned with some form of "Huskers."

Bathrooms, of course, are not the only room in the house that can be decorated in Husker. The Red Zone catalog also typically offers rec room furnishings, a fireplace screen, and various kinds of clocks. Gothenburg, Nebraska, bank president Matt Williams told reporter Bill Plaschke during a phone interview that "he was standing in a room filled with such souvenirs as a piece of Memorial Stadium goalpost torn down nine years ago, and a clump of stadium turf. Outside, in his backyard, a plastic Santa was sitting on a holiday light display fashioned in the shape of a goal post."[52]

For Ann-Marie Duffy, of Ennis, County Clare, Ireland, Husker representations always served as a welcome home sign when she returned to visit family from her work in the Peace Corps or her residence in Ireland. "Whenever I was flying home from Africa or Ireland," she wrote me, "I always knew where my gate was for my flight back to Omaha. All I had to do was look for the red sweatshirts, caps, etc. being worn by the other passengers. No matter what, the Nebraskans are always supporting their team, whether it's football season or not. As I got closer to the gate for the Omaha flight, I would see the red and know I was home already!" Adds Ann-Marie, "My Irish husband gets a kick out of this, and he himself owns at least three Nebraska shirts and a few caps that he wears proudly around Ireland."

No wonder, then, that selling Husker stuff is big business.

Julie Lattimer, marketing director of a Lincoln mall called SouthPointe Pavilions, says, "I can tell you, we definitely see an impact on sales based on the mood of the [game- day Husker fan] shoppers."[53] In short, the more games the football team wins, the more Husker merchandise is sold.[54]

In 1995–96, following consecutive national championships in 1994 and 1995, the University of Nebraska earned an astonishing $3.2 million in royalties alone from the sale of licensed Nebraska products. That year, only two universities earned more in royalties.[55] In 2004–05, the year of the 5–6 record in Bill Callahan's first season, *only* $1.4 million in royalties was earned by the university, a figure that ranked Nebraska 14th in the nation.[56]

All of this Husker merchandise floating around gives Huskerville a bit of a scarlet glow (no wonder photographer Joel Sartore titled his photo essay *Under a Big Red Sky*). This can be daunting, perhaps even annoying, to visitors, as one Huskerviller living in Iowa explains in this anecdote about returning to Iowa with three Iowa State fans following a Nebraska-Iowa State game: "A housefly, that had been with us since Lincoln, started buzzing around again near Des Moines. One of the [Iowa State fans] said, 'Dang Nebraska flies!' Another, whom I don't think had said three words since the game, muttered, 'I'm surprised it's not wearing a red sweatshirt!'"[57]

Huskervillers recognize our limited (if you can call multiple kinds of Husker apparel limited that is) wardrobes. We're not terribly bothered by this, though, as the following joke circulating on the Internet illustrates:

One day my housework-challenged husband decided to wash his sweat-shirt. Seconds after he stepped into the laundry room, he shouted to me, "What setting do I used on the washing machine?"

"It depends," I replied. "What does it say on your shirt?"

He yelled back, "Nebraska."

Alec McHoul, an Australian communication professor, has an explanation for this infusion of sports into our everyday lives. He calls it "doing we's." That is, in jointly performing our sports affiliations, we are also making sports such a part of our group identity that the sport "leaks into everyday life."[58] Thus, we don't think things like Husker bathrooms, motorcycle helmets, and mailboxes are all that odd. After all, our neighbors might well have such things, too.[59]

From birth to death, Huskervillers let football leak into our lives. Pam Rietsch of Michigan testifies to the birth dimension of this leakage: "When I had been in the hospital for a week with spinal fusion, [my] hubby picked me up and since it was cold here in Michigan, he helped me put on my red winter N jacket.... On the way through the lobby of the hospital some young couple called to me and brought me their brand new baby which they were leaving the hospital with, and you guessed it, he was in a really cute little jumpsuit with the Husker logo and a matching jacket all in red."[60] At the other end of the scale, *New York Times* reporter Malcolm Moran tells us that Byron Hock's deceased uncle Dean has a Husker helmet figure on his tombstone; his epitaph reads GO BIG RED.[61]

Collectively, the various types of representation that occur in Huskerville serve to reaffirm our sense of identity and to help transform others' perceptions of our identity. Dismissed as a desert, disrespected as a place of beauty, and diminished through insults, Nebraska has long been constructed as a place of little social value. Huskers know better, though, and we seek to reverse the popular understanding of Nebraska by establishing Huskerville, a place where the values of a rural lifestyle are celebrated.

Cultural studies scholar John Fiske calls these places like Huskerville "locales." Locales, he explains, are the opposite of "stations," places where we are assigned by powerful social structures.[62] So when popular media describe Nebraska as "Hicksville," Nebraskans are stationed. Any direct attack on those who create these stations can be easily dismissed as biased or defensive or sour grapes. We don't write books like *Why We Hate Paul Finebaum* or *Bill Bryson Doesn't Know Squat About Nebraska*, and we can't erase the 50 years worth of maps that labeled our home a desert. As much as I admire the folks who responded to T.J. Simers' column in the *Los Angeles*

Times, I have no illusions that a smart-aleck like Simers—or those who find him amusing—would in any way reassess their opinions of Nebraska and its people after reading our letters.

What we can do, though, is offer indirect arguments for how we do things. Rhetoric and folklore scholar Roger Abrahams points out, "each item of expressive culture is an implement of argument, a tool of persuasion."[63] Our football-related performances—on game days and on every other day for that matter—are arguments for the Huskerville way of life. They offer correctives to a social order in need of correcting.[64]

When others notice these indirect arguments, they can't help but be impressed. Thirty thousand people wearing red in Notre Dame's stadium, over four decades of home sellouts, neighborly fans, down-to-earth coaches, hard-working walk-ons—all of these things highlight what Huskerville is all about. They provide what argumentation scholar Chaim Perelman calls "a *presence* that prevents them from being neglected."[65] When an argument or performers enacting an argument have presence, they "establish control of some space and maintain the attention of some audience," writes Jackson Miller.[66] Rather than having others control and define our space, Huskervillers use our ritual performances to create and define our own community. We create a locale called Huskerville while resisting the efforts of outsiders to station us in Hicksville.

Wearing red, and representing in other ways, becomes particularly important in this respect, for presence is primarily a visual experience. As rhetorical scholar John Murphy observes in his review of the idea of presence, "One comes to 'see' the argument."[67] The performances of the Husker football team and its fans, on game days and every day, thus do much more than meets the eye. They serve as arguments for a way of life as well as expressions of hope that others may recognize, and then adopt, new ways of seeing Nebraska and its people. They tell others, as Don Welch's poem says, to "go back to your home and work on your eyes."

12

It's a Small Husker World

Thursday Night, October 7, 1999. On the phone in the Nebraska Union.

My wife, Christie, is working on her ears; she can't believe what she just heard.

She said that she just called the Travelodge in Lincoln where I told her I would be staying. She asked to be connected to my room, but another man answered the phone. "Roger?" she asked.

"Yes."

"Roger Aden?"

"That's me."

But it wasn't *me*. Turns out two guys with the name of Roger Aden were staying in the same Lincoln motel. What are the odds?

Well, in Huskerville, the odds are pretty good because it's a small world.

I ask Christie where the other guy lives—she had to compare addresses with the desk clerk to figure out who "her" Roger Aden was—but she can't remember.

"Gothenburg?" I ask.

"That's it," she says.

I explain about my trip to Gothenburg, Nebraska in high school and how, as I tended to do then, I looked in the phone book to see if any Adens were listed. To my surprise, I counted something like 17 (Gothenburg, for you non–Nebraskans, holds just over 3,000 people)—none of whom I'm directly related to.

Earlier that night, a Nebraska student named Emilie Wolgan had told me, "Life is a small world, they say, and here in Nebraska, I don't know, it's just an even smaller world." She's right, as I learned over and over again after that night in Lincoln.

The next day, in fact, the first person I interviewed grew up in my home-

169

town of Scottsbluff. Later, I ran across a couple who now managed the radio station in Scottsbluff where I worked while on breaks from college, and their friend, the husband of a woman who was a year ahead of me in high school and now worked at the same grocery store as my dad; we talked like long-lost friends. On the way to the game, I noticed a former student walking ahead of me with her husband. On the flight home, after the pilot welcomed us with, "How about those Huskers!" I learned that the man sitting next to me lived in the same city in Florida as my brother and his family.

Maybe this whole small world thing is why, just prior to running into Emilie Wolgan and her friends, I had a 45-minute conversation with Darren and Monty Seidler, people who felt like good friends even though we had never talked in person before. Or why, on my way to meeting Darren and Monty, I ran into my high school friend Jim Steward in the lobby of the Nebraska Union.

But these sorts of things didn't just happen in Lincoln. They also occurred when I visited watch parties in Chicago and Seattle.

On the subway ride to McGee's in Chicago, I ran into one of my professors from graduate school. He introduced me to a then-current graduate student named Scott who was traveling with him. As we talked on the short walk from the subway stop to McGee's I was impressed with Scott as both a person and a young scholar. Today, I'm happy to say that he's now one of my friends and colleagues at Ohio University.

In McGee's I ran into a young man from Scottsbluff named Greg Cervantes whose family ran a couple of Mexican food restaurants in Scottsbluff.

In Seattle, I found out that the oldest fan at the watch party, 92-year-old Irene Elder, had worked at the Great Western sugar factory in Scottsbluff in 1929. I ran into two former students of mine. I then met Jerry Henderson, whose nephew graduated from Scottsbluff High School. After a brief exchange, I realized that his nephew, Dave Cook, was only a year behind me in school and, in fact, was a friend of my brother's. Later, as the game wound down, Jerry handed me his cell phone and said, "I have somebody here I think you would like to talk to." Not surprisingly, he had called his nephew Dave and put us together on the phone.

I've since discovered that my experiences weren't all that unusual.[1] Beth Townsend, who traveled all over the world during her time in the Air Force, explains: "It also seems that whenever you meet someone from home, they know someone you do. I met a guy who grew up in the next town over when I was in Korea. Once when I was attending a class at UVA [the University of Virginia] in Charlottesville, a man approached me and asked me if I had a sister who taught English in a small town in Nebraska. Turns out, he was talking about my sister who taught his children in Pawnee City."

In a lot of ways, get-togethers of Nebraskans are a bit like extended family reunions. You're bound to run into people you know, people who know people you know, and people you've never met but feel like you know.[2]

That's why I'm more than a little bothered by the use of the word HuskerNation to describe Husker fans. First, it's trying a little too hard to make Nebraska seem big or important; as if using "nation" somehow makes everyone forget that Nebraska is, by technical definition, a desolate state.

In addition, the term nation is so impersonal. Except for their leaders, nations are composed of nameless, faceless, generic people. I'd go as far to say that nations are unfortunate collections of stereotypes. "The French" are rude, "the Americans" are arrogant, "the Japanese" take a lot of pictures, and so on. These caricatures are rarely positive, which is why caricatures of Nebraskans are of the hick and hayseed variety. We don't need HuskerNation to help us perpetuate those stereotypical images.

More importantly, though, the qualities that Nebraskans hold dear aren't typically ascribed to nations. How many nations have you heard described as hard workers, good neighbors, or down-to-earth folks? These are the kind of people we think of as inhabiting small towns and the country around them.

In other words, a 'ville.

So, as we Huskervillers talk about our small world experiences, what stands out is not the idea that we're all part of one nation. No, what stands out is the idea that, in the small world of Huskerville, everyone we meet is a friend, neighbor, or part of the family.[3]

Not surprisingly, then, Huskervillers often speak of fellow Huskers in ways that suggest a family relationship. Says Matt Shurtliff in his HuskerPedia.com story: "You visit with them like extended family."[4]

Notes a HuskerPedia bulletin board user named BlueCreek, who now lives in Orange, California, "One more of the many reasons I am so proud to be Nebraskan—no matter where in the world you might travel, if you meet another Nebraskan you might as well be family."[5]

Listen to these other Huskervillers talk about their extended families:

SANDI DARBY, FEDERAL WAY, WASHINGTON: No matter where [in the world] we may be, we meet someone who is from Nebraska. They immediately strike up a conversation. There remains a "kinship" regardless of how long you may have been away.

JOHN BRUNS, BOISE, IDAHO: Watching a game with others from the "Husker

Family" brings a little of that atmosphere to Idaho. It's also a great way to meet people from my home state and surprisingly find out that we know someone in common.

Chris Tradewell, Hartford, Wisconsin: It is like having an extended family all over the world. We are all interconnected and truly care about each other.

Ed Vinton, Atlanta: Nebraska football is like family.

Matthew Grosz, New Bern, North Carolina: Everyone knows someone who played for Nebraska. You're rooting for your friend, your friend's brother, your neighbor's son—it's like a big family.

Alisa Bredensteiner, Chicago: The emotional connection with the team in Nebraska is more than fandom, it feels much more like family.

Jill Hayhurst, Topeka, Kansas: It is a family and part of who you are.

Arthur Hudson, Yerevan, Armenia: Being a Cornhusker is like being part of one big family.

You don't even need a big crowd to find a Husker family connection. You can, as the following story—told by a Huskerviller on the HuskerPedia Web site—illustrates, even be in a cab in Aruba: "On my honeymoon in Aruba 9 years ago, I get into a cab and our driver was wearing a N[ational] C[hampionship] sweatshirt and a Husker cap. I asked him where he got them and he tells me that his brother sold 'Rumbas'[6] at Memorial Stadium in Lincoln. When he found out that Mama Bear and I were from Nebraska, he wouldn't accept our $ for the ride."[7]

We don't need much of an invitation to start seeking these family connections either. We might overhear a Nebraska town name or notice a family name on a credit card, as the following two stories respectively illustrate:

I'm in L.A. visiting a college buddy (he grew up in Lincoln and is a fellow UNL grad). We went to Santa Monica and ended up in a tiny English Pub packed wall to wall. My buddy overhears some guy say "Grand Island" so we struck up a conversation with him and the two guys he was with. Turns out this guy and one of the other guys currently live in Grand Island and both had worked farming for my grandpa in O'Neill in the early-mid '70s.[8]

We all [the family] grew up on a farm in northeast Nebraska. After high school in '78, my brother moved out to Portland, OR. He ended up pumping gas. One day, an older lady was paying for her gas with a credit card. Brother noticed her last name was the same as ours. It's not an everyday household name, so he struck up a conversation with her. It turns out she is married to my grandpa's nephew. She knew my grandpa, who died in '42, and proceeded to tell my brother all about our homeplace! We never knew these people existed.[9]

Sometimes, the familial connections are a few degrees of separation, but Huskervillers manage to find them anyway. A Huskerviller in suburban

Philadelphia illustrates how: "I grew up in Western Maryland (my parents are both from Neb, lived in MD since 1972—the year I was born). Anyway, my Mom's brother still has a farm in Weston (just outside of Wahoo). My brother's roommate his freshman year in college at the US Merchant Marine Academy in Kings Point, NY, turns out to be the next door neighbor of my Mom's brother (since we are talking farms here, next door neighbor is actually a few miles, but still, pretty strange stuff)."[10]

Another Huskerviller residing in Pennsylvania, Bob Sklenar, remembers looking at a sign-in sheet during a watch party and seeing a familiar name. "I spoke to the lady and her mother and it turns out that the mother is second cousin of my brother's father-in-law from Plattsmouth."

The funny thing is Nebraskans don't even have to plan to get together to experience this small world phenomenon. We often simply stumble upon one another.

One of the more popular items in recent years on the HuskerPedia discussion board was an offseason post asking people to share their "'It's a Small World' Nebraska travel experiences."[11] The first story posted, by LutheranHusker, was illustrative:

> My wife and I were on our honeymoon on Maui, and we took a helicopter tour of the island. During the trip, you have headphones on to cancel out the noise. You can hear the pilot speaking on your headset, and they play music during takeoff, landing, and at a few different points of the ride. Well, as we were taking off, the music they played was Alan Parsons Project's "Sirius" (from the Tunnel Walk).
> My wife and I looked at each other, laughed, and started clapping along like we do at the stadium. The other couple on the helicopter sitting behind us noticed it (they had the same song on their headsets), and the wife pointed to the Husker logo on my watch and mouthed, "We're from Nebraska too!"
> After the trip when we could actually hear each other, we found out that they had grown up in Lincoln, used to live in our neighborhood, but had since moved to Texas because of work.[12]

Of course, all this running into each other is a lot easier when Huskervillers follow the community dress code: some bit of attire, usually red, that says "Nebraska," "Husker," or "Cornhusker" on it. As the previous chapter suggested, we Huskervillers don't have just one Husker hat, shirt, or coat that we dig out to wear on game days. No, we have closets full of Husker clothing and hats that we wear throughout the year and for many different occasions.

People within the borders of Nebraska take these presence-generating practices for granted, so much so that Husker attire becomes part of the scenery for us. Outside of Nebraska, though, Husker attire serves another function: a mobile welcome sign that alerts other expatriate Huskervillers to our presence. "If I'm wearing my Husker jacket," says Terry Kunc of Washington, DC, "I'm often stopped on the street by people who want to talk Husker football."

Marty Martinson of Scottsbluff, Nebraska, notes, "No matter where you go—you can be in New York City in Rockefeller Center—[if you] have a Nebraska sweatshirt on and someone will stop [and ask], 'Are you really from Nebraska?' [They answer], 'yes,' and they'll talk for fifteen minutes about football."

These "are you from Nebraska" exchanges occur throughout the country. Denver resident Leroy Horst, who has lived outside of Nebraska for 40 years, says that—almost without fail—his "are you from Nebraska" exchanges have been pleasant experiences. "When I walk through a mall or on the street here in Denver, and I see someone wearing Nebraska paraphernalia," he says, "I'll say 'Go Big Red!' And you know, it never, there's only been one time that the response has not been positive or the response has not been something to just initiate a conversation."

Connecticut-based Husker Jim Berryman's license plate holder, as his story demonstrates, quite literally worked as a mobile "Hi, I'm a Nebraskan" sign one day:

> Recently I was driving on Interstate 95 in New Haven, Connecticut, when in my rear-view mirror I noticed a guy in a car waving at me in a very strange manner. I was wondering if my car was on fire, my trunk was open, or if I had cut him off.
>
> I became a bit alarmed as I saw him speed up behind me. He began to tailgate me very closely all the while waving his hands like he was nuts. I continued on, knowing that my car seemed to be in working order. I knew I hadn't cut him off in traffic, but for the life of me I couldn't figure out why he was trying to get my attention. In Connecticut, more people tailgate than don't, so it was no big deal. I did what I always do when I'm being tailgated. I started driving slower.
>
> Then he came up beside me in the far left lane. By now, he had rolled down the passenger side window and was leaning across the seat, left hand on the steering wheel, and his right hand was waving and trying to get my attention. Did he have a gun? Was he the stalker I didn't know I had? No.
>
> His right hand lifted up into view. Fully expecting to see his middle finger come up, I almost turned away. But I didn't. He didn't raise his middle finger. He raised his index finger, into a "Number 1" sign. He was mouthing the words "We're Number 1!!"
>
> Ahhhh!! I knew what was up. I remembered the "Nebraska, Go Big Red" license plate holder I had around my Connecticut plate. Instead of a crazy, madman out to kill me, he was a Husker fan, bonding with another Husker fan at 60 miles an hour on I-95. I waved back at him with a number 1 sign as

well. He then got in front of me, and had the same Nebraska license plate holder that I had purchased at the Nebraska Bookstore on one trip back to Lincoln.[13]

When we out-of-state Nebraskans spot these signs indicating the presence of another Huskerviller, we often react with just this kind of excitement. Our almost reflexive response—even among introverts like myself—is something along the lines of "I'm from Nebraska, too!" or, if we're playing it closer to the vest, "Are you from Nebraska?" (Fortunately, most of these exchanges do not happen on interstate highways!) My friend and colleague Alena Amato Ruggerio, for instance, decided to blend in to the Kentuckiana Huskers watch party she attended by wearing a red sweater, which, she told me, "turned into an invitation to every single person there to ask me, 'Are you from Nebraska?'"

After this opening question, we then talk like third cousins at a family reunion, exchanging hometowns to see where the connections take us. Alena reports that after she explained her connection to me, and that she was in Louisville to collect interviews on my behalf, the Kentuckiana Huskers then "wanted to know what part of Nebraska *you* were from." "When you meet someone and find out they are also from Nebraska," Kerianne Kluge of Louisville explains, "you can ask them their hometown, and chances are, they will know someone you know from their hometown; therefore, the state is like one huge community."

Matthew Grosz illustrates how this process works:

> It was after the 1996 season, during the winter and I had my Nebraska sweatshirt on. I was working down in eastern North Carolina as an engineer. I was having lunch with a friend and mentor of mine when a Marine Corps Colonel walks past me and goes, "Grand Island." Without thinking, I said, "Bellevue."
>
> We proceeded to talk about our hometowns and the Huskers, the season, the surprising loss to Texas in the Big 12 Championship, the latest recruiting class, and the outlook for the 1997 season, for about 15 minutes like old friends.
>
> My friend sat there with his mouth open the whole time.
> Afterwards, he asked: "Did you know him?"
> I said, "Nope, never saw him before in my life."

Exchanging hometowns is a vital part of these interactions because, since darn near every town in Nebraska is a small town, chances are pretty good that we'll know someone that they know. "When you're raised in a state with that small of a population," says Brian Winkle of Brooklyn Park, Minnesota, "it seems like almost everybody knows everybody else."

Because so many of us are from small towns, we even think of people in other small towns near us (meaning, roughly, a 60-mile radius) as neighbors. So, when I discovered a student in my class at Ohio University was from the Nebraska panhandle town of Kimball—about 40 miles south of my hometown of Scottsbluff—I thought of her as being from my Nebraska neighborhood.

Nebraska neighborhoods can emerge all over the world. A Husker living in London explains:

> I'm at my local super market here in the Notting Hill area of London with my girlfriend (fellow born-n-bred Nebraskan) who is wearing a Nebraska sweatshirt. The man behind us in line asks if we know where Blue Hill is. (We do— my high school sports teams took on Blue Hill multiple times per year.) It turns out that he was born in Blue Hill and was raised someplace in northeast Nebraska ... Laurel maybe? I can't remember. Apparently he now lives in London and acts as a "supervisor" for undergraduate college students from some school in Oregon ... Pacific Lutheran, I think ... who are doing a year abroad in England.[14]

This story then prompted a response from another Husker with a Blue Hill connection: "My father was born and raised in Blue Hill. I know the town well with all the visits to grandma's house as a kid. While I was on a cruise to the Caribbean I went walking around the ship in my National Champions T-shirt. As I stopped to look around a couple came up and asked where I was from. Turns out they were from Fremont and now lived in New Jersey. All we talked about for 2 hours was NU football. We still talk every once in a while for the last 7 years."[15]

Even big city Huskers share this Nebraska neighborhood orientation, as VABeachHusker illustrates in his HuskerPedia small world story: "When my wife, kids and I moved to Virginia Beach, we purchased our home from a family moving to Omaha! The father of the family was originally from Gretna. Also, when we joined our church in Virginia Beach, the couple that sponsored us was from Lincoln. Finally, we have neighbors 3 blocks down the street who are both from Seward. Huskers—taking over Virginia Beach.... 1 house at a time."[16]

All of these small world connections help us Huskervillers to remember to "all stick together in all kinds of weather" while simultaneously defying the laws of time and space; yesterday and next door are always just around the corner when Huskervillers gather.[17] Physically, we may find ourselves in places such as a helicopter over Maui, a cab in Aruba, or a car on a Connecticut highway, but existentially we're in Huskerville.

We have all congregated in a metaphorical barn for a contemporary cornhusking.

While big events like Husker games do much to bring us together, their residue lingers in such a way that allows us to keep one foot in the barn as we go through our daily lives. The sight of a red Huskers shirt in a North Carolina restaurant is enough to pull the rest of us back into the barn.

The conversations that follow these sightings are a type of everyday ritual for us Huskervillers. We follow the same routine—exchange hometowns and see who we both know—every time as a way of reminding ourselves that, despite the distances among us, we're still all sticking together.[18]

"It's like there's a bond present," says Matthew Grosz of New Bern, North Carolina. "Like in the past where your neighbor was just 50 miles down the road. You're out in the middle of nowhere, and you see someone from home—it's like seeing your neighbor for the first time in a month or so. You've been isolated for so long that it just feels GOOD to meet someone from your neck of the woods. You share common experiences and the Huskers."

We also share an attachment that envelops us, sheltering us from all of the everyday forces such as time, space, and change that work to uproot us and create what ritual scholars Sally Moore and Barbara Myeroff call "indeterminacy in ... human affairs."[19] Husker football provides a sense of security, a sense of order, a small world in which certainty replaces indeterminacy. It anchors us.

As Willa Cather scholar Sue Rosowski explained to me during a walk on the University of Nebraska–Lincoln campus in the fall of 1999, "When you have as they say, a football stadium as the third largest city in the state, it is such a daunting thought. At the same time there is something of a sense of security, I think, with people who go there to be around everyone else like that."

Moreover, the Huskers' continued success and adherence to the heritage of homesteading, or doing things the right way, gives us confidence that our shelter will withstand those forces. As HuskerPedia member sdhusker notes in his praise of the reign of Tom Osborne, Husker football gives "Nebraskans something as sure as the sun coming up every day. And when you live and die by the tractor, that [success] is a mighty, mighty big reassurance to have in your life."[20]

What I've realized, then, is that Huskerville offers us the symbolic equivalent of a gated community. The locale of a Huskerville not only offers us a respite from those whose words and actions attempt to station us as desolate hicks, it also provides us with the security afforded by home. Home, writes geographer Edward Relph, provides "a secure point from which to look out on the world, a firm grasp of one's own position in the order of things, and a significant spiritual and psychological attachment to somewhere in particular."[21]

Such attachments are not to be taken lightly. They are profound connections. They provide a particular kind of security, not just an "I feel safe" or "I feel comfortable here" type of security. No, they offer us something vital to human existence, something that philosophers and social critics such as Anthony Giddens refer to as "ontological security."[22] This is the feeling that our very being, the essence of who we are, is safe and secure in a particular place.

"A stable sense of self-identity," writes Giddens, is at the core of ontological security.[23] This identity, moreover, depends primarily upon our "capacity to keep a particular narrative going."[24] Huskerville offers a place where that narrative continues.[25] This is, undoubtedly, why a fight song with corny lyrics written in the 1930s still resonates among Huskervillers today.

Ontological security, continues Giddens, is an antidote for anxiety. While he writes of a more general, existential kind of anxiety, we experience it in specific forms when we move away from home, feel time pass by too quickly, and notice things just aren't the way they used to be—in general, when we feel forces pulling up our roots.

Thus, when social and economic changes threaten to uproot Nebraska's agricultural traditions, we need Huskerville to remind us of what Nebraska means.[26] When every town in the country with more than 10,000 people has a Wal-Mart and McDonald's, and starts to look like every other town in the country with more than 10,000 people, we need Huskerville to remind us that we have a unique heritage.

This isn't anything new—writer Louise Erdrich notes that "Willa Cather's novels about Nebraska homesteads are elegies to vanishing virtues, which she links with an unmechanized and pastoral vision of agriculture."[27] It also isn't anything specifically unique to Nebraska, of course. But precisely because these forces of uprooting are relentless and pervasive, we embrace the security afforded by Huskerville.

13

Conclusion: To Dwell

When I first began thinking about this book, I was more than a little confused. I was struggling to come up with answers to several interrelated questions. Why did I still feel like a Nebraskan a decade after leaving the state? Why did something like Husker football mean so much to me? Why does it mean so much to other Nebraskans? Why did the idea of being a Nebraskan seem so tied to Husker football? And, most important, why couldn't I—an introspective, educated person—explain the pull of Husker football when asked to explain its uniqueness compared with other team-fan relationships?

Thankfully, my neighbors in Huskerville have helped me sort through these questions. Their insights, offered generously and almost entirely without condition,[1] led me to identify how the rooting process works as an anchor for our cultural identity, how being a Husker fan is a means of collectively (and continuously) enacting the values of the Nebraska homesteaders, and how coming together in the contemporary equivalent of cornhuskings puts the small, unique world of Huskerville on the map.

At the same time, our conversations—as well as the comments of non–Nebraskans who have read drafts of this book—have raised a set of new questions for me. Would we embrace the football program with such fervor if it was not, as some have said, "the only game in town"? Even more technically desolate states have two major state universities and thus potentially divided loyalties among their citizenry.[2] Would be so passionate about a team that won a lot of games but didn't seem to reflect our values? More specifically, how we would we respond to a national championship contending team that ran the West Coast offense, had few Nebraskans on its roster, and seemed to treat the victory as more important than the game? Or, conversely, what would we say and do if a team lost a lot of games while seemingly reflecting our values?[3] Does our reaction to recent seasons of 5–6 and

7–7 say more about us or more about the different people involved with the football program during those seasons?

Here's what I believe: winning helps, as does being the only game in town. Without them, we might struggle to find such a powerful and comprehensive unifying experience, although undoubtedly we would (and, arguably, should) find additional opportunities for communitas experiences. At the same time, the success and prominence of the football program has provided us with an unparalleled opportunity to publicly—and collectively—enact and celebrate ideals which might otherwise remain beneath the surface.

The value of such opportunities is immeasurable, for they provide us with the means to construct, affirm, and re-generate an experience of ontological security sought by humans everywhere: to cherish a sense of place and to richly dwell within it.

The eloquent cultural geographer and rancher Keith Basso calls the notion of sense of place "a universal genre of experience,"[4] but one that often escapes our notice until our attention is drawn to it.[5]

I think my leaving Nebraska, oddly enough, helped me to begin to reflect upon what I am calling Nebraska and Huskerville's sense of place. That's not to say that I did not have some awareness of Huskerville, only that my awareness of its characteristics and its ability to take up space in my own life more fully emerged after moving away.

I don't think I'm alone in this regard.

Some of the most passionate Huskervillers who visited with me were those who no longer lived in Nebraska (or never had the opportunity to live there in the first place). Yet we all remain rooted there.

Basso explains why: "Fueled by sentiments of inclusion, belonging, and connectedness to the past, sense of place roots individuals in the social and cultural soils from which they have sprung together, holding them there in the grip of a shared identity."[6] No wonder Huskerviller Harold H. Hunter describes the experience of returning to Lincoln from Dallas in these words: "You feel grounded again."[7]

Sense of place is more than an appreciation for an area's geography; it is not just scenic. It is also, Basso says, "an expression of community involvement."[8]

Put simply, a strong sense of place also promotes communion with others and vice versa.

So, while Nebraskans have long appreciated the idea of neighborliness given our distance from one another, Huskervillers are also engaged in another very human tendency: to congregate. Writes Huskerviller Darren Carlson, "From coast to coast, Husker fans gather not just to watch the games, but also to surround themselves with other Nebraskans. They do it to feel more at home, no matter where they might be in the world."[9]

Americans, in general, have long enjoyed the company of others. In his famous observations about the fledging American democracy in the 1830s, French writer Alexis de Tocqueville proclaimed, "In no other country in the world has the principle of association been more successfully used, or applied to a great multitude of objects, than in America."[10] Although de Tocqueville was writing about political associations, and well before the advent of college football, his commentary can easily be transferred to the associations evident in Huskerville. Consider, for example, his definition of an association and how well it reflects the characteristics of Huskerville: "An association consists simply in the public assent which a number of individuals give to certain doctrines; and in the engagement which they contract to promote in a certain manner the spread of those doctrines."[11]

The spreading of those doctrines—which in Huskerville include working hard, being neighborly, and remaining down-to-earth—through what de Tocqueville calls "the power of meeting" might well describe the allure of watch parties: "When an association is allowed to establish centres of action at certain important points in the country, its activity is increased, and its influence extended."[12]

The idea that "we'll all stick together in all kinds of weather"—evident in the over four decades of continuous sellouts of Memorial Stadium—to root for a Husker victory and to celebrate a way of life might be illustrated by de Tocqueville's observation that "an association unites into one channel the efforts of diverging minds, and urges them vigorously towards the one end which it clearly points out."[13]

The urgency with which Huskervillers stick together to celebrate our ideals may well have some connection to the difficulty of forming associations these days. We don't live in de Tocqueville's America, nor do we live in Cather and Sandoz's Nebraska. As Harvard professor Robert Putnam pointed out in his 2000 book *Bowling Alone*, during the twenty years encompassing the mid-1970s to the mid-1990s, the number of Americans participating in civic associations and attending public meetings dropped dramatically. (In rural Nebraska, of course, the number of people who *could* participate in associations has declined as the rural population has decreased.)

While some evidence points to increasing civic participation in the first few years of this century,[14] other evidence indicates that we have fewer close friends than we used to. The General Social Survey found that, between 1985 and 2004, the number of Americans who reported having no one to discuss important matters with almost tripled while the number of people who counted their neighbors as confidants dropped by more than half.[15]

At the same time, we are simultaneously fighting a collective battle against the loss of places that have a sense of place. French scholar Marc Augé observes that we are losing meaningful places left and right as what he calls "non-places" proliferate. Non-places, according to Augé, include airport terminals, interstate highways, chain stores, etc.; in short, non-places can be found *any old place* as opposed to *somewhere in particular*.

Non-places may give us benefits such as efficiency and predictability— we know what kind of food we'll get at McDonald's and how fast we'll be served[16]—but they deprive us of the unique experiences that should come with dwelling in a particular place. The result, argues writer Philip Sheldrake, is "a crisis of place in Western societies—a sense of rootlessness, dislocation or displacement."[17]

My hometown of Scottsbluff, for example, now contains the kinds of fast food eateries and chain grocery stores that populate all the other towns its size across the country. Yet, one of the most popular fast food establishments in town is a locally owned place called Scotty's, which appropriately features an item called the Big Red Burger. Sadly, Scotty's is more the exception than the rule in Scottsbluff—and the same holds true in other towns and cities across the state.

In a University of Nebraska study of 52 rural Nebraska counties, locally owned retail establishments have seen their share of "the retail pie" halved over the last 20 years.[18] Yet Scotty's continued existence points to a crucial characteristic of places that have a particular "sense of place": they are, says Basso, "stoutly resistant to change."[19]

At least, they seem that way to those who inhabit them.

The advantage of Huskerville is that the place itself lacks particular physical boundaries. While it is rooted within the borders of Nebraska, and it reminds us of the connection to the land that falls within those borders, Huskerville is *more than a* physical location; as an imagined community it can also collect, preserve, and enact a particular way of life.[20]

"The link between imagination and place," Eugene Victor Walter reminds us, "is no trivial matter. The existential question, 'Where do I belong?' is addressed to the imagination."[21]

When we imaginatively address the question, "Where do I belong?" we begin the process of creating what German philosopher Martin Heidegger called places for "dwelling." To be human, Heidegger noted, is to dwell, to turn undifferentiated space into a meaningful place.[22] To dwell is to inhabit some place in particular, for as the late cultural anthropologist Clifford Geertz astutely observed, "No one lives in the world in general."[23]

From vast landscapes to unfurnished apartments to slabs of sidewalk, humans of all kinds encounter spaces and seek to inhabit them, to dwell in them, to transform them into places of meaning and value. I recall, for example, hearing my friend Natalie Dollar talk about her interviews with young people living on the streets of two U.S. cities.[24] These young people refused to accept the label of homeless because, in their world, the public places where they took up residence were their homes.

To *take up space*, then, might also be thought of as dwelling. That young couple huddled on the sidewalk by the same bus stop day after day might be merely taking up space in the minds of passersby, but they are symbolically taking up the space around them, calling it home, and making it a dwelling place.

Heidegger's ideas, notes rhetorical scholar Michael J. Hyde, are grounded in the work of the ancient Greeks, who used the term *ethea* to refer to "'dwelling places' where people can deliberate about and 'know together' some matter of interest. Such dwelling places define the grounds, the abodes or habitats, where a person's ethics and moral character take form and develop."[25] Hyde focuses upon argumentation and public deliberation as the means by which dwelling places are constructed, but Huskerville—as I hope this book has demonstrated—is a dwelling place constructed both through collective, ritual performances and individual, everyday enactments.

Consider, for instance, how Hyde's explanation reflects the idea of Huskerville if we substitute the bracketed words in the following quotation. We are, Hyde writes, "[fans] whose symbolic constructions both create and invite others into a place where they can dwell and feel at home while thinking about and discussing the truth of some matter that the [fan] has already attempted to disclose and show-forth in a specific way with his or her [rooting]."[26]

Our rooting and our team's performance ultimately *do* serve as arguments for, and rhetoric about, a particular way of doing things.[27] In this respect, what happens in Huskerville is the same as what happens in the dwelling places that Hyde identifies: we articulate what we believe to be ethical and right. We demonstrate it to skeptical others who do not see what we experience, in hopes of both gaining their respect and, potentially, their adherence.

At the same time, our collective and individual performances in Huskerville address a second audience: ourselves.

As we negotiate the tensions between the physical surroundings that signify our uprootedness and the imagined place we call home, we act in ways that help us to belong. "We need to be capable of affirming our origins, a place, a people, a way of life, a set of relationships," writes Jim Wayne Miller. "Not to acknowledge these freely is to lose a part of one's self."[28]

Without this mooring, we not only are not sure of where we are, we are also equally uncertain about what we should do. "People everywhere *act* on the integrity of their dwelling," claim Steven Feld and Keith Basso.[29]

No wonder, then, that when the University of Nebraska's Bureau of Sociological Research asked Nebraskans to come up with positive characteristics of the state, the most prominent response was "good place to live."[30] Both halves of that phrase are important, for the "good place" is where we dwell and "to live" is how we "act on the integrity of" that dwelling.

What we do every day, how we enact our values, how we perform collectively—all of these are wrapped up within the phrase "to live." Dwelling is living in a way that is meaningful. As Basso adds, our dwelling can generate a "sense of place" so intense that its "social and moral force may reach sacramental proportions"[31]—which is why we Huskervillers often compare our devotion to something like a civic religion.

This is also why we work so hard to preserve that which seems to be changing—and why we do so through the conduit of football. "Sports," observes religious writer Bob Welch, "remains one of the arenas in which lives are shaped, courage is tested, faith is steeled. In an ever-changing world, it's a place of permanence."[32]

So, like our homesteading forebears, Huskervillers continue to struggle with circumstances outside of our control—even as we like to think that we can control them through our rooting. While the early homesteaders once followed the bizarre dictum "rain follows the plow" (that is, if the land was plowed, the climate would change) because they steadfastly believed that if they worked hard enough they could control seemingly uncontrollable circumstances, we continue to root today.

Today, we can't control socio-economic forces that are de-populating rural Nebraska, and we can't control what the Husker coaches and players do on the field, but we work hard to keep alive the way of life that has been enacted in the fields and on the field. This struggle is in many ways unique to Nebraskans, but it is also one that in other ways reflects an ongoing struggle of all human beings: the desire to dwell in meaningful places and to act with integrity.

So, as we act, we continue to keep these dwelling places alive and vibrant. Rather than thinking of imagined communities like Huskerville or incorporated communities like Scottsbluff as static entities, we should remember that "communities are living creatures, nurtured and nourished by rhetorical discourse."[33]

In particular, we tend to our communities by telling stories about them, for "a place without a story is really nowhere at all."[34] The story of Huskerville told within these pages points out how Nebraskans nourish, nurture, and tend our sense of place by rooting it in a collective memory, defining it through enactment of homesteader ideals, and maintaining it through ritual performances of contemporary cornhusking.

You see, we're still doing agricultural work. It's not *only* or *just* symbolic work; it's meaningful, purposeful work that helps us stay rooted—even if the winds of change raise new questions for us to consider. This story of Huskerville illustrates that—to borrow from the late Sue Rosowski, an expert on the literature of Willa Cather—"a sense of place can serve as an anecdote, reminding us that a sense of place is not a lesson to be learned and set aside, but a habit that will support a lifetime."[35]

Appendix: Stories from Huskerville

Kevin J. Bourn

I was born in O'Neill, Nebraska, in 1974, and then my family moved us to York when I was three years old. As a young child I spent most of my time with the neighbor kids playing football, and dreaming of becoming a Nebraska Cornhusker someday. Then when I was nine my father was transferred to Webster City, Iowa, and we moved once more.

Even though we moved to another state my family members were still proud Nebraskans. We were still fixed on the television on Saturday game days. I can still remember my father and I yelling at the TV during those Oklahoma battles. When I was thirteen, tragedy struck our family. My father, who had been battling cancer for years, passed away at age 41. We buried him back in Nebraska, in his hometown of Niobrara.

Life continued for my family and I as Iowans, but I never lost that Husker spirit. Going through junior high and high school was tough sometimes during the fall and football season. Everyone knew I was a loyal Nebraska fan and I took a lot of ribbing from my friends. It usually didn't get to me too often though because Nebraska won most of the time (I still have not heard the last of the Iowa State upset of the '92 Husker team in Ames).

I graduated in 1992 and my mother decided she would have a better chance of finding a better living if she moved to Florida and lived with her sister. I moved down with her that summer and I lasted about thirty days. I became very homesick, and decided to move back to Iowa and go to Iowa Central Community College in Webster City. It was very hard to leave my mom since we became so close through the years without my dad around. The first semester of junior college was really bad. I ended up with a 1.6

grade point and decided that I was not smart enough for college, so I quit. I got a job in town at Murray McMurray Hatchery where I worked full-time. They treated me great and also gave me a hard time about being a Cornhusker (the Lawrence Phillips incident did not help me at all).[1]

When I was twenty-one I decided it was time to get educated. So I enrolled back into Iowa Central Community College. I learned how to study and pulled my grade point back up to a 3.3 before graduating with my associate of arts degree at age twenty-four. After this I wanted to tackle my next goal, and that was attending a university. I decided to follow my dream and attend the University of Nebraska. I got accepted and that summer I picked up and moved here to Lincoln. I have completed a year and a half of school and it still has not sunk in that I have made it here. Even though I never made it as a football player, I still am very proud to walk the campus and wear the red-and-white. It feels good to be back to my roots here in Nebraska. I know my mother is proud of me, and I know my father would be too if he were here to see me. I remember when my friends used to give me a hard time about being a Husker fan. I would just tell them, "You just don't understand, I have Big Red blood flowing through my veins." There is no place like Nebraska.

E. Steve Cassells

I now live in Colorado, but have parents still in western Nebraska, so I go back regularly, often stopping by the Big Red store in town to replenish supplies of clothing, etc. Many of us do wear our hearts on our sleeves, regardless of the atmosphere where we happen to be. Having taught in Illinois for about 15 years, the heart of the Big When (I mean 10/11), I regularly had to take heat from the locals for my loyalties out West. Part of the fun. I always had a big red N coffee cup I took to lectures.

Now, living in Colorado, there is a mix of migrated Nebraskans here who are friendly, and a large collection of Buffs fans who are not. Local sports shows really hammer us regularly with Husker jokes and references to criminality. The occasional problems with players at CU and CSU lately have quelled the criminal charges for the moment, though they tend to have a short memory.

When I was a kid in the '50s, the biggest day of the year was Thanksgiving, when we would schedule T-Day Dinner at grandma's around the NU-OU game on TV. I kind of miss that, with it being moved to the next day, as well as the decline in the OU rivalry and the replacement with CU.

Years later I can remember turkey hunting near Chadron, NE, on Saturdays, and taking time out during the hunt to sit under a tree and catch the game on the radio. In the '80s, sitting in the visitors' stands at Boulder, I can remember the crowd being taunted by a drunken frat boy when CU was threatening to go ahead, and seeing an NU farmer in the stands, complete with red coveralls, walk down and flatten him with a single punch.

I have been to Memorial Stadium only once, but it was Turner Gill's debut as quarterback, and I still remember thinking he looked like a ballet dancer out there, the way he juked around. I think we scored about 60 points that day vs. CU, a point a minute!

As far as "Being Nebraskan" goes, I know I've probably idealized it a bit since becoming an adult and moving away. I had an idyllic childhood there, yet couldn't wait to get to the big city after growing up. I do know I appreciate the slower pace there when I go home now. Drivers seem more willing to help stranded travelers, and are less rude on the roads. There seems to be more trust of strangers, which may or not be good.

Economics keeps me living elsewhere now, and my wife, from Denver, will keep me from moving back in the future. However, I'll be bleeding Nebraska red until my canoe turns upside down for the last time.

Lt. Col. Mike Caudle (retired)

Our trip to Lincoln via Omaha was a truly enjoyable experience (even though we were scalped on the football field). Everywhere we went we were treated as special guests. People on the streets of Omaha would single us out and welcome us to Nebraska. They were very complimentary of our bandsmen as they met them in town. On Saturday prior to the game, our band buses unloaded beside the baseball stadium and formed up for the march-in to Memorial Stadium. Hundreds, perhaps thousands, of Big Red fans lined both sides of the street and cheered and applauded as the [Texas A&M] Aggie Band marched proudly toward the stadium in military fashion. It was such a great feeling to be entering into "enemy" territory with such a warm welcome. During the half time performance, I watched from the upper level of the press box as the Nebraska fans gave the Aggie Band a standing ovation throughout their drill. I understand the noise meter pegged out to the maximum from your fans. Then, I noticed several members of the Nebraska Band standing in line to shake the hands of several of our band members. I assure you that wouldn't happen at the University of Texas. After the game in which we had our heads handed back to us, fans at most schools would taunt us when leaving the stadium. Not your fans. I heard comments like, "Thanks for bringing your band" ... "You have a wonderful band" ... "Great halftime show" ... "Thanks for coming to Nebraska" ... "Have a safe trip home" ... and on and on. The entire weekend we spent in Nebraska, I never heard one bad comment from any of your fans. How refreshing to visit a place that understands that the game is just that ... a game. Everything I had heard about your fans was true. You really are the class of college football fans. The only other school that I have witnessed that ranks close to you is Penn State. But you are better. Thanks for making our visit to your state and university a pleasurable and memorable one.[2]

Annette Frain

I was born and raised in York, Nebraska, until the age of 17. Then I thought it was time to "get out." Much to my surprise I was back six months later, getting ready to attend the University of Nebraska–Lincoln for my freshman year. I knew from the time that I was young that UNL was where I wanted to go to college. But, what I didn't realize was the impact that it would have. The school pride was tremendous.

I had attended many Husker games with my father, but nothing compared to the preparation for the first game kick off in '96 when I was in the stands with my fellow students, rather than my father. It was exciting as well as sad when it all sank in. I didn't have to drive an hour to get to Memorial Stadium. I also didn't stop at Burger King for my usual chicken sandwich and Dr. Pepper, which had been a 10-year tradition.

Instead I was experiencing Husker football at a whole new level. I stood throughout the game with pride, I was a part of this sea of red. I was officially a student and this was my team. But something was missing—my father. He wasn't sitting next to me with his headphones on, mumbling when a "mistake" was made. He wasn't updating me on the new players and stats. Instead, I was hitting around a beach ball (until security took it away), and drinking out of someone's flask. This was football, UNL style!

I attended UNL for a year and a half, two football seasons, and then I decided to take some time off from college. I moved to New Jersey sporting my Husker pride. I wore a Nebraska national championship sweatshirt and jeans. From that point I didn't realize how my life was going to change. When asked where I was from I would say Nebraska with pride, and amazingly enough most knew about my famous football team that I supported.

I would get a gleam in my eye and have a flashback to "tunnel vision." The goose bumps would almost appear instantaneously before I'd jump back to reality. As the months passed, the urge to come home progressed in my heart. It was August when I decided that I needed a football fix. I called up my dad and told him I was coming home; much to his disappointment it was not for good. Rather my decision was to come home, for a game. He was ecstatic, as was I. Plus I managed to convince Meredith, a friend of mine (originally from Vermont), that she needed to experience a football Saturday in no place other than Lincoln, Nebraska.

It was set! I called Midwest Express Airlines and booked two round trip tickets for Omaha. We were going to homecoming. I counted down the days until I was going to be sitting in Memorial Stadium. Waiting for the day that I too could be in our stands, cheering on my team. I did have to wait till October, and I had to get caught up on the stats for myself since I lived so far away. I watched the games that actually were televised in New Jersey, and my boss had *The New York Times* waiting for me after game day. I was determined to be ready.

Meredith became just about as excited as I was to go to Nebraska. I could tell she was as eager as I was to enter Memorial Stadium on game day. Her eyes were wide and she did not realize the intensity that the game would cause. We were freezing cold, but that didn't damper the fun that was to be had by all. Then tunnel vision, I got goose bumps, and brushed a few tears out of the corners of my eyes. I was overwhelmed and speechless. I was so happy to be a part of that day, and happy that Meredith was just as moved by the whole experience.

Now a year later, I am counting down the days once again. This time my dad and I are going to homecoming, for old times sake. I will be on cloud nine, until it is time to leave and the clock has hit 00:00. But I can take away the memories and joy of taking part in another game. Not to mention I will be watching the team progress through the season from afar. But my support will always be with the team called the "Nebraska Cornhuskers."

So the next time I am asked, "Where are you from?" I will reply, "Nebraska" with the same gleam in my eye. Because there is no place like Nebraska, and for some reason that is the only way I can explain it.

Fritz Gottschalk

I am a US Army Special Forces officer and have deployed to some of the garden spots on earth. During the initial invasion of Haiti, I ended up in the city of Cap Haitien (the second largest city in the north part of the country). My team (Special Forces Detachment) ran missions from the city, to smaller towns in the countryside, showing presence, talking to folks making sure everything was going OK.

After everything settled down the US military started to get some of the nice things in life. This was about November, 1994. One day, right prior to Thanksgiving, I was returning from a patrol. As we approached the town, I saw two missionaries walking back from a roadside market. They kind of stood out, they were American (white) and dressed nicer than most Haitians.

We (me and the other guys on the team) stopped off to talk to them. That was one of our habits, if you see a friendly face, stop off and talk to them. They were both Catholic missionaries and had been running a nursing school in the area for several years (15–20 or so). One was about 50, the other was 74. Both were happy as heck and we had a good time talking. After about five minutes of talking, the conversation turned to hometowns. They were from just south of Lincoln! All three of us went nuts, and started to reminisce. After about 20 minutes of that, the guys on the team were starting to get bored (they were not from Nebraska, and were pretty tired of me bragging about the state), so the ladies invited us to dinner the next night to talk some more.

Dinner was very pleasant and Husker/Nebraska memories were exchanged. I invited them to the base camp for Thanksgiving, but they had other plans. We had just had Armed Forces Network TV installed at the base camp, so I invited them down for the OU/NU game. They couldn't make that one either, but did take up my offer for the Orange Bowl that year.

If you remember, Nebraska was playing the dreaded Miami Hurricanes, a constant thorn in the Huskers' side, so it promised to be a good one. The ladies showed up at the base camp and we went to the TV tent and took over. Being Special Forces, we were in the minority of the base camp, most of the other soldiers were from a regular infantry unit and thought we were pretty strange folks. When they saw us escorting these two ladies in, they started to harass us a bit about security. After a few quick words (rank helps), we proceeded to the TV tent to watch the Orange Bowl.

The older missionary was pretty much blind, but she more than made up for that in rowdiness. We all three were singing Nebraska songs, cheering every play. Awesome time. Middle of Haiti, combat zone, not the most pleasant of surroundings, sitting in an army tent, watching a fuzzy TV screen and the Huskers. It doesn't get any better, the surroundings kind of disappeared and we were just three folks from Nebraska sharing a good game. Neither of the ladies had seen a Husker game in the past 10 years, but they knew all about Tom Osborne and the boys.

After the first round of songs and rowdy cheers, the conventional army sergeant major (senior NCO, responsible for good order and discipline) ran into the tent and started to tell us to settle down. When he saw the two missionaries, he started to get a bit excited about the security posture (after all, they could have been spies!!!!). He gave me a stern look and started to light into me, but the older missionary cut him off (74 years old!). "I don't know who the heck you are, but these are the Huskers, and I am watching the game. Either settle down and watch the game with us, or get out." A sweet old Nebraska fan, partially blind (her eyes sparkled all the time, though), lighting into a big gruff infantry sergeant major. Priceless. He backed off, and we went back to the game.

If you remember correctly, the first quarter of the game was all Miami, so we were all a bit tense. Believe me, by that time, we had attracted a ton of naysayers and folks interested in teasing the captain (me) as his football team was struggling. Every year, I get real worked up about the Huskers, and brag a lot to the guys in the unit. Prior to that year, I had to take a ton of teasing when the Big Red Machine faltered during the bowl season.

The three true Husker fans in the tent more than answered them. As the game moved into the second quarter, Nebraska strength and conditioning started to show, and they started to give better than they were getting. Every time a Nebraska defender tackled a Miami player, the older nun would jump up and scream "Hit him again, remember '83!" Hilarious. I couldn't stop laughing. (1983 was the year that the two-point conversion didn't connect, and Nebraska went down to the Hurricanes. Side note: After that pass was deflected, you could hear the state sigh; honest, nobody talked in the house the next day.)

During the TV coverage, there was a picture of the Miami bench (3rd quarter or so, I think). The picture was of Warren Sapp (his senior season), on the bench with his head between his knees. He had an oxygen mask stuck to his face and ice packs all over his neck and head. He was plumb done in. Nebraska strength and conditioning. When the missionaries saw that, they told me the game was over.

The Huskers went on to win the game, the national title and all of the glory that went with it. I stayed in Haiti for another month or so. Whenever I saw the two missionaries, I always stopped, said hello and reminisced about the homeland, the game, the Huskers and life in general.

If you want to know about the essence of Nebraska, imagine two Catholic nuns, smiling away, eyes sparkling, in the middle of Haiti prior to the intervention. Putting themselves at risk, daily, to establish and run a nursing school. Neither one of them had been back to Nebraska for 10–15 years. One of them was 74, practically blind. Every time I saw them they had huge smiles on their face. Doing something nice for people who really needed it.

Matthew G. Grosz

We moved to Florida during the summer of 1980 and haven't been to a 'Huskers game since. This Oct. 7, against Iowa State, myself, my two brothers Milton and Dr. Michael, and my brother Milt's ex–UNL roommate Tim will be going to see the Cornhuskers play. To say we're EXCITED is to say the Sun is kinda warm!!! Every Football Saturday—REGARDLESS of where we are: New Bern, North Carolina (me), Tallahassee, Florida (Milt—a pilgrim in an UNHOLY land!!!) or Savannah, Georgia (Dr. Mike)—it's like pre-game. We're nervous, a little tight in the stomach, hope the boys play up to their capabilities, little bit of sweat on the forehead. Everything done that morning is done just to kill time until the game—MASSIVE amounts of chores get done to work off some of that energy, plus it kills time. Of course the Nebraska Sweat shirts and T-Shirts come out for the game—hat if it's off to a sports bar—don't even notice the waitresses in their REALLY TIGHT shorts and t-shirts—HEY, THE 'HUSKERS ARE PLAYING!!!

Ok, so we're in Tallahassee, Florida—Big Deal, Greenville, NC (East Carolina plays football? since when…. really! That long? I didn't know that) or Savannah (Georgia, Florida—I've heard of them … they play football?).

My brother Milt had his house photographed in Tallahassee, Florida. I was down there at that time. Every photograph taken had a Nebraska Helmet, NATIONAL CHAMPIONS 'Huskers Illustrated issue (all three—1994, 1995 and 1997) or something that said Nebraska on it. We were wearing our White Nebraska Back-to-Back National Champions Sweat Shirts the entire photo shoot. When the photos came out in the paper (the *Tallahassee Democrat*) I was wearing a Garnet Florida State Sweat shirt—go figure.

No matter where I go, if I've got my Nebraska stuff on or if someone else has Nebraska stuff on—INSTANT FRIENDSHIP!!! It's like NOTHING I've EVER SEEN BEFORE or SINCE. I've had a Colonel in the Marine Corps who came up to me and just said "Grand Island," I returned "Bellevue" and we talked like we'd known each other since we were little kids. My friend, Ray, asked me later: "Did you know him?" I said "No." He said, "The way you two were talking, I thought you guys knew each other for twenty years!" I said, "Nope, just met the man, but that's how it always is when people from Nebraska get together." I've met people from Nebraska in Durham, NC, at the new stadium—gave them directions to get to where they were going, some places to stop and eat, radio stations to listen to: sports, rock, country, Christian, top 40 ... whatever. Of course, we ALWAYS talk about the 'Huskers. It's like there's a bond present. Like in the past where your neighbor was just 50 miles down the road. You're out in the middle of nowhere, and you see someone from home—it's like seeing your neighbor for the first time in a month or so. You've been isolated for so long that it just feels GOOD to meet someone from your neck of the woods. You share common experiences and the 'Huskers. Everyone knows someone who played for Nebraska. You're rooting for your friend, your friend's brother, your neighbor's son—it's like a big family.

I have an internet business—I got into business in Eastern North Carolina with a man from Spalding, Nebraska—Mr. Ed Cunningham. The moment he told me about growing up on the plains of Nebraska—I KNEW THIS WAS THE GUY to get into business with. I KNEW he would be a GOD-fearing, straight forward, honest and trustworthy man, NO DOUBT WHAT SO EVER!!!! To say that he is, would be an understatement. He and his bride Sharon (who's from Iowa) remind me of my parents in so many ways it's almost scary. Both my parents are still alive, thankfully. He didn't know I was from Nebraska and was TOTALLY surprised when I told him I was from Bellevue, Nebraska. I take his word as Gospel. I have a TREMENDOUS AMOUNT of respect and love for them. What they learned, started on the plains of Nebraska and Iowa.

Tim Hindman

Nebraska.

The word brings many different images to mind.

The name is attributed to the native Oto, who called what is now the Platte River "Nebrathka," meaning "flat water."

To the early American pioneers, Nebraska was part of the "Great American Desert," unfit for settlement by the white man.

To modern-day travelers, Nebraska is often nothing more than 455 miles of Interstate highway, consisting of corn fields broken only by the state Capitol skyline of Lincoln and the Great Platte River Road Archway near Kearney.

Still others identify Nebraska by the Cornhusker football team, beloved by many, reviled by others, but generally regarded as one of the premier collegiate athletic programs in the country.

For many of us, though, Nebraska is home, a place we carry in our hearts and memories wherever we go and whatever we do.

To understand why Nebraskans hold their native state so dear to their hearts, one must first consider the factors that make the state unique. Many people consider Nebraskans as a homogeneous group of conservative white Christian farmers. In fact, Nebraska presents a surprising range of diversity: geographic, cultural, ethnic, economic, and political.

Geographically, Nebraska is located near the physical center of the continental United States. The state's borders encompass a transition region between the eastern deciduous forests and the Rocky Mountains to the west. Along the Missouri River, the landscape is in many ways similar to the Great Lakes and Ohio River regions. To the southeast are remnants of tall grass prairies extending up from Kansas. The west and southwest are part of the high plains dominant in western Kansas and eastern Colorado. The tree-lined Pine Ridge and the stark Badlands extend into northwestern Nebraska from neighboring South Dakota. And of course, one cannot forget the Sandhills, the largest region of stabilized sand dunes in the world and a geographic feature that is uniquely Nebraskan.

Economically, Nebraskans have historically relied on farming for a living. Although agriculture and related industries still dominate the state's economy, manufacturing and financial services have established a significant presence, especially in the Omaha and Lincoln areas. Tourism has also become a major industry, especially in areas where the decline in the agricultural economy has hit hardest.

Culturally and ethnically, the population of Nebraska continues to be overwhelmingly white. But other ethnic groups have become a significant part of the cultural landscape, from the African-American, Asian, and Arab communities of Omaha and Lincoln, to the growing Hispanic communities scattered across the state, to the Native American people located mostly in the northeast and northwest. Even the white population of the state is broadly diverse, from the Czech population of Wilber, to the Swedish settlers of Gothenburg, to the Irish heritage of O'Neill, and the many German settlements throughout the state. Each of these groups has left a unique and lasting impression on the heritage of the state.

Politically, Nebraskans are generally viewed as strongly conservative. This landscape as well is becoming increasingly diverse, from the traditional conservatism of Omaha's business community, to the more progressive academic and social center Lincoln, to the grassroots populism of rural Nebraska. The state has historically been a leader in implementation of progressive reforms, ranging from the only unicameral legislature in the United States to the only fully publicly owned electrical power system in the country. Nebraska politicians are often branded as mavericks, reflecting the unique character of their constituency.

With such a broad range of diversity and an increasing dichotomy between urban Omaha and Lincoln and the rural areas of the state, one might wonder what could bind the people of Nebraska together. The answer: Cornhusker football.

The University of Nebraska has a rich history of college football. From a humble beginning in 1890 as the Bugeaters, the Cornhuskers have faced some of the greatest teams of all time: the Four Horsemen of Notre Dame, the Red Grange teams of Illinois, the great Oklahoma teams of the 1950s. But it wasn't until Bob Devaney's arrival in 1962 that the Huskers achieved national status. Now after 39 consecutive winning seasons, five national championships, a record 31 consecutive bowl appearances, 233 consecutive sellouts at Memorial Stadium, and more Academic All-Americans than any other college program, the Big Red has become a rallying point for people across the state.

So why are Nebraskans so eager to find a common bond? The answer, I believe, lies in something most politicians know all too well: Bad press.

As early as 1820, Col. Stephen Long noted that Nebraska was "the Great American Desert ... unfit for human habitation." Throughout the next half-century pioneers passed along the Platte River on their way to more promising locales in Oregon and California. Even today many travelers see Nebraska as "in the road to everywhere." The Cornhusker football team is evidence that there is more to Nebraska than what can be seen from the Interstate. Indeed, as anyone who has ever lived here can tell you, there really is "no place like Nebraska."

Go Big Red!

Arthur Hudson

Our first overseas assignment was in Kuwait in August of 1991 (right after the invasion and Gulf War). As we flew out of Lincoln, Nebraska, to go to Kuwait, we both had tears in our eyes. My wife's tears were because we were leaving our two college-age daughters behind. I have never told anyone this, but my tears were because as we flew out of Lincoln we could see the Nebraska game in progress. I have not been able to attend a BIG RED game since.

I have devoutly followed the HUSKERS by whatever means were possible during the football seasons. My daughters have always had strict instructions to call me immediately after the game with the score. Since we are usually 12 to 14 hours ahead this usually means an expensive phone call in the middle of our night. Nevertheless, they know they had better be prompt with that phone call. They have forgotten only once. Once in awhile, if it is a close game and score, they will call and let me listen to the ending on the phone.

It is impossible to describe some of the funny situations surrounding the Nebraska games overseas. While in Kuwait, we had many friends from Texas, Arizona, and Oklahoma in the American International School of Kuwait. Teachers were known to have radios in their possession to listen to the games as they might be broadcast over the Armed Forces Radio Station. It didn't matter who was playing and teachers would gather in little groups during the day to hear the final results. The host country nationals could never figure out why we were so crazy.

While we were teaching at the International School Singapore for three years, my wife had her 4th grade students trained to always make the principal happy on Monday morning by bringing in the Nebraska score. She had one faithful little Chinese girl that always knew the Nebraska score on Monday morning. Her students also know which of the states in the United States is most important. They also know what a "CORNHUSKER" is and what we mean by a sea of red and white.

We now of course have access to scores immediately through the internet. We are teaching in Yerevan, Armenia, at the present time. But, we anxiously await the sports news on CNN each Sunday afternoon for a quick replay of the scores and highlights of college football.

Harold H. Hunter

It's more than the game, really. I think it means more for out-of-staters, too. At least for those who don't live in or get to Lincoln much. It's more than simply going back home. It's a sense of renewal, of reinvigoration, of reconnecting to things in life which drive you and make you wait for this day like a child waits for Christmas.

It's about flying in, descending slowly over the yellowing cornfields, gazing out the window, looking at your watch impatiently, until you get close enough to see the Missouri River, and you start to feel at home again. You land, and wait anxiously to deplane and upon the first burst of light in the terminal as you leave the tunnel, you instinctively look at the faces, as if you'll see someone you know, even though no one is there waiting for you.

You take the familiar walk to your rental car, and drive down past Carter Lake, a drive you've made 300 times before—at first, as a teen to go to the drag races out on the old, distant, dark lanes ending out beyond Dodge Park when nothing else was there, and now, the other way, down a nicely manicured road, and as you do, you catch your first glimpse of the downtown skyline. You see the Woodmen Tower and other familiar trappings of a city nicely grown up, one you're proud of and seems both imposingly new yet still familiar to you since you left for good 20 years ago.

You drive past the new Qwest Center and Hotel, feeling proud that the city that couldn't attract major shows now is a destination for them. You think of the Old Civic Auditorium, the old barn where you took in your first NBA game, watching Nate Archibald work his magic, and where you saw your first concert, on Crosby Stills Nash and Young's last tour together. Your mind drifts to watching Baron Von Raschke vs. Mad Dog Vachon wrestling for the Heavyweight Championship, the first time your mom ever let you ride the bus downtown by yourself to go somewhere.

Suddenly, something yanks you back to the present, driving down Dodge St. past all the old familiar 2 A.M. destinations when you had to cover one eye to read the signs in days of yore. Past the old Ready Mix Plant, past UNO and Memorial Park, and you're almost there, in your old neighborhood. You get to 72nd and Dodge, which to you, is still the Center of the Universe, as it was for you growing up, even though today, it's considered "east Omaha" almost.

Then the familiar drive past the old house, by Crossroads and down where Peony Park used to be, the Goodrich Malt store and Roberts Park. You think of family and friends you'll see at some point during the visit, and of family you miss and that you can only see in your heart. You wish they could be there with you, and with you share the eager sense of anticipation, that special pre-fall ever so slight cool in the air at night as September approaches. A touch of sadness comes and goes as you remember how long it has been since you last shared such feelings with them.

You feel grounded again.

On Saturday, though, your step is light, your senses sharp, your emotions bubbling up and a sense, again this year, of renewal, that whatever happened in the past year, you're turning the page today, because it's time for a new year, a new season. At least that's the way it is for Huskers.

Then, the drive. It's 45 minutes, but seems like an instant. You savor it yet it seems to pass too quickly. The first drive of the fall down I-80, past Sapp Brothers, weaving through whatever construction they've put in your path this year. You notice the rural country side and landscape, and how much more comfortable it feels to you than other places. You cross the Platte River in what seems like no time, signifying that you're half way there, time to turn on KFAB, just because that's what you do and have done for decades before. Then, you hit the familiar "Waverly Curve" where I-80 kisses Highway 6, and you know you're in the home stretch.

You finally get to Exit 401, and that's when your pulse starts to quicken. You can feel it again, the adrenaline. Your mind races with all the times you've made this drive before, and what you saw when you did.

Tearing down goalposts after conquering the Sooner Jinx. Mike Rozier slashing bowlegged through what seemed like statues then. Johnnie Mitchell making fingertip catches on a day when you couldn't feel your hands. Tommie Frazier and LP making you realize that, all those years when you said "some year"—well, that year was here. Blackshirts' wreckage strewn across the astroturf. Eric Crouch bringing you to tears hauling in the pass on a day you thought would never happen again.

All those things run through your mind as you watch your speed carefully, down the highway, until—look—there it is, to your left, that huge, gray, sturdy, impenetrable facade, with the huge N, telling you that, indeed, you were home again.

In days past, you'd park in yards or alleys for 5 bucks. Now, you park in parking garages and see the same folks, every year, who welcome you back and take your money. You get out and start walking, almost trotting anxiously, because you want to be on the street. You want to see older folks wearing the hats, and overalls, and other things that you swear you'll never wear, but laugh to yourself because you're thinking in the back of your mind, someday you probably will too. The traffic cops, the lines at Barry's, the people window shopping or just sight seeing. The smell. The feel. You can close your eyes and see it as it is today, and as it was in 1975 too.

And finally, the best part of all, the walk. From wherever you choose to prepare before the game, the walk is what you feel in your blood, what you think about on the plane, what you've waited for all winter, spring and through the dead of summer. You try to see and sense almost everything, but cannot. But as you walk down 10th St. seemingly en masse with hundreds of others, you see the party tent on your right with the same van and satellite dish you've seen for 20 years. You hear music, and fight songs, and GO HUSKERS and GO BIG RED. Your heart skips a beat, or two. You catch yourself smiling. You get closer until, on your right, there it is.

Memorial Stadium.

And as you walk up the tunnel to get inside the stadium, as you walk up the stairs and get closer, you can see the sun and hear some of the pregame on the field, and when you finally emerge into the stadium, you take a deep breath and absorb what seems like a transfusion of life force. You stop, if only momentarily, to simply stare and see everything again. You swell with emotion, yet strangely try to hide it, because that's what Nebraskans do.

And when you're finally seated, and the Pride of All Nebraska finally bursts onto the field, you let it go ... 8 months of frustration, waiting, boredom, drain—everything, and you soak in "Hail Varsity," "March Grandioso" and "There is No Place Like Nebraska" like the desert soaks up a cloudburst.

Life is full and good again. And then, "Sirius" starts....

Jon Johnston

Rewind my life to November 14th, 1992. I am at the Nebraska-Iowa State game in Ames. It's a beautiful day, sunny, not much wind—rather rare for November in Iowa. Sitting next to me in the first row of the upper deck on the east side of the stadium is my wife. She is seven months pregnant with our first child. Next to her are my sister and brother-in-law, and next to them is my good friend Todd and his wife. Todd got his undergrad degree at Nebraska, and his master's at Iowa State. Tammy is an Iowa State alum.

Nebraska is ranked seventh in the nation, fresh off blow-out wins over eighth-ranked Colorado 52–7 and thirteenth ranked Kansas 49–7. We're expecting another Nebraska blow-out, as Iowa State was 3–6 coming into the game and starting Marv Seiler, a fifth-year senior quarterback who'd never started a game. As was expected, Nebraska was leading the nation in rushing at 351 yards per game, but today the offense is incapable of moving the ball. Early in the game John Parrella sacks Seiler and is flagged for a fifteen yard personal foul penalty for excessive celebration when he points both his fingers at him as he's lying on the ground. It's a borderline call, but it sets a certain tone for the game—a tone you could feel ripple throughout the stadium. Little did we know it was foreshadowing the day.

We snuck alcohol into the game. "Snuck" is a difficult word to use here, because as I'm looking around at the other fans, I see a woman sitting in the front row who has a wine cooler bottle in her hand, out in the open for anyone to see. I see an ISU student below us stand up straight, lift a bottle of whiskey high to drain the last drop, and then throw the fifth-sized bottle into the ISU band. A few moments of glancing around gives me the idea that Iowa State really doesn't care what people have brought into the stadium.

On the kick-off after a Nebraska score the ball sails all the way through the uprights. In a moment of glee, with a beer can in my hand, I stand up, signal touchdown, and scream "Field Goal!" at the top of my lungs. At that instant an Iowa State policeman who is ten yards to my left yells at me.

"Buddy, you and YOUR CAN are outta here!"

"For what?"

"You can't bring alcohol into the stadium."

"And I'm the only person with alcohol?"

My voice is rising.

"You're the only one I see."

So is his.

"You must have pretty selective vision."

At this point, he's moved toward me and I have moved toward him to the point that we're just about in each other's face. My buddy Todd saves me when he moves between us and begins pushing me towards the exit. The cop follows us, yelling more warnings about jail, fines, charges, and my heritage.

"You come back into the stadium, you're going to jail."

I realize at this point that I have to calm down and leave because the alternative is very bad. I try some witty banter like, "Where can I listen to the game?" and it works because the policeman calms down and we have a short, but civil conversation about football as he follows me to the bottom of the upper deck ramp.

As I'm leaving, the thought enters my mind that there are at least 60 exits—there is no way he can guard all of them. I begin to walk out of the stadium, and at the North end, I spot a porta-potty. I have no intention of leaving a game like this, and figure the porta-potty break will give me a moment to see if he's still watching me. Besides, I need the break.

As I'm stepping out, an ISU student bumps into me and says something to the effect of, "Hey, come and sit with us," so I do. At that time, there wasn't a building at the North end, but there were temporary aluminum bleachers. I wander up to the bleachers with him and encounter an entire section of drunk students from ISU. They're all very friendly, and we are all standing together yelling at the game. They share their snuck-in beverages with me—we're all having a helluva time.

The game goes on. Nebraska's potent offense can do nothing, ISU leads at half 12–10. With each ISU first down, the announcer is becoming more excited. As we hit the fourth quarter, the guy is screaming so wildly you can barely understand anything he's saying. ISU leads, and on a key play early in the fourth quarter, Seiler breaks free and is running towards us. The guys around me are screaming that he's going to score and I'm screaming, "He's not going to make it," and he doesn't. He's tackled at the two yard line, after a 78 yard run. The Cyclones score to make it 19–10.

The students around me start to make plans to storm the field. I inform them that after a win like this, they have to take down the goal posts. The game is nearly over, and the students start to mill about the field, just outside a short wire fence. Being an expert at tearing down goal posts (I was on the field during the 1982 Oklahoma win, but that's another story), I start screaming instructions at them.

"Make sure you all get over the fence at once, otherwise the cops will pick you off if you go one by one! Make sure not to go onto the field. Stand at the edge of the field, but don't go on it!"

So sure enough, about 30–40 guys jump the fence simultaneously. As the last one goes over, he looks up at me and says:

"Aren't you coming?"

I pause for a moment and answer:

"Hell yes, I AM!"

I am wearing Nebraska red clothes, a Nebraska hat, and I jump the fence and get to the edge of the field. The game ends, and I'm on the field with a mob of students, trying to tear down the goal post. It's pandemonium. It's like festival seating at a rock concert, with everyone smashed together in a mass and moving in the same direction. A student next to me sees me, and says "You're Nebraskan?" I nod yes and he laughs and I realize how odd this must look

Apparently, a week or so before the game someone had driven onto the field and used a car to tear down the real goal posts, so they've put up some pretty fake, wimpy goal posts in their place. They come down pretty easy, fortunately, so no one gets injured.

The students are running around the field, and I'm running around with them for a moment until I see the Huskers, dejected and walking off the field. I run up to Tommie Frazier, and I hit him in the chest, tell him to get his head up and that we still need to beat Oklahoma and get to the

Orange Bowl. I run up to every Nebraska player I can find and do the same, hit them, tell them to get up, and keep going for the season.

I turn and see that the group carrying a goal post are the same group of guys that I've just spent most of the game with. I run up to the head of the procession and yell at them:

"What the hell are you doing? You can't just parade around inside the stadium! Get the goal post out of here!"

"Where do we go?"

"I don't know, go to the bars, use it to pick up women, go to somewhere where you can cut it up and keep a piece, just get it out of the stadium!"

And off they go, out of the stadium. I heard later that the goal post was found thrown in a fountain or something like that—the perfect place for a goal post graveyard.

I have my camera with me, so I walk around on the field, taking pictures. The other goal post has been confiscated by Iowa State policemen, and they're guarding it as if it's Fort Knox. As I'm taking their picture, I turn around so see my buddy the policeman coming towards me. He's coming towards me with a look on his face like cops had when they went after hippie protesters during the Vietnam War. He has his hand on his nightstick, and he's pulling it out. I'm not thinking about jail at this point, I'm thinking about brain damage.

I feebly lift my camera to show him I'm just taking pictures, and then I turn away from him and take another picture, thinking I'm about to be bludgeoned from behind. I turn to him again when he's close enough and say:

"Did you really think I would miss Iowa State's only victory over Nebraska since forever? I'm just taking pictures, man, just taking pictures."

At the last moment, he calms, laughs and says "Go ahead and take your pictures."

I try to maneuver him into a picture, because I don't ever want to forget him, but I'm not successful. I take a few more pictures, and then I suddenly remember that my wife is very pregnant. I make my way out of the stadium to find my wife, sister, brother-in-law, Todd, and ISU alum Tammy. After a few minutes with Tammy, I decide that being thrown out of the game was divine intervention because if I'd spent the whole game sitting next to her I might have committed murder.

Iowa State's '92 victory over Nebraska was the only loss that Tom Osborne suffered against a team with a losing record. It was the first time since 1978 that Nebraska had lost to another Big Eight team besides Okla-homa or Colorado. It was the only Big Eight loss for Nebraska quarterback Tommie Frazier, the greatest quarterback in college history. After the Iowa State loss, Nebraska didn't lose a regular season conference game for another six years (the only non-conference loss being the 19–0 "Debacle in the Desert" loss to Arizona State in 1996).

I'm still married. I still tell this story. I leave out the part about my wife being very pregnant, as it's her part and she never forgets to tell people how pregnant she was at the time. I don't tell it as much when she's around because it ticks her off all over again—how bad my behavior was. We're rais-ing kids, and I guess I can understand that response.

Jon Johnston

The road to the 1994 Colorado-Nebraska game began many months before with a phone call from my brother-in-law Doug. He called to let my wife and I know that he and his fiancée, Sarah, had finally set a wedding date. He proudly announced they were going to be married on October 29, 1994.

I yelled to my wife, Heidi, to inform her of the date for the upcoming wedding.

"Does he know what day that is? It's the day of the Colorado-Nebraska game!"

I asked Doug, "Why did you pick this particular date?"

"It was the only day the church was available."

In other words, my brother-in-law Doug was the only person in Nebraska who was crazy (or desperate) enough to get married that particu-lar day. I've never asked him, but I wonder if he was worried about whether or not Sarah would suddenly jump up one day and run off on him, unless they got married before that could happen.

Given Doug's reluctance to change the wedding date, we relented from bothering him too much, as we were happy for Doug that he had finally found someone to love (and more importantly and surprisingly, someone who would love him back). We stopped bothering him about it, until it became clear as the season continued that the 1994 Colorado-Nebraska game was going to be something special. This was especially bothersome for me since I accepted the responsibility of being a groomsman. Short of a seri-ous illness or death, there was no way out of attending the wedding and being involved as an official member of the wedding party.

The church Doug was referring to is St. Mary's Catholic Church in Lincoln, Nebraska. St. Mary's is a beautiful old church that is right across the street from Nebraska's State Capitol building. It happens to be only eight or nine blocks away from the home of Husker football, Memorial Stadium. Not only would I be in Lincoln and unable to attend, I would be close enough to hear the roar of the crowd and wonder what the hell had just happened.

The 1994 Nebraska offense featured the best offensive line in school history—the "Pipeline." Behind the line stood the greatest college quarterback to ever play the game, Tommie Frazier. Nebraska had worked their way to third in the rankings, one spot behind Colorado.

Led by soon-to-be-NFL-starting quarterback Kordell Stewart, the Buffs had more than their share of NFL-level talent. A number of the Buffs would later play on Sunday, including Michael Westbrook, and Heisman Trophy winner Rashaan Salaam. Colorado featured an offense that no one had stopped so far that season, so not many people outside Nebraska figured that the Cornhuskers had much of a chance in the game.

Throughout the 1994 season, I listened to the "Fabulous Sports Babe" on her nationally syndicated radio sports show. The Sports Babe talked about nearly any kind of sport that callers would bring to the show, but had a special love for college football. Each week, fans would call raving about this or that with regards to the teams they hated, those overrated, and the outdated.

The "Babe" had a theme every Thursday in which fans could pick their "Geek of the Week." The "Geek of the Week" was the sports figure, organization, or event that had done something the previous week to deserve the ire of the fans.

Doug has been one of my best friends throughout my life, but the idea that he'd chosen to be married on the day of one of the most important games in Nebraska football history was something that I could not let go unpunished. Doug deserved to be nominated for the "Geek of the Week."

On the Thursday one week before the Colorado game, I sent a fax to the "Babe" show, explaining my dilemma and pointing out Doug's choice of a wedding date and that he deserved "Geek of the Week" nomination.

During that Thursday's show, I feared that the "Babe" wouldn't recognize Doug's geekiness and he would go unpunished. My fears were put aside when Craig James (a member of ESPN's College Gameday crew at the time) came on the show, and the "Babe" read my fax to him on the air.

"What do you think of that? This guy is going to be at his brother-in-law's wedding eight blocks away from the greatest game of the season, and he can't even go!"

Revenge had begun. ESPN called my office shortly after the Babe's on-air rant. I promptly returned the call, and a person there explained that they loved the nomination and wondered if it were possible to interview Doug before the game. The Friday morning before the game, Doug went on the Babe show to get grilled, and I followed him on a few minutes later. The Babe and I professed our love for each other, but mostly for our love for jabbing Doug.

Doug and Sarah had set the wedding time at 4:00 P.M. The game was to start at 1:30 P.M., and this meant that if the game were close going into the fourth quarter, we had a good chance to miss out on the ending. Another problem: since I was chosen to be in the wedding party as a groomsman, and therefore would be part of the picture taking, I would expected to be dressed nice, look nice, act nice, and stay that way at least until the wedding was over—a truly difficult task for me.

The day of the game, er, wedding, had finally arrived—October 29, 1994. My first thought of the day (after finding aspirin) was to get some of the "cornhead" head apparel for pictures. The early model "cornhead" looked more like a pointy bald skull cap, like *Saturday Night Live*'s "Coneheads" wore, with corn kernels painted on them.

While the game started, the wedding party gathered at the State Capitol building for picture-taking. We had tried to time everything so that pictures would be finished by the time the game started so that we could watch it on a tiny nine inch portable battery-powered TV I'd purchased for the occasion.

So there we were, a bunch of guys in tuxedos, some sporting dorky-looking cornheads, huddled around an itty-bitty portable TV on the steps of the state capitol building. Nebraska was playing inspired football. As our buddy Terry said at the time: "It's like we're telling them where we're going, and they still can't stop us."

It was true. Nebraska's "Pipeline" spent the day blowing holes in the Buffs' defense. The Blackshirt defense terrorized Kordell Stewart, not allowing a third down conversion through the game. By the time the wedding started, we knew the game was a win, so we abandoned most of the hi-jinx we'd planned, such as the old "paint the score on the bottom of the shoes so people see it when they kneel" trick, hidden radios and pre-arranged hand signals from guests to let us know the status of the game.

It helped the wedding go smoothly. Doug and Sarah said their vows, we exited the church, and—as a traditional wedding party—we stood outside St. Mary's waiting in line for the wedding guests to congratulate us. As we waited, we heard the roar of a crowd growing louder—a crowd from the stadium that had torn down a goal post and decided that the steps of the state capitol was the perfect place to deposit it.

The draw of the crowd was too much for me—I wasn't going to stand in line waiting for someone to congratulate me as a groomsman for not showing up drunk or falling over or screaming out loud when the priest asked if anyone should stop the wedding. Congratulating Doug and Sarah, I and the other groomsmen took off to celebrate with the crowd. When people saw us, they wanted pictures taken with us, and we wanted pictures with them and the goalpost.

And there we were, tuxedos, cornheads, goalpost on the state capitol steps, like a big Happy Husker Wedding stew with all ingredients complete including happy bride and groom. Doug and Sarah got their perfect wedding picture, standing on the capitol steps holding up the goalpost along with a throng of fans.

Rather than being one of those stories about how some guys missed a great Husker game because of a wedding, we found ourselves part of the greatest part of it—the celebration of carrying the goal posts to the steps of the capitol building.

Epilogue

A few years later, I found out that the ESPN College GameDay crew had tried to get in touch with the wedding party so that we could come down to Memorial Stadium and get on the College GameDay show. I'd considered heading to the stadium early that Saturday morning, but was informed of my need to remain clean, calm, and in general good order and decided that it was best I not go. It would have been fun, but the day turned out to be nearly perfect as it was.

Cristine Miller

As a born and bred rural Nebraskan, I can tell you what it means to me to be from that state. I can appreciate the:

• wonder of going to high school athletic events, whether my child is playing or not

• beauty of a flat landscape, seeing nothing but corn or soybeans for miles and miles

• kinsmanship of small town loyalty and friendship as they rally around their own in time of need or celebration

• fabulous Cornhuskers, whether they win or lose, if I see them in person, on television or hear them on the internet or radio.

• instant connection I have with fellow Nebraskans, regardless of where they now reside.

I grew up in Shelby, Nebraska, population seven hundred and twenty. My high school class graduated eighteen students in 1975 and we were in Class D for sporting activities. I was able to participate in anything I wanted, not having to worry about being "cut." I participated in track, volleyball, basketball, cheerleading, band, theater, speech and, oh yes, I did attend class.

We always had great crowds at our sporting events, regardless of whether we were winning or losing. In fact, my senior year, Shelby won the Class D Nebraska state volleyball championship and when we returned from Scottsbluff, we had a police escort into town and the entire population of Shelby turned out to welcome us back.

My mother has recently (three years ago) had a stroke. This event has left her disabled in physical ability and judgment. The community has rallied around her and my father to make sure that she is rarely alone. She participates in bridge tournaments, has coffee at the Senior Center and the A&B and attends all community events. Without the friendship of Shelby, my family and I would be poorer. I appreciate all that they have done to make my mother's life full after this debilitating stroke.

I hope this letter fits with your other submissions. It is difficult to put into words what growing up in Nebraska has done for me. My husband is from Montana and shows none of these feelings for Montana.

Regardless of where I live, I will always be a Nebraskan and a Cornhusker.

C. Thomas Preston, Jr.

I grew up during the 1960s and 1970s in a suburban, Southern environment somewhere between *Leave it to Beaver* and *The Andy Griffith Show* and with a wonderful and loving family. In fact, from higher ground in my home town of Winston-Salem, NC, you could catch a nice view of "Mt. Pilot" in the distance on a clear day.

I know some of this narrative may not seem like much to many, but I have to give it in order to try to explain my own experiences in Huskerville.

My father (the senior C. Thomas), from Winston-Salem, played on the state championship basketball team in high school—although US 52 at 25th street runs today over where he grew up and where he practiced. He worked very hard, and earned a scholarship to play at Wake Forest College from 1952 to 1955. His 1953 team won the Southern Conference basketball championship, the only team besides North Carolina State to win the conference over a seven-year period. He also played as a reserve on the runner up team of the first two ACC men's basketball tournaments. He was quite happy when Wake Forest moved its entire campus to Winston a year after he graduated. He and my mother had met at Wake Forest and shortly after graduation, married in '55 and moved to Winston-Salem. I was born in '57. That's the sports tradition in which our family and many others in North Carolina are steeped, with the generation before mine having been there for the "birth" of the great Atlantic Coast Conference (you have to be from the mid–Atlantic to understand fully).

My sports allegiance, therefore, was to loyally (and, admitting my individual character flaws, not so loyally sometimes) pull for the Deacons in football and basketball during the late 1960s and early 1970s (around the time Steely Dan penned the song "Deacon Blues" with the line, "they call Alabama the Crimson Tide, call me Deacon Blues").

What were my most poignant sports memories?

1. Rooting for the dedicated Deacons with my Dad, at courtside, as they struggled valiantly through a 9–18 rebuilding year for Wake under a new head basketball coach—but experiencing the Division II national championship of Earl "The Pearl" Monroe and the Winston-Salem State Rams that same year. To a ten year old Caucasian child growing up in Winston during 1967, the Rams provided the "substitute team" to admire during the Deacons' off year. Only years later would I more fully appreciate the rare nature of this privilege—to attend a southern sporting event with the African Americans at courtside and in the best seats, with a smaller but noticeable number of whites sitting in the rafters and at the end of the court of the old Memorial Coliseum. Everybody in Winston who attended these games admired the dignified way Coach C. E. ("Bighouse") Gaines, a basketball legend, would bring his team onto the floor, and the joy for life Monroe and his teammates exhibited after the ball was tossed. Watching the "Pearl" work his magic was healing for everybody in this Southern town who had the privilege in this time of turmoil and change in our region and nation. It was also a moment that remains to this day the only time during which a team from Winston-Salem has won a national basketball championship.

2. The '70 football Deacons (with their ground game).

That first basketball fan memory brings us to the year 1970 and eventually leads to a football memory—actually my most memorable moment at any sporting event. This coincidentally was the year of Nebraska's first national championship in football. That year, the hated Tar Heels and Blue Devils were predicted to fight it out for the ACC championship in football; Wake Forest was picked to finish dead last, although Wake had a set of loyal supporters who faithfully attended every game. But first, how would the Deacons deal with the opening game—a "cash cow" game—against the mighty Huskers in Lincoln? 0–63? 0–77? Would a single player on Wake's first string escape Lincoln uninjured?

Nonetheless, "Deaconville" rejoiced as the Old Gold and Black finally went ahead 3–0. The Deacon Blues set in as the halftime score became 5–29, but a moral victory could be claimed with a 12–36 loss. After all, a school of only 3,000 students had both LED and SCORED three ways with a touchdown, a field goal and a safety against this nationally ranked behemoth picked correctly by some to win the national title. And, it did not go un-noticed in Deaconville that the Deacons received a standing ovation when leaving the field, despite Tagge's having rained a bit on the party.

Later, after two more losses in "cash cow" games at Florida State and Tennessee, the Deacons would go on to win their first—and until the 2006 dream season, their only—ACC football championship.

Along this journey was the rivalry game with North Carolina that year. UNC quickly took a 0–13 lead, and Wake closed to 7–13. Then, Wake got the ball at its own seven yard line with about two minutes to play.

The Deacons scored the winning touchdown with :07 on the clock, and the image of the quarterback (who also held for the place kicker) embracing the referee and jumping up and down after the game-clinching extra point was always, and will always be, the best memory of my lifetime of watching sporting events at venues from Wrigley to Wembley.

Of course, not everybody on either side of the family was happy—after all, my mother's older brother had attended Duke (the conference runner-up that year), my father's older brother had been a member of the Tar Heels band back in the early 1950s (Carolina was the other runner up), my mother's younger brother attended East Carolina (the "little red headed stepchild" among athletic programs in our state, often overlooked), and my grandmother had taken courses at North Carolina State (to this day, the "cow college" or "the best engineering university in the world" depending on one's allegiances). Such divided allegiances among North Carolina families were not at all uncommon.

Well, with the family encouraging my brother and I to go away for college, both my brother and I later enrolled at North Carolina—not as "pres-tigious" as Duke or Wake, but not a "dive" like the so-called "EZU" of those days either (we easterners can be a little elitist, you know).

There, I became a pure Tar Heel fan over a six-year stay while I earned my baccalaureate and Master's degrees—although a little of me to this day doesn't mind when UNC loses to Wake Forest. But the memories are a part of me as a sports fan, and with [basketball coach Dean] Smith on the side-lines, not only were you rooting for your school, but you were rooting for the "good guys"—the ones who graduated, and the ones who played by the rules. On top of that there was the atmosphere of the home basketball court, Carmichael Auditorium. Well, you had to have been there to really appre-ciate this cracker box arena where 10,000 individuals cheered as one, with the students surrounding three sides of the court. Aside from the many ACC rivalries I witnessed there, I saw the likes of Indiana under Knight, Michigan State with Magic, the Soviet national team, and many, many oth-ers fall to the now beloved Tar Heels.

And, after I graduated and left the state for the graduate program in Lincoln, when I returned home for the holidays, I remember returning to the magical Carmichael as an alumnus to see a team with some first-year guy named Michael play. I suppose that none of us totally appreciated what we were watching until a special night in New Orleans in '82 (which I remem-ber watching vividly on an old black and white TV from a worn out old couch I shared with three roommates at my apartment on G street in Lin-coln—yes, a part of Blue Heaven that evening). For readers who have lived in Chicago for awhile, perhaps your memories of "that '90s pro basketball team" can help you to relate.

Those days in Chapel Hill—with the lush foliage, the manicured cam-pus, and, yes, the hills, the tall trees which blocked the horizon—were all good, and fun, days.

Getting back to football, with this background, how can I remember Nebraska so fondly, especially when the villainous Osborne put Garcia in during the fourth quarter of the 1977 Liberty Bowl and turned a 17–7 Tar Heel football win into a 17–21 "moral victory" for the Heels? After all, even as I attended many Nebraska football games from 1981 to 1984 as I pursued my PhD there, my eyes kept shifting when the scoreboard flashed scores of other games. How were the Deacons doing? The Tar Heels? Ha, Duke lost again, and so on and so forth.

What on earth ties cheering for the Deacons, Tar Heels, and Huskers together? To me it really has been more than the "when in Rome, do as the

Romans" notion, much more than went into my pulling for the St. Louis Cardinals or St. Louis Rams just because they were located where I was living at the time, or winning. Rather, as I alluded earlier, these college programs represented cheering for the very best qualities humans could possess. I was among a group pulling for not only a hometown school, not only the flagship university where I received two degrees in my home state, not only the winning football team at a school that was so inviting to me to attend its communication Ph.D. program. Rather, I was pulling also for honesty, for integrity, for the good guys—neither program was ever on probation, and all three had high expectations for their student athletes to excel in the classroom as well as on the playing field. And, even the athletes that left during those days shortly after earned their degrees.

What continues to set the Big Red experience apart even from these common elements is the unity. The opposition is more distant—there will never be too many opposing fans in Memorial Stadium, unless the Huskers start losing games over an extended number of years. Go to any in-state game, even men's basketball, in NC. Now that the intimate, and raucous, Carmichael has given way to the cavernous, and sterile, Dean Dome with its large donors rather than the students sitting in the front rows, you'll usually find many opposing fans in arenas for in-state rivalry basketball games, with the exception of Duke's Cameron Indoor Stadium. Furthermore, were a poll taken, a vast majority of North Carolinians would vote resoundingly "no" to cheering for the University of North Carolina in any sport, even women's soccer. Rather, most college sports fans in the state go to games for ECU, NCSU, Wake, and Duke—and shout "go to hell, Carolina, go to hell"—with organized free throw distractions, catcalls based on computer searches for anything bad about a player's family, and screaming slogans like "the home of the Pack" at the end of "The Star Spangled Banner." In all fairness, North Carolina fans such as myself are seen as smug and elitist by fans from rival in-state schools. In short, part of the fun on Tobacco Road is that there are many "-villes" in North Carolina and east coast fandom—each I suppose reflecting the values of each institution—but none representing an entire STATE such as Nebraska and its diaspora of fans throughout the nation.

So, why did I up and drive all the way from St. Louis to Lincoln more recently this decade—without a ticket, no less, to a Nebraska football game—NOT to meet any friends, but on the spur of the moment just to see a game—and against a Division II opponent?

I think the answer both leads me not so much to a home, but rather further on a journey. So, here are my thoughts about my own journey through Big Red country:

1. Each new day of life is a blessing. We cannot take it for granted. After 9/11 (which devastated me emotionally more since New York too has always been a special place in my journey), we were all faced as never before with the cold, hard notion that none of us are promised tomorrow. I remember having stood beneath the twin towers on one of my many visits and saying to myself, "these will never fall," and how the movie *AI* (Artificial Intelligence) reflected their permanence over centuries by showing them still standing a million years from now. So, my visceral logic went, if these can fall, anything can fall, and we need to enjoy our blessings while we can. I was in Billings, MT, teaching at Rocky Mountain College while on sabbatical from the University of Missouri-St. Louis on 9/11/01. Yet had the first Nebraska game after that day not been rescheduled for a class night, yes, I would have been there for the Rice game and probably cried my eyes out along with everybody else when they played "There is no place like Nebraska."

2. Until I recently became full professor of Communication at Gainesville College near Atlanta, I was for 21 years employed at the University of Missouri-St. Louis. Over those 21 years, every other year in Columbia, Nebraska visited Mizzou, preceded by my dreaded invitation to a St. Louis friend to join me for the drive. And, unless I could find a person from Huskerville, I would get a look like I was crazy, but conversation is always found with the many others wearing red at this away game. But, after 9/11, I will follow my impulses more. I realized in 2002 that although I had visited Lincoln for academic meetings on occasion, I had not been to a football game there since 1984.

So, on a Friday afternoon back in St. Louis, I said to myself, you know, they're only 4–2, and I bet I could get a ticket if I showed up an hour before the McNeese game. So, on a whim my cerebrum would have prevented and did on occasion prevent before 9/11, I got in a car, drove as far as I could stay awake, camped out somewhere near St. Joseph, MO, that night, and arrived in Lincoln an hour before kickoff. Sure enough, I got a ticket on the fifty yard line, and only paid face value! For old times sake, I even parked the car in my beloved Near South neighborhood—near the basketball court at 16th Street and G, across from the apartment where I had lived the last year '83-'84.

Why park so far away? Because I wanted the whole experience again—of passing the old Korn Popper (which was still there), of walking past the State Capitol just as I had done so often as a younger man on my way to class, of seeing a few people in red by the time I got to K street, to seeing red east and west as far as the eye could see when I got to O street. Yes, I was upset to see some old hangouts in downtown Lincoln no longer there or in different places. I may not have been home. Nevertheless, I was in a wonderful place in life's journey, no longer an officer of anything, a director of anything, an author of anything, or an academic rank. I suppose that I was nobody at all in a sea of red. Regardless, I felt very, very happy.

And, I felt young again.

What made the day was not so much the game (a good game in a mediocre season, just a win over a Division II team), but just knowing that this place was still there. The identical announcement made at the beginning of the pre-game show from 20 years earlier, something like, "It's football Saturday, and on a football Saturday, there is no place like Nebraska," followed by the famous fight song, in and of itself made the entire trip worthwhile, and would have even had the game that followed immediately been cancelled. To some this may sound strange, even a bit neurotic as only the viscera can describe it. This emotion persisted as the game wore on, even as the Tar Heel beneath the surface and the Deacon beneath that were watching still as the scores from back East flashed across the scoreboard.

But there's something about that song—no, the moment that it is announced—that is the most special, that reassures you that even if there is some sort of calamity tomorrow—if Camelot somehow falls—that there was such a spot where people from all walks (including two of Nebraska's newer immigrant residents who also got tickets outside and sat next to me) could celebrate as one. And, on a fragile and divided planet, that is worth celebrating.

Erik

Let me tell you my Husker story.

It began in September 1958. My mom was 3 months pregnant with me. In those days women in a "delicate condition" didn't attend sporting events. While my dad drove from Omaha to Lincoln for each home game, mom sat in a rocker and listened to "the game" on the radio. Whereas it is now vogue for expectant mothers to listen to Mozart, hoping for the next great genius, my mom hatched a die-hard Husker fan. I have memories from early childhood, my first pet, the Kennedy assassination, my first day of school and yes—those Saturdays when we piled into the Chevy and drove to Lincoln. I remember a carload of Kansas State fans driving by in 1968 and pointing to their hats. My dad said, "I hope they have to eat those hats tonight." It was not to happen that day and was in fact, the last time Kansas State won in Lincoln.[3]

My dad wouldn't let me go to the games until I understood what was going on. In 1970 I impressed him with my knowledge of the game and he took me to my first contest. I will never forget it, Nebraska vs. Wake Forest. I remember the color, the excitement, the March of the Cornhuskers all as if it happened yesterday. I was sitting next to my dad and had just gone through one of the wickets that a boy goes through on his way to being a man. Nebraska triumphed 36–12 and I felt good about myself. I felt good about my state.

I attended most of the home games during the national championship years in the early seventies and until I was a teenager. I then rebelled and lost interest in going to the games. It seemed to be much ado about nothing at the time, kind of "square." I'm sure my dad was disappointed that he didn't have his son by his side for at least one or two games each year. What I wouldn't do to get in a time machine and go back so we could go to an Oklahoma game in the mid-seventies (even though the result would be a Cornhusker loss in the last minute of the game).

I joined the Marine Corps reserve in 1977. While in bootcamp and truck driving school, I noticed that everybody was from somewhere and part of your identity included where you were from. When the guys found out I was from Nebraska, they automatically wanted to talk football because they assumed I would be interested. I learned that the guys that followed most teams would consider a 9-win season as a great achievement rather than a disappointment. My fellow recruits respected me because I was from Nebraska and a lot of that had to do with football.

After the Marines, I returned to Lincoln to become a UNL student. When I went to my first game it was in the same old stadium but now I was in the student section. It was exciting. How wonderful to be young, optimistic about life ahead and sitting in Memorial Stadium watching a game with a pretty girl. I attended every home game throughout college. One of the best weeks of my life included celebrating my girlfriend's birthday, scoring several good marks on tests and watching Nebraska beat Oklahoma for the first time in the Osborne era. The next week my girlfriend dumped me, I flunked a calculus test and sitting "alone" in the stadium, Nebraska got whipped by Missouri. I had to that point never felt so low in my life.

After four years at good old NU I graduated and accepted a job in California. It was a tough decision and one of the reasons was that I was leaving my beloved Huskers behind. I watched them whenever they were on TV, listened to all the games on the radio and went to see them when they played in or near California. I dated several girls in California but something was always missing. That something was that they all thought my interest in a college football team was silly. I happened to be at a beach party one day and I met a girl that "understood" about the Cornhuskers. After further conversation, it turned out that she was from Grand Island. We began a relationship and though she is not a Husker fanatic, she understands my need to be close to my team.

We were married at the Rose Bowl on September 10, 1988, at the Nebraska-UCLA game. The Rose Bowl staff had saved a couple box seat sections for us down by the field and we even got our 30 seconds of fame on national TV. Despite a big Nebraska loss, it was a pretty good day. We celebrated our 10-year anniversary in San Francisco in order to attend the Nebraska-Cal game. We spent the first days of 2000 in Tempe for the Fiesta Bowl where Nebraska whipped Tennessee.

Well, the marriage made at a Nebraska game is still going strong. My mom is 80 years old back in Omaha and still works a 40-hour week. My old girlfriend is a famous artist. My dad passed away several years ago, several months after the Cornhuskers were crowned national champions.

Throughout my life, my birth, my youth, my loves, my sorrows, my service to my country and the deaths of loved ones, Nebraska football has always been there. A dozen times a year, all responsibilities, appointments, commitments and other stressful things melt away for a few hours on Saturday afternoon as the Scarlet and Cream does battle. I can't explain my devotion to their cause other than to say it is, and always will be, a part of me.

Loren Wagner

How I feel about this whole deal has very little, if anything at all, to do with winning and losing. I could care less what Bill Callahan's record is at Nebraska or anywhere else for that matter. I don't hate him, I just disagree entirely with his offensive philosophy. It didn't matter who Pederson hired after he fired Solich, I wouldn't have liked him because he shouldn't even be there.

For forty-two years "NEBRASKA" had a system and a program. Football games are won and lost with a stout defense and a running game that can punish people (Friday night's game was a prime example). They did it for forty-two years. They won five national championships with the same basic philosophy. They won more conference championships than I care to take the time to count. They did this all with the same mix of a great running game and a great defense. When nearly everyone else in the country was throwing the ball all over the field from spread sets and everything else, "NEBRASKA" was still doing the same thing, playing tough defense and pounding the ball down the opponent's throat, physically beating them and preparing to win the fourth quarter. They played with this philosophy for forty-two years, against all kinds of national powers and offensive geniuses. Who won a great majority of those games? "NEBRASKA!"

"NEBRASKA" was different from everybody else. They didn't change offensive systems, try to "keep up with the times," be trendy or find a quick way to a championship. They did what they believed in, stuck with it and won three national championships in four years. Has anyone else ever done that? I don't think so.

The other thing that made them different was the longevity of coaches. Not just the head coach, but the entire staff. I was uneasy when Solich cleaned house after 2002. I quietly questioned what was going on. This just wasn't a "NEBRASKA" thing to do, but even I felt like it was time for Craig Bohl to go. However, his success at North Dakota has made me question if even that was the right thing to do. But Solich's success the next season tells me there were some personal problems between coaches if nothing else and it appeared to be working out well for all involved. Then Pederson fires Solich after a 9–3 regular season. The man goes 9–3 and has a good start on what looks to be his best recruiting class in his six years as the head coach and he gets fired. Why? Because the AD wants the opportunity to hire "his" coach and put a mark on the program. He put his mark on the program alright, a great big BLACK mark.

It was a sad day when Solich got fired. It was the end of "NEBRASKA" football. Now it is just Nebraska football. We are just like everybody else. We run the same trendy offensive schemes. We hire and fire coaches on a whim. There is nothing any different than anybody else in the country. We were DIFFERENT and we were DOMINANT for forty-two years because of it. We will never see the likes of that again, EVER! It is over, it is gone and there is nothing we can do about it.

I have not quit going to games because of the losing and pathetic offensive showings. I have not turned negative toward the coaching because of those things. I have the attitude that I have because what was done was wrong! I have not gone to a game because what was done was wrong!! I have quit giving to the Touchdown Club because what was done was wrong!!! I don't know any other way, in this money hungry industry we call collegiate sports, to make my voice heard than to quit buying their product. I still have my season tickets because that is a "tradition" that I don't want to see die. The sell out string is a tradition I don't want to see die. It is the only on-going record that the Huskers have left. I will continue to do my part to keep that alive. But I will keep as much of my hard earned money as I can out of the hands of Steve Pederson. When this whole thing blows up in his face and he gets fired, I'll still have my tickets and I will again visibly be the diehard Husker fan that I always have been. Until then I have no interest in going to games. I just hope he doesn't stay long enough for the sell out string to end, because he is working on killing that too. How in the heck is he going to sell 3 to 5 thousand more season tickets when he is putting the kind of product on the field that we have seen the last two years? He isn't!

Brian Walton

About 20 years ago, a good friend and former Nebraskan decided to be married. His wife-to-be and her family were Californians, living in the desert in a small town called Lake Elsinore. To facilitate the many family and friends who would be traveling in from near and far (mostly far), they decided to hold the gala festivities on Thanksgiving weekend.

Unfortunately, none of them, other than the groom, who was totally without voice in the entire matter, realized or cared that the biggest Nebraska game of the year, the one against hated rival Barry Switzer and Oklahoma, was scheduled to start during the wedding reception.

Since I was in the wedding party, I had no other choice but to comply with the bride and groom's request and travel to California instead of to Lincoln. However, I was not going to miss that game. So, we arrived in Elsinore a day early. I found the only video store in the area that had rental VCRs (remember this was a long time ago, long before Blockbuster) and convinced them to let me take a machine out to attach to my motel television. (I had previously checked that the motel had ABC-TV before making my reservation.) Once I tested out the set-up, I could at least sort-of participate in the wedding at-ease. My only mission was to stay away from any news reports of the outcome so as not to spoil the replay.

As luck would have it, the story ended differently than planned. As the wedding completed without a hitch and the reception began, the father of the groom (a Nebraskan, remember) grew increasingly nervous as the various lines were manned and photos were taken. As the reception began in earnest, he completely disappeared.

After awhile, this became obvious, and I was among the tuxedo-clad individuals who were called upon to form a search party. Turns out, we disappeared, too, once we found Dad. He was holed up in the back room of the reception hall, huddled up against a 10" black-and-white television screen watching the NU-OU game live! I can't remember if he knew about our rented VCR or he just couldn't wait. It didn't matter. There ended up being at least a dozen of us hooting and hollering in that little room as we jockeyed for position to see that little-bitty screen. I remember it just as if it were yesterday.

Eventually, the bride and her family grudgingly forgave us for our transgressions. And, believe it or not, the next day, the day after his wedding, who showed up to watch that game tape at our motel, but the groom himself, who was quite put out by his Dad. Not that he slipped away. Not that he ended up with most of the Nebraska guys with him. No, his son was angry that he had to miss the action himself!

Joe Winkler

I first thought of TO as a Nebraskan through and through when he went for two in the Miami game. After all the fussing and shouting was over and he had explained a hundred times that you play football to win, not tie, and everything else, finally he said, "Well, you know it is just a football game, not anything really important, not a life or death issue." The fact that he said the same basic thing after winning the National Championship made it even better.

I also remember when we were playing Oklahoma State one year, the coach had hyped the game up to the highest level (it was there) and was saying things such as, "They are going to have to keep the women and children off the streets," and TO just kept to the basics, said that it was an important game, but just a game, and that all games are important, but they are just football games, not wars or once in a lifetime opportunities, but just games.

I feel that this is a lot of what Nebraskans are, down-to-earth realists. They don't hype things to the sky (ask a New Yorker what it is like to live in New York if you want hype), they don't over dramatize their job, their relatives, their church, or their kids (ask almost someone from Southern California about any of the above). They can be risk takers without being stupid about it; they figure out ways to improve things through trial and effort.

Like Tom, most of them enjoy the outdoors, spend time with their family when they can, pay taxes without complaining about it all the time, and believe in God without preaching all the time. I have not really met Tom very often, just a couple of times, but I will share one of those times.

When I was working in a factory, they sent me to Chicago for a workshop. It was in February or so, after the football season but during the recruiting season. There is only one late plane from Chicago to Lincoln, and Tom was waiting in the same lobby or gate or whatever you call it. I walked up to him and asked him for an autograph for my son.

He asked me my son's name, and signed a note to him. As he handed it to me, some other guy walks up and says, "Tom, let me tell you what you need to do with your pass defense," and begins jabbering away. Tom just stood there and listened, and after the guy was done he turned away and looked out the window at the dark until we loaded on the plane.

Now if it was me, after a long week or so of recruiting, and waiting for a late night flight and wanting only peace and quiet, I would have first told the guy I wasn't interested, and then punched his lights out if he didn't go away. But Tom has too much class, and is too down-to-earth, and is true blue Nebraskan, through and through.

Chapter Notes

Preface

1. I have attempted to enact, in the writing and revising of this book, a practice that Steven Feld calls "dialogic editing." I first encountered this phrase in Daniel Cavicchi's book about Bruce Springsteen fans, *Tramps Like Us*. As Cavicchi explains the process, dialogic editing is "sharing one's scholarly writing with those written about and incorporating their comments and corrections into the text" (19).

Introduction

1. As historian and geographer David Lowenthal ("Nostaliga") explains, "Nostalgia today is less often prized as precious memory or dismissed as diverting jest. Instead it is a topic of embarrassment and a term of abuse. Diatribe upon diatribe denounce it as reactionary, regressive, ridiculous" (20).

2. For a list of college football stadiums and their seating capacity, see: http://homepages.cae.wisc.edu/~dwilson/rsfc/stadiums.txt

3. For a list of Notre Dame's alumni chapters, see: http://alumni.nd.edu/clubs/clublist.html

4. See Rushin ("Hockey's Miss Havishams") for more on these fans, and others who still "follow" defunct hockey teams.

5. Price, *Dry Place*, 27.

6. As my college friend Tim Hindman notes in his story in Appendix A, Nebraska is a diverse state—more so than outsiders would expect—yet its residents are bound together by Nebraska football.

7. To know a place and its people requires that we should pay attention to what those people value—and to look beyond what may seem superficial or ridiculous to others. "The outsider," observes cultural anthropologist Keith Basso, "must attempt to come to grips with the indigenous cultural forms that the landscape is

experienced *with*, the shared symbolic vehicles that give shape to geographical experience and facilitate its communication" (109; emphasis original). In Nebraska, football is one of our primary indigenous cultural forms.

8. In Lowe, *Johnny Goes Home*. Thanks to John Strope for alerting me to this quotation and to Andrea Faling of the Nebraska Historical Society for tracking it down for me.

9. Basso, *Wisdom*, 109. See also, Relph, *Place*, 43, for a discussion of orientation through association with places.

10. I owe a thank you to Mohammad Auwal, who suggested that I visit with his colleague Bob Kully.

11. Mikhail Bakhtin, *Dialogic Imagination*, refers to the collected fragments as chronotopes, or symbols that condense time and space fragments to "stand as monuments to the community itself, as symbols of it, as forces operating to shape its members' images of themselves" (7). Similarly, sociologist Joseph R. Gusfield, an expert in the field of symbol usage and collective meanings, writes of the need to be "aware of the importance which history has for community identity" (35). Austrian researchers Rudolf de Cillia, Martin Reisigl, and Ruth Wodak add that "the construction of national identity [and cultural identity, I would argue] builds on the emphasis on a common history" (154).

12. Lippard, *Lure of the Local*, 24–25.

13. While many folks now refer to the congregation of Husker fans as HuskerNation, I shy away from that phrase primarily because the small town qualities that are evoked by the name Huskerville seem, to me, to better reflect the values, beliefs, and behaviors of those who call themselves Husker fans. I hope, over the course of this book, that I explain this idea more fully. I should also note that the name Huskerville is by no means an original creation. Long-time residents of Lincoln, I imagine, recognize the name as one applying to a neighbor-

hood outside the Lincoln Air Base. As the 1999 Arnold Heights Comprehensive Plan (http://www.geocities.com/bigrob685/AH.html) explains, "At the conclusion of World War II, an influx of returning soldiers caused a significant shortage of housing in the Lincoln area. Many of those returning from active duty were enrolling at the University of Nebraska, Lincoln under the G.I. Bill. The University converted 65 former army airfield hospital buildings, located on the west side of NW 48th Street, to married student housing. Known as 'Huskerville' the area roughly covered 4 square city blocks and encompassed a grocery store, drug store, barbershop, beauty shop, laundry, nursery, movie theater and church. The Lincoln Housing Authority assumed management of Huskerville for the University in 1949 and later ownership of the buildings; the land remained in city ownership." Additionally, a number of Web sites (e.g., http://groups.yahoo.com/group/huskerville and http://huskerville usa.tripod.com/nebraska/), newspaper articles (e.g., Hamar), and Web site participants have used the term over the years. Interestingly, I first stumbled upon the name, and then decided it fit, when my wife asked me one day in the fall of 1999, "So, how's your Huskerville project going?"

14. Scholars use phrases such as "imagined community" (Anderson, *Imagined*) or "diffused audience" (Abercrombie and Longhurst, *Audiences*) to refer to people who envision themselves as sharing the same community even though they may find themselves in different locations. As St. John (*Rammer*) notes, this idea probably dates back to French psychologist Gustave Le Bon's 1895 book, *The Crowd*, in which he introduces the idea of a "psychological crowd" or a collective dispersed in different physical locations.

15. I asked the Husker fans with whom I spoke whether they wanted me to use their real names in this book. Thus, when quoting other Husker fans, I will either use the real name of the fan or refer to those who wanted anonymity by calling them a "Husker fan." In addition, I often refer to the fan's city and state of residence (although, invariably, a few folks have moved since they talked to me).

16. A watch party is an event in which Husker fans gather, usually at a sports bar, to watch the football team's game on television.

17. Low and Altman, "Place Attachment," 10.

18. In fact, I found excerpts from these books to be quite helpful in my own research. Thus, references to them will be sprinkled throughout the pages that follow.

19. I devote much space in this book to telling my story, and the stories of other Husker fans because, as Belden Lane (*Landscapes*) urges, "The role of the storyteller is essential in grasping the power that place exerts on the religious imagination" (x). As the rest of the book explains, the idea of the Huskers is something of a civic religion among a great many Nebraskans.

20. "Place attachments," Barbara B. Brown and Douglas D. Perkins observe ("Disruptions"), "are integral to self-definitions, including individual and communal aspects of identity" (280).

21. Pierre Nora (*Realms*) uses the phrase "realms of memory" to refer to "any significant entity, whether material or non-material in nature, which by dint of human will or the work of time has become a symbolic element of the memorial heritage of any community" (xvii). The University of Nebraska football team, for many Nebraskans, is just such an entity. The remaining pages of the book attempt to explain why.

22. See John Bodnar's *Remaking America* for a historical account of how some social groups challenged official and traditional versions of collective memory.

23. Brown and Perkins, "Disruptions," 280.

24. Fred Davis explains in his book, *Yearning for Yesterday*, that "the past is never something simply there just waiting to be discovered. Rather, the remembered past like all other products of human consciousness is something that must constantly be filtered, selected, arranged, constructed, and reconstructed from collective experience" (115-116).

25. See Lowenthal ("Fabricating"), in which he argues that heritage is different from history in that the former is generally closed to outsiders, selective, and provides a sense of cultural identity to those who adhere to it.

26. As Doreen Massey (*Space*) points out, "the identities of place are always unfixed, contested and multiple" (5). For example, in the survey conducted for this book by the Scripps Survey Research Center at Ohio University, 28 percent of the Nebraska residents who responded to the statement, "I closely follow the Husker football team," indicated either disagreement or strong disagreement. In addition, as I talked about my ideas with a couple of prominent Nebraska scholars, who will go unnamed here, both told me that they were disappointed and even frustrated with the amount of attention given to Husker football, especially in light of how many academic units associated with the university struggle for funds and, in their opinion, are more beneficial for Nebraskans. Similarly, I received a letter from a Hastings, Nebraska, resident in the spring of 2000 who

wrote, "As you have probably guessed I am not a lover of football, and the extremes people go to just to go to a game—buy season tickets when need other things a lot more—neglect their children, jobs, livestock and sick relatives just to be there. Go Big Red!"

27. Holbrook, "On," 96.

28. Christopher Lasch discusses the distinction between memory and nostalgia in his book, *The True and Only Heaven*: "Nostalgia appeals to the feeling that the past offered delights no longer obtainable. Nostalgic representations of the past evoke a time irretrievably lost and for that reason timeless and unchanging. Strictly speaking, nostalgia does not entail the exercise of memory at all, since the past it idealizes stands outside time, frozen in unchanging perfection. Memory too may idealize the past, but not in order to condemn the present. It draws hope and comfort from the past in order to enrich the present and to face what comes with good cheer. It sees past, present, and future as continuous. It is less concerned with loss than with our continuing indebtedness to a past the formative influence of which lives on in our patterns of speech, our gestures, our standards of honor, our expectations, our basic disposition toward the world around us" (83).

29. See, for example, Crawford (*Consuming Sport*), Guttmann (*Sports Spectators*), and Wann, Melnick, Russell, and Pease (*Sport Fans*).

30. See, for example, Warren St. John's *Rammer Jammer Yellow Hammer* (Alabama football), Will Blythe's *To Hate Like This is to be Happy Forever* (North Carolina basketball), and Sean Glennon's *This Pats Year* (New England Patriots football). Their insights, as well as those of other sports fan writers, can be found throughout the rest of this book.

31. For interested readers, I drew from three academic bodies of literature. First, I collected most of the material contained within this book through ethnographic methods. In those instances where I asked people to complete interviews, share stories, and complete questionnaires, I followed the guidelines outlined by Ohio University's Institutional Review Board. This project was approved by that board on August 31, 1999, approval number 99E110. Second, I interpreted this material with an eye toward how Husker fans performed our identities as Huskers. As performance scholar Dwight Conquergood ("Ethnography") noted, "Far from frills and fakery, performance events and processes, according to [cultural anthropologist Victor] Turner, are the very stuff and heart of culture... Performance—powerfully conceptualized—is the borderlands terrain between rhetoric and ethnography" (84 and 80). Third,

since the notion of place lies at the heart of this project, I relied extensively on the insights of geographers—cultural, humanistic, and philosophical—in making sense of the collected material. I have used these three academic influences in the service of writing what I hope is a story that is at once intrinsically interesting, culturally enlightening, and theoretically invigorating.

32. Thanks to John Strope for the inspiration behind this idea.

Chapter 1

1. As of 2002, sugar beets were grown on about 74,000 acres of Nebraska panhandle farmland (Alswager, "Researchers").

2. In the 18th and 19th centuries, Russia's czars offered land and autonomy to ethnic Germans. When the Russian leaders then began to take back some of that autonomy in the latter part of the 19th century and into the early 20th century, these German Russians emigrated to the United States. Many settled in the Great Plains (see Williams, *The Czar's Germans*).

3. Welsch, "Germans," 205.

4. Irrigation, in general, is largely responsible for the growth of my hometown of Scottsbluff. The Federal Writers Project's 1939 history of Nebraska (*Nebraska*) observed that Scottsbluff "is the leading Nebraska city that has grown up because of irrigation. What was an irrigated alfalfa field in 1899 is now [40 years later] the chief trading center for a large area of Panhandle Nebraska and eastern Wyoming" (387).

5. Tom Osborne writes in his book, *More Than Winning*, that his paternal grandfather, also named Tom Osborne, "homesteaded some land in western Nebraska with the help of my grandmother" (14).

6. Smith, *Forever Red*, 103.

7. Sandoz, *Old Jules*, 39.

8. In "An Overview of the Great Plains" (available at: http://libr.unl.edu.2000/plains/overview.html), Wunder writes: "The Plains environment encourages community and retention of traditions."

9. Hickey, *Nebraska Moments*, 115. Hickey used 1980 U.S. Census data to draw this conclusion. He examined how many Nebraskans indicated awareness of our ancestry.

10. Luebke, "Ethnic," 427.

11. Found at: http://www.huskerhysteria.com/HuskerPlates.htm. This site is apparently no longer active.

12. *Homestead National Monument*. Washington, DC: National Park Service, 1998.

13. Deleuze and Guattari, *Thousand Plateaus*, 7.

Chapter 2

1. Cather, *My Ántonia*, 218. Interestingly, Cather based her description of this fruit cave upon a cave owned by the grandmother of Kent Pavelka, a former Husker football radio announcer (see Rosowski, *The Place*, for a brief description of this connection).

2. Following the 2006 season, the sellout streak stood at 282 consecutive games. A stadium expansion completed for the 2006 season increased the stadium's seating capacity to over 85,000. The sellout streak comparison is noted by Starita and Tidball, *Day in the Life*, 8.

3. Fujioka, "Sustaining," 23.

4. See www.hiplain.org/states/index.cfm?state=3 and Hickey, *Nebraska Moments*, 277.

5. Hickey, *Nebraska Moments*, 277.

6. According to Moseman ("Nature's"), "About 94 percent of the water used for irrigation in Nebraska comes from groundwater" (13).

7. My roots in Scottsbluff help me to appreciate the value of nourishing the ground through irrigation. As Olson and Naugle point out, Scotts Bluff County's emergence as an agricultural center depended upon the development of irrigation. "By 1940," they write, "the city of Scottsbluff, which in 1900 had been only a little huddle of tar-paper shacks, ranked sixth in the state [in population]" (342–343).

8. Moran, "Where Football," 18A.

9. Federal Writers Project, *Nebraska*, 112-113.

10. This 2006 figure is derived from a listing on the University of Nebraska Alumni Association Web site: www.huskeralum.com/events/radio_and_tv.htm

11. Smith, *Forever Red*, 7.

12. Posted on HuskerPedia on January 16, 2004, by bentNblue.

13. Posted on HuskerPedia on January 15, 2004, by sdhusker.

14. Stein, "Cult and Sport," 35.

15. Posted on January 17, 2004, by jdsabin1.

16. To read all of Matthew's story, please see Appendix A.

17. Starita and Tidball, *Day in the Life*, 9.

18. This 2006 figure is derived from a listing on the University of Nebraska Alumni Association Web site: www.huskeralum.com/events/radio_and_tv.htm

19. Starita and Tidball, *Day in the Life*, 9.

20. Ibid.

21. In Smith, *Forever Red*, 124.

22. This figure is found on the University of Nebraska-Lincoln's Sports Information Office Web site: http://www.huskers.com/SportSelect.dbml?DB_OEM_ID=100&DB_LANG=&KEY=&SPID=41&SPSID=185. Retrieved February 10, 2005.

23. Watch party locations are listed on the University of Nebraska Alumni Association Web site: www.huskeralum.com/events/radio_and_tv.htm. Over the years 2001–2004, the *Nebraska Alumni Resource Guide* reports the following figures: In 2003–2004, 645 watch parties and Founder's Day dinners occurred under alumni association sponsorship; they were attended by 30,000 Huskers ("2003–2004 Event/Activity Participation," *Nebraska Alumni Resource Guide, 2004-2005*, p. 5). In 2002–2003, there were 645 events with 34,105 attendees ("2002–2003 Event/Activity Participation," *Nebraska Alumni Resource Guide, 2003-2004*, p. 7). In 2001–2002, there were 691 events with 52,125 participants ("2001–2002 Event/Activity Participation," *Nebraska Alumni Resource Guide, 2002-2003*, p. 6). I have used approximate figures above because of the inclusion of Founder's Day events, which are held only once a year but still make average watch party figures difficult to assess with any degree of precision.

24. I received the following e-mail from the Capital of Texas Nebraskans on September 16, 2004, which—of course—was displayed in a red font: "The Core [committee] members of the Chapter and JC's [the watch party site] would like to THANK everyone for a record attendance at the first Watch Party of the Season. We rocked the house with 320 Husker Fans."

25. Ballard, "Finding," 74.

26. Susan Tyler Eastman and Arthur M. Land ("Best") observed sports fans watching games at sports bars and noted that fans enjoyed the social interaction as well as the feeling of being part of a community.

27. O'Neil, "Home Away," F2.

28. Osborne, "Big Red Planet," 37.

29. *Sports Illustrated*, 24.

30. Borchers, "Netsurfers," 3.

31. The longer version of Fritz's story may be found in Appendix A.

32. The longer version of Arthur's story may be found in Appendix A.

33. Snook, *What It Means*, xvii.

34. Winkler, *My Big*, 1.

35. In Snook, *What It Means*, 116.

36. Ibid., 89.

37. Maisel, "Coaching Carousel," 75–76.

38. Mitchell, "Seeing Big Red," 3.

39. "California gets big taste of Big Red" (January 2, 2002). Associated Press. Retrieved from Lexis-Nexis on March 1, 2005.

40. In Snook, *What It Means*, xvii.

41. Rosenblatt, "HuskerNation."

42. The students' letter can be found at: http://www.nd.edu/~observer/09122000/Viewpoint/3.html. Retrieved July 15, 2004.

43. Notre Dame's alumni base, for instance,

is simply immense compared with other U.S. universities with major college athletics teams.

44. St. John, *Rammer*, 1–2; emphasis added.

45. Tom's reminiscences of his life as a fan of Wake Forest, North Carolina, and Nebraska can be found in his story in Appendix A.

Chapter 3

1. Wright, "NU Grad Oversees."

2. Sano, "Sower Sees All."

3. Gruchow, "Thinking of Home," 344.

4. Edward Casey, a philosopher-geographer, provides a fascinating explanation of *how* places do these things in his 1996 essay, "How to Get From Space to Place in a Fairly Short Stretch of Time: Phenomenological Prolegomena," in Feld and Basso.

5. Momaday, "Native American Attitudes," 80. Momaday explains that the idea of reciprocal appropriation works at three levels. He writes, "I tried to express the notion first that the native American ethic with respect to the physical world is a matter of reciprocal appropriation: appropriations in which man [sic] invests himself in the landscape, and at the same time incorporates the landscape into his own most fundamental experience... Second, this appropriation is primarily a matter of the imagination. The appropriation is realized through an act of the imagination which is moral and kind ... he [the native American] is someone who thinks of himself in a particular way and his idea comprehends his relationship to the physical world, among other things. He imagines himself in terms of that relationship and others. And it is that act of the imagination, that moral act of the imagination, which I think constitutes his understanding of the physical world. Thirdly, this imagining, this understanding of the relationship between man and the landscape, or man and the physical world, man and nature, proceeds from a racial or cultural experience.... I mean that the Indian has determined himself in his imagination over a period of untold generations. His racial memory is an essential part of his understanding" (p. 80). This linking of identity to land is found among indigenous peoples throughout the world, including the Maori in New Zealand and the Aborigines in Australia (see Malpas, *Place*, 3–4).

6. Explains Simone Weil (*Need For Roots*), "To be rooted is perhaps the most important and least recognized need of the human soul. It is one of the hardest to define. A human being has roots by virtue of his real, active and natural participation in the life of a community which preserves in living shape certain particular expectations for the future" (41).

7. Catherine Middleton ("Roots and Rootlessness") outlines the importance of different kinds of rootedness: "It is essential to stress the importance of factors other than purely physical ones in this idea of rootedness, for attachment to a particular place is compounded of many different relationships: a person who is 'rooted in some sort of a native land' is rooted not only in a geographical landscape but also in a social landscape (in a community), in an emotional landscape (in a family or in intimate relationships with a few individuals) and in an intellectual landscape (in the knowledge and ideas which he has acquired)" (101).

8. Nagel and Williams, "The Prairie Below," 44.

9. Ibid., 45.

10. *Homestead National Monument: Official Map & Guide*. Washington, DC: National Park Service, 1998.

11. Dick, *The Sod-House*, 112.

12. Novak, *Joy*, 143. Additionally, Alec McHoul ("On Doing") notes that sports and everyday life "leak into each other on particular and specific occasions" (320). A number of surveys and studies have confirmed this blurring. Rachel A. Smith and Norbert Schwarz ("Language") discovered that students use "big game" rivalries as a means of emphasizing their school and team's positive qualities. Not surprisingly, other studies have demonstrated that winning teams tend to promote the strongest feelings of representation and affiliation (e.g., Bizman and Yinon; Cialdini, Borden, Thorne, Walker, Freeman, and Sloan).

13. In Nack, "Bang for the Bucs," 68.

14. Blythe, "Blue Blood," 69.

15. In Elliott, "Field of Dreams," 34.

16. Quoted in Geyer, *Part I*.

17. Starita and Tidball, *Day in the Life*, 7.

18. Posnanski, "Nebraska Fans," C1.

19. *Warsaw* [IN] *Times-Union*, 16C.

20. Israel, *Cornhuskers*, 7–8, 10-11.

21. See the June 14, 2004, issue of *Sports Illustrated* for Nebraska information (37). The July 12-19, 2004, issue contains information regarding all 50 states (42). The top five states were Nebraska (89.1), Alabama (88.8), Kentucky (88.6), Massachusetts (88.3), and Texas (87.7).

22. See Kaipust ("Spring") for Nebraska and Colorado attendance figures, Thomas ("Defense") for Florida State figures, and Klein ("USC") for University of Southern California figures. Thanks to Matthew Grosz for suggesting that I compare spring scrimmage attendance numbers.

23. Nolan, "Huskers."

24. This figure is from 2004 and was

retrieved on February 11, 2005, from the University of Nebraska Alumni Association Web site at: www.huskeralum.com/events/radio_and_tv.htm

25. I want to thank Devendra Sharma for helping me locate some of this information. All numbers reported here come from the universities' alumni association Web sites and were retrieved in January and February 2005.

26. This category does not include international chapters.

27. This number refers to the number of watch parties listed for the USC-Oklahoma national championship game in January 2005. Ten watch parties were listed for the December 2004 USC-UCLA game.

28. This figure refers to the number of watch parties listed for the September 10, 2004, game between Miami and Florida State University.

29. Texas and Ohio State, of course, enroll and graduate many more students than the other schools listed here. The enrollments at Nebraska, Alabama, USC, and Miami are similar.

30. Mike Nolan introduces this idea in a column in the *Lincoln Journal Star* newspaper ("Huskers").

31. Quoted in Geyer, *Part III*.

32. One hundred twenty-five people responded to this statement; 80 of them indicated either agreement or strong agreement with the statement.

33. These figures were determined through a cross-tabulation of answers performed using SPSS statistical analysis software.

34. The question was phrased, "What is the difference between a Nebraskan and a Husker fan?" The pollsters, who were working at computer terminals and keyboards, were then asked to enter the responses of the Nebraska residents verbatim.

35. Heather Gibson, Cynthia Willming, and Andrew Holdnak ("'We're Gators'") point out that University of Florida football fans refer to the idea of "being a Gator" (398)—as do other fans, no doubt. They do not discuss, however, any possible connection between "being a Gator" and "being a Floridian."

36. Darren's comments are found on his blog. The word blog is a shortened version of web log; it is akin to a public diary in that writers share their thoughts on a Web site. I was alerted to Darren's letter through a friend at Kansas State University, Chuck Lubbers. I retrieved the letter on November 1, 2004. The URL, or Internet address, for Darren's blog is http://friedmeatandsugarwater.blogspot.com/

37. Matt's posting occurred on December 3, 2003, in response to a questions, "What makes Nebraskan different [than other football pro-

grams]?" I encourage you to read his entire response, which received much praise from its readers. It can be retrieved from http://groups-beta.google.com/group/nebr.sports.unl/brows e_frm/thread/e8772127a66c0e53/c2f584ea454 2f158?tvc=1&q=why+Nebraska+is+different&_done=percent2Fgrouppercent2Fnebr.sports.un lpercent2Fsearchpercent3Fgrouppercent3Dneb r.sports.unlpercent26qpercent3Dwhy+Nebrask a+is+differentpercent26qt_gpercent3D1per-cent26&_doneTitle=Back+to+Search&scroll-Save=&&d#c2f584ea4542f158. I retrieved the posting on December 6, 2004.

38. Cather, My *Ántonia*, 14.

39. Cather, O *Pioneers!*, 50 and 118.

40. Ibid., 179.

41. Sports fan scholarship indicates that identification with a team and its players is a common experience among fans (see Guttmann, *Sports Spectators*; Wann, Melnick, Russell, and Pease, *Sport Fans*).

42. This idea was initially suggested to me by Alena Amato Ruggerio following her visits with members of the Kentuckiana Huskers.

43. Kevin's remarks are part of his longer story, which can be found in Appendix A.

44. The rest of Erik's story can be found in Appendix A.

45. Basso, *Wisdom Sits*, 75.

46. While alumni association groups label themselves in a number of different ways, another popular version is "XXX for Nebraska" (i.e., Arizonans for Nebraska, Minnesotans for Nebraska, Coloradans for Nebraska).

47. These quotations are found, in order, on the following pages of Snook's book: 4, 11, 16, 22, 223, 289.

48. In *Kentuckiana*, 1.

49. Brennan, "Solich," 1C.

50. Brennan, "Solich," 2C.

51. Coleman, "Letter."

52. See Guffey, "Nebraska Going," and Claussen, "Coach."

53. See http://www.huskersforohio.com

Chapter 4

1. "In some very fundamental but inexpressible way," explain geographers Roger M. Downs and David Stea (*Maps*), "our own self-identity is inextricably bound up with the knowledge of the spatial environment" (27).

2. Carlson, *New Agrarian Mind*, 203–204.

3. David Hendee, "Century of change leaves its mark on farms, ranches." *Omaha World-Herald*, May 23, 1999, Lexis-Nexis (accessed April 12, 2005).

4. Hanson, *Fields Without Dreams*, xv.

5. Ibid., xvi.

6. Scott Bauer, "Tax Break Benefits Retiring Farmers Who Help Up-and-comers." *Associated Press*, August 9, 2002. Lexis-Nexis (accessed August 20, 2002).

7. See Krantz, *Jobs Rated*, 6. Farming is listed as the 243rd "best" (out of 250) available job.

8. Reported in McFeatters, "There Can."

9. See Nebraska Databook at: http://info.neded.org/stathand/esect1.htm.

10. Based on population data provided by the U.S. Bureau of the Census; calculated and made available by the Nebraska State Data Center, Center for Public Affairs Research, University of Nebraska-Omaha. See: http://www.unomaha.edu/~cpar/census.htm

11. See Center for Public Affairs Research at the University of Nebraska-Omaha at: http://www.unomaha.edu/~cpar/agriculture.htm

12. *Nebraska Magazine*, 9.

13. Write Allen, Vogt, and Cordes (*Quality of Life*), "Only 19 percent of the farmers and ranchers think they are better off compared to five years ago. In comparison, 44 percent of the persons with professional occupations say they are better off" (p. i); "59 percent of farmers and ranchers are dissatisfied with their current income level, compared to only 30 percent of the persons with professional occupations" (p. ii). Additionally, less than half of the farmers and ranchers polled believe they will keep their farm or ranch in the family (Kawar, "Rural").

14. In Egan, "Amid."

15. Tyson, "In Rural Nebraska," 9A.

16. In Kawar, "Rural Poll Finds Concern."

17. Humanistic geographer Anne Buttimer observes, "It appears that people's sense of both personal and cultural identity is intimately bound up with place identity. Loss of home or 'losing one's place' may often trigger an identity crisis" (167).

18. Rooney, "Nebraska Faces Identity Crisis."

19. Chatelain, "Ickes."

20. Belsie, "New Frontier," 10. Nebraska has thus been caught between its past and its future. As its metropolitan areas sprawl, its rural areas become more desolate. In addition, as more of Nebraska's residents can make a living without agriculture—"In the 1950s, two-thirds of the nation's nonmetropolitan counties were farm-dependent (at least 20 percent of business earnings came from agriculture). Today, only a seventh of nonmetro counties remain farm-dependent" (Belsie, "Little Farms," p. 12)—the values associated with agriculture may seem increasingly outdated.

21. Agrarianism, notes Timothy W. Kelsey ("Agrarian"), is a "moral rhetoric," but, he continues, "the values of agrarianism conform to the realities of neither late 19th-century agriculture nor modern agriculture" (1172).

22. In Hassebrook, "State of Rural America."

23. See Eviatar Zerubavel's book *Time Maps* for a thoughtful explanation of the process of collective memory.

24. See Lasch's distinction between memory and nostalgia in footnote 28 in the Introduction.

25. Belsie, "New Frontier," 10.

26. Tyson, "In Rural Nebraska," 9A. See also an Associated Press article by Courtney Lowery, "Dropping Enrollment," for a fine feature on the emergence of six-man football in Nebraska. As Lowery points out, the sport was invented (or adapted) in 1934 by a Nebraskan named Stephen Epler.

27. "Without commemorative vigilance," writes Pierre Nora (*Realms*), "history would soon sweep [preserves of memory] away. These bastions buttress our identities, but if what they defended were not threatened, there would be no need for them" (7). Husker football is critically important, as this and the next four chapters illustrate, to preserving the memory of an agrarian way of life.

28. Huskervillers tend to overlook the fact that, early in his head coaching career, Osborne nearly left the University of Nebraska to take the head coaching job at the University of Colorado. He was, understandably, frustrated by how a number of Husker fans were responding to his changes in the program and his lack of success in defeating rival Oklahoma.

29. Of the 75 fans who responded to this particular statement, 24 indicated either agree or strongly agree; 17 of the 24 responded with "agree." Pollsters were instructed to clarify "real," if necessary, by using phrases such as "as it ought to be" and "as Nebraskans expect." The results of the survey seem to reflect phenomena identified by social psychologists as BIRGing (Basking in Reflected Glory) (see Cialdini, Borden, Thorne, Walker, Freeman, and Sloan, "Basking") and CORFing (Cutting Off Reflected Failure) (see Snyder, Lassegard, and Ford, "Distancing"). These concepts describe situations in which fans strongly identify with winning teams and decrease their identification with losing teams. A summary of this research can be found in Wann, Melnick, Russell, and Pease (*Sport Fans*).

30. In the 2003–04 season, Nebraska was defeated by Missouri 41–24, Texas 31–7, and Kansas State 38–9.

31. See http://www.usatoday.com/sports/college/football/big12/2003-11-30-nebraska-solich_x.htm.

32. See Olson, "Big Red."

33. Bob Devaney was an "outsider" when

hired. In 1968, following consecutive 6–4 seasons, he was nearly run out of town. As Corcoran (*Game*) notes, "Full-blown grumbling and second-guessing commenced, followed by the drumbeat of opinion that Devaney should be fired" (41). Osborne, now revered perhaps more than Devaney, was also the target of much criticism in the 1970s, and considered leaving Nebraska to become the head coach at the University of Colorado after the 1978 season.

34. Some Husker fans welcomed the idea of an offensive system that passed the ball more frequently. I was not among them.

35. Chen, "Extreme Makeover."

36. Sports reporter Eric Olson ("Big Red") writes that Callahan's decision to reduce the size of the walk-on program was "because he [Callahan] doesn't have enough locker space for them and that his coaching staff would be stretched too thin if there were 180 to 200 players on the roster."

37. In Pluto, "Small Town," C1.

38. In Sherman, "Group." Osborne estimated that the walk-on program gave the team an estimated 5–8 scholarship-worthy players each year.

39. These numbers were based on my counting of the rosters posted on the University of Nebraska athletics Web site (huskers.com), the *Omaha World-Herald*'s Web site (omaha.com), and http://nationalchamps.net/NCAA/ncaa_previews/nebraska_preview.htm.

40. Frost's comments are part of a long posting on the *Lincoln Journal Star*'s Husker football Web site. They were posted on November 10, 2005, and can be found at: http://www.journalstar.com/huskerextra2/blogs/always_husker.php.

41. The former player quoted was Jason Baker. In Merrill, "Some Former Huskers."

42. The former player quoted was Gregg Reeves. In Rosenthal, "What Anxiety?."

43. As University of Nebraska sports historian John Wunder ("Change") remarks in his discussion of changes in the football program, "Nebraskans take pride in their football, and they like to win and, if they must lose, to lose in the 'right way.' They do not like the win-at-all-costs mentality they see at other universities" (11).

44. Loren's full story can be found in Appendix A.

45. Posted on Huskerpedia on January 15, 2004 (shortly after the hiring of Bill Callahan). The excerpt printed here is part of a much longer story posted by BlueCreek.

46. In Merrill, "Osborne Vents."

47. In Olson, "Big Red."

48. Ibid.

49. Organizational change scholars George L. Daniels and C. Ann Hollifield ("Time") note that successful changes in organizations require managers to involve employees in the change process. "Also critical," they point out, "was insuring that employees shared the company's attitudes and interests, and could see the ways in which the changes related to the company's overall goals" (662).

50. This letter was posted on Darren's Internet blog, which can be found at: http://friedmeatandsugarwater.blogspot.com/

51. Former Nebraska coaches have also expressed their support of Callahan while suggesting that those concerned have nothing to worry about. Milt Tenopir, a long-time offensive line coach with the Huskers who retired (apparently with some encouragement) following Solich's 7–7 season, has vocally supported the new coaching staff. "People worry about the old traditions," Tenopir said. "Nebraska's tradition will never leave, I don't care who's coaching. This is a tremendously capable staff. They'll get 'er done" (Olson, "Retired").

52. Cather, *O Pioneers!*, 17.

53. Preservation efforts of all kinds, writes Eviatar Zerubavel (*Time Maps*), offer "some sense of permanence [and] help promote the highly reassuring conservative illusion that nothing fundamental has really changed" (41).

54. In Bohlke, *Willa Cather*, 37.

55. The remainder of Annette's story can be found in Appendix A.

56. Tim's story about Nebraska and being a Husker fan can be found in Appendix A.

57. Burke, *Philosophy*, 293–304. Burke is referring to literature, but his ideas have been applied to other popular forms of communication as well.

58. See, for example, Larkey and Morrill, "Organizational," 209.

59. Eisenberg, "Building," 534.

60. Berry, *Unsettling*, 9.

Chapter 5

1. Welch, *The Platte River*, n.p. Welch's poem emphasizes the physical things we live by while also implying the "way of life" we live by.

2. See http://www.unl.edu/pr/notables/alumni.shtml

3. "The quality of a place," notes Eugene Walter (*Placeways*), "depends on a human context shaped by memories and expectations, by stories of real and imagined events—that is, by the historical experience located there" (117). Adds Eviatar Zerubavel (*Time Maps*), "where communities locate their beginnings tells us quite a lot about how they perceive themselves" (101).

4. Who claimed the first homestead is far from a settled issue, especially since multiple offices were opened around the country to process homesteaders' claims. See, for example, Plante and Mattison ("The 'First'"), who examined the competing claims of Freeman, William Young, and Mahlon Gore. They conclude, "It cannot be safely said that the 'first homesteader' was any of these three because there is no reliable means today to determine whether some of the other land offices were open at midnight [on January 1, 1863] for acceptance of applications" (5).

5. Hickey, *Nebraska Moments*, 102.

6. See Nebraska Databook at: http://info. neded.org/stathand/esect1.htm. These population growth figures, of course, may not reflect the many Native American tribes who lived in Nebraska prior to, and during, the homesteading period. As Knopp (*Nature*) notes, fifteen treaties "opened the future state of Nebraska to homesteaders one piece at a time between 1825 and 1882" (144).

7. Olson and Naugle, *History of Nebraska*, 198.

8. Federal Writers Project, *Nebraska*, 74. A number of other problems surrounded the Homestead and Kincaid Acts, including insufficient land, fraudulent filings, and different standards for Native American homesteaders who, ironically, had to complete more stringent requirements to claim land that was taken from them (see Knopp, *Nature*, 142-145).

9. The sampling error range for this survey is +/- 8.4 percent. Thus, even assuming a worst-case scenario reduction of 8.4 percent, well over 70 percent of the phone respondents agreed with these statements.

10. Allen, Vogt, Cordes, and Cantrell, *Attributes*, 7.

11. Percentages for these values were, respectively, 61, 61, 62, and 72. Importantly, these percentages were derived through questions that asked rural Nebraskans whether they believed rural Nebraskans to be "most like" one of two opposite items or neutral. So, while 61 percent indicated work-oriented, only 12 percent selected leisure-oriented; the remainder of the responses were neutral. For self-sufficient or dependent on others, only 13 percent selected dependent on others. For tough or resilient or weak, only 14 percent selected weak. For friendly people or unfriendly people, only 11 percent selected unfriendly people. See Allen, Vogt, Cordes, and Cantrell, *Attributes*, 7.

12. Compared to what the survey defined as "laborers," farmers and ranchers believed that rural Nebraskans were more work-oriented (72 percent–54 percent) and friendly (82 percent–68 percent).

13. This question was asked in slightly different forms as I refined versions of the questionnaire during my research. In early versions of the questionnaire, I asked respondents to define a Nebraskan. In the latest version of the questionnaire, I asked for five characteristics that best define a Nebraskan. Given these different approaches, calculating percentages for each characteristic seemed problematic, especially since some characteristics may overlap with others.

14. Again, this question was asked in slightly different forms, but hardworking was the most frequent answer overall.

15. Starita and Tidball, *A Day*, 10.

16. This message was posted on the epinions.com Web site (www.epinions.com/con tent_39485935236) by a Husker fan using the name Ms. Hooterville.

17. These three themes emerged through an analysis of interview transcripts, questionnaire responses, and—in particular—later questionnaire questions that asked Husker fans to identify five prominent characteristics of the team and of Nebraskans in general. Some responses were incorporated into these three themes (e.g., tough and dedicated into work ethic; helpful, friendly, and loyal into being neighborly; simple, straightforward, honest, genuine, and plain into down-to-earth), while others were not mentioned as frequently. These three themes, then, represent the characteristics mentioned most prominently but they are by no means intended to represent all of what I was told by Husker fans. These three themes share much in common with Garreau's (*Nine Nations*) observation that "all over the Breadbasket, especially in urban industrial contexts, people genuflect in the direction of values they believe are taught by the family farm. Rarely are they articulate about what they mean, but as people stumble toward an explanation of what they value in their friends and neighbors around here, the words are *always* 'open,' 'friendly,' 'hardworking,' 'there when you need them,' 'down-to-earth'" (350). My experience differs from Garreau's in that I found many people able to articulate what they mean, and they were able to do so in ways that marked Nebraska as different from other surrounding states. Thus, while the region may share some value orientations, each state's understanding, and enactment, of those values is understandably different.

18. Speer, "Communication," 89.

19. Basso, *Wisdom*, 146. This kind of contemporary homesteading is described by Edward Casey, a philosopher with a geographical orientation toward the world. Homesteading, he says, is the establishment of "co-habitancy" with the landscape. Co-habitancy,

a term Casey borrows from Thoreau, "signifies a special kind of settled coexistence between humans and the land, between the natural and the cultural, and between one's contemporaries and one's ancestors" (Casey, *Getting Back*, 291).

20. Judy was speaking generally about Nebraska values rather than referring specifically to what I have identified as the primary values of Huskerville.

21. Timothy B. Gongaware ("Collective"), observes, "Collective memory also implies a sense of unity for a group as remembrances are shared and interactively integrated in one way or another" (487). In Huskerville, such integration occurs through Husker football.

22. Nolan, "Huskers."

Chapter 6

1. Furay, "Small Town," 53.

2. This expectation also reminds me—though sadly, it did not cross my mind at the time—that, as a good neighbor, I should have *volunteered* to shovel the snow from Mr. and Mrs. Baggs's driveway and sidewalk.

3. Gates, *Free Homesteads*, 2.

4. While promoted as "free land," persons claiming the homestead did have to pay a filing fee, have the capital to make something of the land, and then pay a final filing fee at the conclusion of the five-year period.

5. Dick, *The Sod-House*, 118-119.

6. Hanson, *Fields Without*, 17.

7. Welsch, *Sod Walls*, 17.

8. As Campbell (*Prairie*) notes, "The Homestead Act of 1862 was something new. It catered to the farmer who was neither a member of an exclusive group, nor connected, nor wealthy" (p. 3).

9. Welsch, *Sod Walls*, 22.

10. Cather, *My Ántonia*, 7.

11. Sandoz, *Sandhill Sundays*, 21

12. Ibid., 10.

13. As Paul B. Thompson notes in his book *The Spirit of the Soil*, farming in general espouses "a work ethic that converts production into a sign of the farmer's moral worth" (68).

14. Grumbach, "Foreword," xviii.

15. The percentages of rural Nebraskans who identified these characteristics are, respectively, 61, 61, and 62. See Allen, Vogt, Cordes, and Cantrell, *Attributes*, 7.

16. Allen, Vogt, Cordes, and Cantrell, *Attributes*, 8.

17. Miller and Benz, "Conceptions," 229.

18. Information retrieved from huskers.com (home of the University of Nebraska athletics department).

19. The NCAA offers another academic award for student-athletes called the Top Eight Award. Fifteen Nebraska student-athletes, nine of them from football, have been honored with this award—more than from any other university in both categories. All information retrieved from huskers.com.

20. Snook, *What It Means*, ix.

21. Ibid., 144-145.

22. Ibid., 12-13.

23. Sandoz, *Old Jules*, 43.

24. In Snook, *What It Means*, 7.

25. Sandoz, *Old Jules*, 45.

26. Retrieved from http://www.livinghistoryfarm.org/farminginthe30s/life_14.html. Accessed on July 12, 2005. The Web site is sponsored by Wessels Living History Farm in York, Nebraska.

27. Olson and Naugle, *History of Nebraska*, 160.

28. As historians have noted, the Homestead and Kincaid Acts did not work as well in practice as they did in theory. Many homesteaders did not have the capital to make a go of it for five years, and the laws were full of loopholes that allowed business interests to claim much of the land set aside for homesteaders. In addition, as Knopp (*Nature*) points out, the "public domain" lands parceled out to homesteaders were once the living spaces of Native American tribes. Their requirements for homesteading, she notes, were significantly more stringent: a 25-year residency rather than the five years required of non-Native American homesteaders.

29. Sandoz, *Sandhill Sundays*, 132. Olson and Naugle (*History of Nebraska*) concur, "That some did succeed is testimony to their courage, fortitude, and sheer determination to triumph against the odds" (163).

30. Sandoz, *Old Jules*, 120 and 256.

31. As Huskervillers are well aware, the team scored a touchdown in the final moments of the game to pull within one point of the University of Miami. An extra point would have resulted in a tie game, and very likely—given their undefeated record and dominant performances in other games during the year—would have ensured that the team would be recognized as national champions. Instead, in a move that cemented his legend and made Husker fans proud, coach Tom Osborne elected to try to win the game with a two-point conversion rather than play for a tie.

32. The score was 17-9.

33. Although this belief is prominent in Huskerville, Nebraska football players have had much success in the professional ranks recently. In 2003, for example, the National Football League (NFL) reports that only nine other colleges had more of their players in the NFL (see:

http://www.nfl.com/news/story/6628372).
More recently, *The Wall Street Journal* developed
a formula to measure the success of college players in the NFL. Nebraska was ranked 13th in
that analysis (see: http://online.wsj.com/pub-
lic/resources/documents/retro-collegefootball
0608.html).

34. Osborne, *More Than*, 138.

35. Moran, "In Nebraska."

36. Quoted in Geyer, *Part III*.

37. Cather, *Kingdom of Art*, 213. I owe a
thanks to the late Sue Rosowski for pointing
me to Cather's writing on football.

38. Schaller, *I Played*, 43.

39. One of the program's most famous walk-
ons, I. M. Hipp, came to Nebraska from
Chapin, South Carolina. One year after his
arrival, in his first start, he set a then-school
record for rushing in a single game. As of 2005,
he ranked sixth on the school's career rushing
list (see Olson, "I.M. Hipp").

40. Moran, "In Nebraska."

41. In Merrill, "Walk-on Schroeder."

42. Ibid.

43. Chatelain, "Ickes."

44. In Snook, *What It Means*, 191.

45. Ibid., 201.

46. Kaipust, "Callahan." In his 1985 book,
More Than Winning, former coach Tom Osborne
estimated that 35–40 percent of each year's
starters were former walk-ons (138).

47. Olson, "Small Colleges."

48. I'm referring to Travis Turner, who
started at quarterback for the Huskers in 1984.

49. Osborne, *More Than*, 139 and 147.

50. Osborne, *More Than*, 147.

51. Ibid., 262.

52. Merrill, "Walk-on Schroeder."

53. I want to emphasize that Callahan has
not eliminated the walk-on program, but
reduced its size. As of May 2006, in fact, he had
awarded 11 scholarships to walk-ons; eight of
the 11 were from Nebraska (Olson, "Big Red").

54. Kaipust, "NU."

55. Shatel, "Wild Finish."

56. In Olson, "I. M. Hipp."

Chapter 7

1. Sartore, *Under*, 7–8.

2. As my friend Natalie Dollar, an LSU
football fan, observed after attending a Husker
watch party in Portland, Oregon, Huskervillers
seem to feel comfortable simply being in each
other's presence. Socializing, she noted, did not
need to include talk, perhaps because being
social was different for people who grew up in
wide-open spaces.

3. Sandoz, *Old Jules*, 81. In another part of

her book, Sandoz observes, "There was always
news at Jules's dugout, companionship, good
talk" (71). These connections were vitally important for the homesteaders, for the loneliness
drove some to suicide or mental breakdowns.
As Susanne George-Bloomfield ("Happiness")
points out in her exploration of how the prairie
is portrayed in fiction set in Nebraska, "The
physical isolation of the open prairies creates
... what Diane Quantic, in *The Nature of the
Place*, terms a 'psychological entrapment' that
produces 'an acute sense of displacement,' caus-
ing individuals to withdraw from normal
human society or try desperately to escape"
(143). For example, in Cather's *My Ántonia*, the
father of the title character commits suicide in
response to being overwhelmed by the prairie.
Sandoz's *Old Jules* also makes multiple references to homesteaders suffering mental illness.

4. Posted on the Huskerpedia Web site on
January 16, 2004.

5. Sandoz, *Old Jules*, 253.

6. See Bob Greene's *Once Upon a Town* for
stories about the canteen.

7. *Pride*, 14.

8. Shapiro, "Why I Like," 14.

9. Shapiro, "Some More," 4.

10. Hickey, *Nebraska Moments*, 262.

11. Ibid., 259.

12. Ibid., 263.

13. Kobayashi, "Responding," 3. Dr. Kobayashi offered his comments while praising the
University of Nebraska for its efforts to welcome students displaced by Hurricane Katrina
in 2005.

14. Clarke, "The Year," 29.

15. Caple, "Red Alert."

16. Accessed on June 21, 2005, through
http://www.epinions.com/sprt-review-1956-
BE6895-39EEEF50-prod1

17. Anderson, "Road Trip."

18. Dick, *The Sod-House*, 248–249.

19. Morrison, "Where," 21.

20. In "Replanting Rural Nebraska," an
Associated Press series of articles. I accessed the
articles through: http://www.starherald.com/
Newfront/pages/Rural%20Nebraska/leads.htm

21. In Snook, *What It Means*, 36.

22. Furay, "Small Town," 43.

23. Dick, *The Sod-House*, 249.

24. Sandoz, *Old Jules*, 180.

25. Jon's full account of his experience can
be found in Appendix A.

26. Robert Cialdini and colleagues ("Basking") call this phenomenon "cutting off from
reflected failure." Fans who do not want their
identity tied to a losing team thus "cut off"
their connection to the team. "True fans," of
course, are supposed to exhibit loyalty.

27. Ibid., 100.

28. Sandoz, *Old Jules*, 248.

29. Dick, *The Sod-House*, 247.

30. The remainder of Cristine's story can be found in Appendix A.

31. Moran, "In Nebraska."

32. Posted on January 15, 2004. At the same time of this posting, the HuskerPedia Web site featured a discussion about being a "good fan" versus being a "bad fan." The undercurrent of this discussion was "how does a Husker fan enact loyalty when s/he doesn't agree with the changes made in the football program?"

33. In Snook, *What It Means*, 232. In addition, some Husker fans booed Nebraska quarterback Scott Frost during the 1997 Central Florida game—again, an occurrence so unusual that many Husker fans vividly recall it (see a discussion on the Husker List Internet discussion board, for example).

34. This survey was conducted by Ohio University's Scripps Survey Research Center. To determine percentages, those survey respondents who indicated either agree or strongly agree with the statement "I closely follow the Husker football team" were counted as fans. As a reminder, the error range on this survey is +/- 8.4%, meaning that we can confidently assume that between 79.6 and 96.4 percent of Husker fans living in Nebraska agree with this statement.

35. Babcock, *Go Big Red*, 253.

36. Anderson, "Road Trip."

37. Tom's memories, which include being a fan of Wake Forest, North Carolina, and Nebraska, can be found in his story in Appendix A.

38. St. John, *Rammer*, 56.

39. Ibid., 140-141.

40. In Frei, "Place."

41. Posted on the Husker List Internet discussion board on November 12, 2001.

42. To be fair, Mark Olson responded on the Husker List that he had a different experience with Kansas State fans when they visited Lincoln. "As we walked up 9th St. to the game, we encountered quite a few KSU fans. One fan had his hand up the entire way, high fiving every Husker fan he encountered with wishes for 'good luck.' We spoke with a couple behind him, they wished us well and expressed their desires for a good game. As we waited for traffic, we struck up another conversation with a couple decked out in their purple shirts. They said that the hospitality in Lincoln was tremendous. They said that they hoped that they would win, but they knew that they would have a tremendous mountain to climb in order to do so. We parted with wishes of good luck. The fans that we encountered were quite gracious."

43. The column, written by Sandeep Rao,

was published on October 19, 2001, in the newspaper then known as the *University Daily*. It can be accessed at: http://www.dailytoreador.com/vnews/display.v/ART/2001/10/19/3bcf9c0e542f1?in_archive=1

44. Lt. Col. Caudle's entire note can be found in Appendix A. This note was originally sent to the Capital of Texas Nebraskans alumni chapter, whose e-mails I have received as part of this project. Lt. Col. Caudle gave me permission to reprint his letter in this book.

45. Cotten, "100% Cotten." Thanks to Jack Kovacs for this article.

46. Taylor, "No. 1 Fans," 3. Taylor wrote following a visit to Lincoln in 2004.

47. This article, written on September 10, 2001, and headlined, "Salute to Nebraska Fans," is not available through an online archive. Mr. Prister confirmed its accuracy through e-mail correspondence. I originally encountered the article when it was sent to me by a high school friend, Soni Smith. The article can also be found online at: http://www.missingnebraska.com/Fun_Jokes/fj00701.html

48. Reprinted in *Nebraska Magazine*, Winter 2003, 14.

49. The column, written by Sandeep Rao, was published on October 19, 2001, in the newspaper then known as the *University Daily*. It can be accessed at: http://www.dailytoreador.com/vnews/display.v/ART/2001/10/19/3bcf9c0e542f1?in_archive=1

50. Ibid.

51. Cotton, "100% Cotten."

Chapter 8

1. Smith, *Forever Red*, 102.

2. Dick, in *The Sod-House Frontier*, notes that "the cottonwood tree was generally selected" by those attempting to improve their land, and thus prove their claims, under the Timber Culture Act (130).

3. Football would rank second among my survey respondents if "Lincoln on game day" was added to the total for football.

4. In her collection of stories, *Memories Are For Sharing*, Vivian Roeder recalls that she attended a one-room sod school near Bayard, Nebraska.

5. Cather, *O Pioneers!*, 12.

6. Smith, *Forever Red*, 119.

7. Berens, *Power*, 1.

8. Thanks to Candy Hodge for sharing this joke with me.

9. Steve offers a thoughtful account of being a Husker fan in Appendix A.

10. Dick, *The Sod-House*, 364.

11. Due to governmental bungling, the Pon-

cas' land in Nebraska had been mistakenly given to the Sioux. To solve the situation, the federal government moved the Ponca to Oklahoma. When Standing Bear led a group of Poncas back to Nebraska to bury Standing Bear's son, they were arrested and held by the U.S. Army. In their *History of Nebraska*, James C. Olson and Ronald C. Naugle note that "federal judge Elmer S. Dundy declared that 'an Indian is a person within the meaning of the law'" (120). Olson and Naugle explain that, as a result of the trial, those Poncas who wanted to return to Nebraska were allowed to do so. The government then provided land along the Niobrara River for the Poncas.

12. Sandoz, *Love Song*, 242.

13. In 1892, for instance, George Flippin took the field for the University of Nebraska football team as the first African American athlete at Nebraska. Later, he was voted captain of the team. This, of course, was an unusual occurrence in late 19th century America (see Mark Fricke's article, "The Beginning of the Huskers," at www.huskernews.com). Yet, no African Americans played on the football team for a long stretch in the early 20th century; a university policy enacted in 1917 forbade African Americans from participating in extracurricular activities (Babcock, *Go Big Red*, 6). Even Flippin was the target of bigoted remarks from his coach (Babcock, *Go Big Red*, 6). Later in life, Flippin filed Nebraska's first civil rights lawsuit when he was refused service at a restaurant in York, Nebraska (see www.unl.edu/pr/notables/alumni.html). Notre Dame stopped its games against Nebraska in the 1920s because of anti-Catholic slurs shouted by fans. As I have tried to emphasize throughout the book, any community's memory of its history is selective. In this case, Huskervillers can rightfully point to many splendid examples of treating others as equals, even if we overlook contrary examples in doing so.

14. Denney, Limprecht, and Silber, *Go Big Red*, 137.

15. Starita and Tidball, *A Day*, 8.

16. Stew Price also observed this connection between the Huskers' former option offense and the down-to-earth qualities of Huskervillers. The offense, he said, is "described by some people as repetitive and mundane—not flashy. The same can be said about the typical Nebraska citizen."

17. For the full story behind the saying, visit http://www.huskernews.com/vnews/display.v/ART/1999/03/15/36ec23e95

18. Jones wrote his account in the January 1, 1999, edition of the *San Diego Union-Tribune*. This portion was reprinted in the Spring 1999 issue of *Nebraska Magazine* on page 31.

19. Posted on January 15, 2004.

20. On pages 150-151, Osborne talks about two approaches to sports, one referring to Vince Lombardi's notion that winning is the only thing (though Osborne, characteristically, does not mention Lombardi by name) and the other based upon sportswriter Grantland Rice's adage that "how you played the game" is most important. Thanks to David Max for pointing out this connection.

21. In his book about the 1971 Nebraska vs. Oklahoma football game, Michael Corcoran also observes, "Osborne personified the state of Nebraska. He was a sincere and stoic man, courteous and well-mannered, who combined great intelligence with the knowledge that the best way to get something done was to put your shoulder to it without complaining" (45).

22. Osborne, *More Than*, 141.

23. Osborne was not the first coach to earn such respect from the citizens of Nebraska. Former coach Biff Jones has been called "the personification of many of the values that Nebraskans treasured most. He was ethical, hard working, and well-disciplined. In football he liked to win in a classic, straightforward, Nebraska way: with a strong running game" (Geyer, *Part I*).

24. In Schaller, *I Played*, 26.

25. Ibid., 42.

26. Ibid., 70.

27. When Osborne declared his candidacy, the sitting governor, Mike Johanns, was precluded from running for re-election. Johanns was then appointed U.S. secretary of agriculture and Lieutenant Governor Dave Heineman took over, declaring that he would seek to retain his seat. For an analysis of the campaign, see Tysver ("Heineman Benches Osborne").

28. Hendee, "Osborne."

29. Shatel, "In Defeat."

30. As Huskervillers will quickly point out, Osborne was not just a football coach. In 1965, he earned a Ph.D. in educational psychology while serving as a graduate assistant coach under Bob Devaney. He now holds the title professor emeritus from the University of Nebraska.

31. In a later e-mail message, Jack added that he would send congratulations notes to Osborne and Frank Solich following a successful season. "Both," he said, "took the time to send a short handwritten thank you note for my mail."

32. The rest of Joe's story about Osborne can be found in Appendix A.

33. Both of these offenses were committed by Nebraska football coach Bill Callahan during the 2005 season.

Chapter 9

1. Paul Tebbel, quoted in *National Geographic*, 1.
2. Holloway, "Great," 102.
3. Johnsgard, *Crane Music*, 43.
4. Bly, "Saga," 2D.
5. Moran, "In Nebraska."
6. Starita and Tidball, *Day in the Life*, 7–8.
7. Gruchow, *Necessity*, 29–30. Cranes, generally, are "the most ancient species of bird on earth" (Bly, "Saga," 2D) and the sandhill cranes have been making their pilgrimages for thousands of years.
8. Bly, "Saga," 2D. Considering that the lifespan of a sandhill crane is approximately 25 years, their partnerships last longer than those of many humans. Nebraska's divorce rate is the 17th lowest among the 50 states and the District of Columbia (see: http://www.cdc.gov/nchs/data/nvss/divorce90_04.pdf)
9. Cornhuskings were by no means unique to Nebraska. Indeed, farmers throughout the U.S. would hold such gatherings. One of the Six Nations of the Iroquois Confederacy, the Tuscarora Nation, describes a cornhusking in one of its newsletters: "an annual husking bee ... is a social event that bridges the gap between utility and festivity... The time spent husking the farmer's corn is always filled with education, laughter, and traditional music. In older times, many farmers would have a dance in the barn after the corn was completely husked." Retrieved from: http://www.hetfonline.org/pages/T4summe2001.htm on February 15, 2005.
10. This definition comes from Volume 1, A-M, of my 1996 *Funk & Wagnalls Standard Desk Dictionary* (143).
11. Historian Everett Dick explains that husking bees were more common in the New England states than in the western states, primarily because the corn crops in the west were too large to take care of in one night. In addition, farmers across the U.S. eventually discovered that, in the words of an Ohio settler, "it was less trouble to husk it in the field, direct from the stalk, than to gather in the husk and go over it again" (Howells, "William Howells," 61).
12. Sandoz mentions "literaries in the schoolhouses, husking bees, a feather-stripping party or two, and socials, sings, masquerades, and dances" (115).
13. Meredith, "Cornhusking," 20–21.
14. Ibid., 21.
15. Daniels, *Puritans*, 94. Daniels writes about New England bees, but his description fits bees of all kinds held throughout the U.S.
16. Dick, *The Sod-House*, 365.

17. Notre Dame football player turned English professor Michael Oriard (*Sporting*) notes, "A 'game' marks the meeting of 'play' and 'work' in the social world" (xiii).
18. Carbaugh, *Situating*, 57.
19. Scholars contest various definitions of what counts as ritual; I am using a fairly loose definition of ritual consistent with those offered by Sally F. Moore and Barbara G. Myeroff ("Introduction") and Tom F. Driver (*Liberating Rites*). Moore and Myeroff use the term "collective ceremonies" as synonymous with contemporary rituals, while Driver writes in an appendix to his book, "I chose to view *all* cultural performances as belonging to the ritual mode" (236).
20. Driver, *Liberating Rites*, 98.
21. Huizinga, *Homo Ludens*, 37.
22. Smith, *To Take Place*, 28.
23. Huizinga, *Homo Ludens*, 31; emphasis added. See Lawrence ("Transcendence") and Hufford ("Thresholds") for examples of transcendent places enacted through ritual participation.
24. Deegan and Stein, "American," 33; emphasis added.
25. Deegan and Stein's approach may have something to do with the fact that they had lived in Lincoln for just "over two years" at the time they wrote the article (33). I should also emphasize that Michael Novak's *The Joy of Sports* overtly recognizes the ritualistic dimensions of many sporting activities.
26. Anthropologists Eliot Dismore Chapple and Carleton Stevens Coon wrote in 1942 that what they term "rites of intensification" serve "to reinforce the habitual relations within the society" (528), especially in light of disturbances to those relations (as was discussed in the Uprooting chapter earlier in this book). Thanks to my friend Tom Preston for alerting me to this concept.
27. Driver (*Liberating Rites*) notes that the three functions of ritual are order, community, and transformation (132). While similar, I believe that the three functions I identify are different, especially given their orientation toward place borrowed from Smith (*To Take Place*).

Chapter 10

1. Driver, *Liberating Rites*, 159.
2. Ritual scholars note that rituals move their participants into places they call a "special world" (Schechner, *Performance*, 11), "alternative world" (Driver, *Liberating Rites*, 80), or "larger setting" (Tuan, *Passing*, 183).
3. Goodall, *Divine*, 119.

4. Turner, *Dramas*, 238.

5. In Starita and Tidball, *A Day*, 23.

6. Annette's story can be found in Appendix A.

7. Wherever Husker fans gather, be it in Memorial Stadium, in watch parties, or with friends at home, we collectively converge into what Chidester and Linenthal ("Introduction") call "sacred space": "a location for formalized, repeatable symbolic performances. As sacred space, a ritual site is set apart from or carved out of an 'ordinary' environment to provide an arena for the performance of controlled, 'extraordinary' patterns of action" (9).

8. Posted on the Husker List Internet discussion board on December 4, 2003.

9. Posted on the HuskerPedia Web site on January 16, 2004, by Calla.

10. Bourland, "Huskers," 8.

11. Ritual scholars note that the language of religion is often borrowed to explain the ritual experience. See Rothenbuhler (*Ritual*) and Moore and Myeroff ("Introduction"). Additionally, devoted fans of all sorts often invoke a comparison to religion to explain their behaviors and attitudes. Daniel Cavicchi, a professor and Bruce Springsteen fan, notes, for example, "My fandom feels to me far more like religion than politics" (*Tramps*, 8).

12. Novak, *Joy*, 218.

13. Ibid., 149.

14. Welch, *Stories*, 157.

15. Bill and Barbara's entire ode to Nebraska is available from http://www.geoci ties.com/Colosseum/Pressbox/3707/index. html. I found it on August 22, 2005.

16. This sports-religion comparison is by no means unique to Nebraska. In *The Joy of Sports*, Michael Novak positively gushes about the spiritual dimensions of sports. In addition, two extensive summaries of sports fan experiences (Guttmann, *Sports Spectators*; Wann, Melnick, Russell, and Pease, *Sport Fans*) report that fans often describe their devotion using religious terms and analogies. *Sports Illustrated* writer Josh Elliott ("Field") observes that for Green Bay Packer fans, attending a game is "like going to church" and that on Sunday game days "the two car-choked interstates leading to Green Bay resemble the twinkling proselyte-filled highways in *Field of Dreams*" (33). Moreover, as Nebraska fan Steve Smith notes in his book *Forever Red*, Husker fans exhibit a nearly religious devotion to our team, though he decries overt comparisons between Husker football and religion as unoriginal (23).

17. Stein, "Cult," 30.

18. Smith, "The Plainsman," 21.

19. In Fallik, "There's No Place."

20. In Snook, *What It Means*, 60.

21. Matt, a reporter for the *St. Petersburg* (FL) *Times*, gave me permission to reprint his story. He distributed it to his friends electronically; it was never published in another form.

22. I received this list on March 8, 2000, in an e-mail message from Candy Hodge.

23. The longer version of this crisis can be found in Jan's story in Appendix A.

24. Brian's story is in Appendix A.

25. *Daily Nebraskan*.

26. Posted on the HuskerPedia website on January 15, 2004.

27. Sampier, "Letter."

Chapter 11

1. In Hickey, *Nebraska Moments*, ix.

2. Baggarly, "Sweet." Thanks to John Strope for sharing this article with me.

3. Posted on the Husker List Internet discussion board on December 4, 2003.

4. Sartore, *Under*, 7.

5. In Rooney, "Nebraska." Interestingly, during the Cold War, Nebraska was very visible—within the Soviet Union. Offutt Air Force Base, home of the Strategic Air Command, was located just outside of Omaha—and was one of the Soviet Union's primary targets in nuclear war planning. Thanks to Matthew Grosz for reminding me of this fact.

6. Olson and Naugle, *History*, 1. To be fair, as Glasser notes, "it appears from a study of tree ring width that at the time of Long's expedition, the region was undergoing extreme drought, possibly worse, in relative terms, than the great drought of the 1930s" (37). Later explorers, such as John C. Frémont, were quite taken with the beauty of the Nebraska prairie (see Volpe, "Prairie Views," 98). Even Nebraska hero J. Sterling Morton, founder of Arbor Day, thought of the state as barren. Morton's tree-planting initiative, in fact, was designed to make Nebraska look more like the tree-filled eastern part of the country (Knopp, *Nature*, 19).

7. Gruchow, *Necessity*, 36.

8. Ibid. Adds Steve Smith in his account (*Forever Red*) of being a Nebraska football fan, "Nebraska's just sort of there, in the nation's blind spot, serving no compelling purpose except to keep Iowa, Colorado, South Dakota, and Kansas from bumping into one another" (89).

9. Hickey, *Nebraska*, ix.

10. Even President Bill Clinton apparently had trouble finding his way to Nebraska; it was, as Nebraskans noted, the last of the 50 states he visited. The visit did not occur until the end of his second term. Geographical ignorance, of course, is not limited to Nebraska. University

of Delaware athletic director Edgar Johnson, for example, reports being asked where he was from while vacationing in the Grand Canyon. "'When I told him Delaware,' recalls Johnson, 'he wanted to know where that's located'" (in Pearlman, "Worth," 34).

11. See U.S. Census Bureau statistics at: http://www.census.gov/population/www/census data/density.html

12. Bellevue, LaVista, and Papillion are considered part of the Omaha metro area. In addition, only four of Nebraska's 535 communities have a population above 30,000 (and one of those is Bellevue). See http://www.census.gov/popest/cities/tables/SUB-EST2004-04-31.xls. Even Lincoln, Nebraska's second-largest city (with a population of nearly a quarter of a million people) has been referred to as "the biggest small town in the country." See page 1 of the document Considering Lincoln's Future, available at: http://ppc.unl.edu/program_areas/documents/2005_LincolnDelibrations/Deliberation%20Backgrounder%20Layout%20Final.pdf

13. See http://www.census.gov/popest/counties/tables/CO-EST2004-01-31.xls

14. See http://www.unomaha.edu/~cpar/documents/nebpopulation_05.pdf

15. See Popper and Popper, "Buffalo Commons."

16. They, in fact, visited numerous places throughout the Great Plains following the uproar created by their Buffalo Commons idea.

17. See http://www.buffalocommons.org/docs/bcsf_history.html

18. See Denzin's (Interpretive) discussion of the disadvantages of learning by seeing—what he calls "ocular epistemologies."

19. In Olson, "Big Red."

20. Bryson, Lost Continent, 207–208.

21. Finebaum, I Hate, (no page numbers listed).

22. See Warren St. John's Rammer Jammer Yellow Hammer for more on Finebaum, especially the vitriol he directs at fans in Alabama. Such denigration is not all that unusual, of course, among sports fans. Wann and Grieve ("Biased Evaluations") indicate that fans who highly identify with their favorite team are likely to evaluate other fans less favorably, while O'Donnell ("Mapping") points out that television announcers pulling for their national soccer teams also stereotype opposing teams and countries.

23. Simers, "Putting." Simers once again returned to this theme before the 2006 Nebraska-USC game in Los Angeles. Speaking for many Nebraskans, Omaha World-Herald columnist Tom Shatel ("Tom") replied, "That's such a lame, tired lounge act. Is that all you got, T. J.?"

24. All comments retrieved from http://www.huskerpedia.com/football/tjsimers.html on February 24, 2004.

25. Garreau, Nine, 337.

26. Questions and answers were recorded by the Scripps Survey Research Center at Ohio University during the 2003 telephone survey conducted for this book. Many Nebraskans, I should note, do not believe that others look down upon us. In response to the survey items "Nebraskans are respected by non-Nebraskans" and "Nebraska is viewed favorably by others," only 17 percent and 22 percent of the respondents, respectively, disagreed.

27. Wahl, "Wilt's," 40.

28. Harris, "Black," 36.

29. Norman, "Bear," 40.

30. See St. John, Rammer, for an account of the Auburn-Alabama rivalry. In this relationship, Alabama fans seem themselves as "classy" and the Auburn group as "backward."

31. Blythe, "Blue Blood," 69.

32. Queenan, True Believers, 97.

33. As Allen Guttmann (Sports Spectators) points out, the outcomes of sporting contests may well have political dimensions as one "tribe" competes against another (180-182). Adds sociologist Anthony Cohen (Symbolic), "The most striking feature of the symbolic construction of the community and its boundaries is its oppositional character. The boundaries are relational rather than absolute; that is, they mark the community in relation to other communities" (58; emphasis original).

34. A Nebraska Educational Television special, Husker Century, Part I (Geyer), notes that nineteenth century students at the University of Nebraska wanted the university to establish a football team to show others that it was a "real" university rather than simply a place for "hicks" and "hayseeds."

35. A number of academics, inside and outside of Nebraska, have reminded me that Nebraskans' elevation of football above other characteristics of the state and its people is troublesome. I agree—to a point. If the University of Nebraska football program were perceived by its fans as being about nothing more than winning and losing, then we could be rightfully seen as shallow. That the team clearly represents what we see as our best qualities, however, mitigates a good deal of the concern that I might otherwise have. That said, we Nebraskans have much to value and promote that, in an ideal world, would be as well known as our football team.

36. In Corcoran, Game, 101.

37. Respondents were asked to agree/disagree on a 1–5 scale with the statement, "The Husker football team generates respect for Nebraska."

38. Posted on the HuskerPedia Web site on June 3, 2004, by FeelLikeAStranger.

39. Ramsey, *Long Path*, 112.

40. According to the Nebraska Blue Book, found online at: http://www.unicam.state.ne.us/bluebook/, the lowest elevation is 840 feet in Richardson County and the highest elevation is 5,424 feet in Kimball County.

41. Welch, *Platte*, (no page numbers). Welch's poem goes on to speak about the natural wonders of Nebraska that visitors can see if they work on their vision. This theme is also evident in two letters to the editor published in the *Lincoln Journal Star* the Sunday morning after the 1999 Iowa State homecoming game. Apparently, someone named Andy Nash had written a column the previous Sunday bemoaning, from his "new guy" perspective, the supposedly dull Nebraska landscape and the state's dearth of things to do. Roger Hilliker of Beaver Crossing replied, "If you don't leave the interstate highway, Nebraska does look flat ... [but] before people put our beautiful state down they need to see it all." Similarly, Tracy Rathe of Lincoln challenged Nash "to visit the many natural and man-made gems that [Nebraska] has to offer."

42. Conquergood, "Homeboys," 40.

43. In Babcock, *Go Big Red*, 1.

44. Meredith, "Cornhusking," 24.

45. Frei, "Place."

46. Pluto, "Red Menace," D1.

47. Caple, "Red Alert."

48. Smith, *Forever Red*, 47.

49. Morrison, "From Farm," 1B.

50. Plaschke, "Corn."

51. Posted on the Husker List Internet discussion board on December 4, 2003.

52. Plaschke, "Corn."

53. In Hord, "Bad Season."

54. Sports fan researchers have, not surprisingly, discovered that "fans high in team identification are more likely to attend games, pay more for tickets, spend more money on team merchandise," etc. (Fink, Trail, and Anderson, "Examination," 195–196).

55. Alexander, "Big Red." Alexander's article lists the top 10 royalty-earners for 2001–2002. During that fiscal year, Nebraska was ranked fourth, ahead of universities located in more populous states (i.e., Florida, Penn State, Texas, Florida State).

56. These figures were provided by Michael Stephens, director of licensing at the University of Nebraska-Lincoln.

57. Thanks to Ehren Mitzlaff for sharing this Internet-posted story.

58. McHoul, "On," 315. Garry Crawford (*Consuming Sports*) also notes that a much-overlooked dimension of being a sports fan is how sporting allegiances are represented in everyday life.

59. "Deliberately and otherwise, people are forever presenting each other with culturally mediated images of where and how they dwell," explains Keith Basso (*Wisdom*, 109).

60. Posted on the Husker List Internet discussion board on December 4, 2003.

61. Moran, "In Nebraska."

62. Fiske, *Power*, 12.

63. Abrahams, "Introductory," 146.

64. Ritual scholars emphasize that cultural rituals are intended to re-order social structures through comparisons with other groups and orders (de Coppet, "Introduction"; Rothenbuhler, *Ritual*). In particular, Jonathan Smith (*To Take Place*) explains, "Ritual is a means of performing the way things ought to be in conscious tension to the way things are" (109).

65. Perelman, *Realm*, 35.

66. Miller, "'Legal,'" 78. Miller is writing about protestors seeking presence, which—I believe—is not far removed from what Huskervillers are doing: protesting social and cultural depictions of our home.

67. Murphy, "Presence," 5.

Chapter 12

1. In fact, as I was preparing to write this chapter, my mom told me that she had written a story for the Scottsbluff newspaper outlining her small world experiences at the Baseball Hall of Fame in Cooperstown, New York. She was accompanying a high school singing group on a tour through Cooperstown when they discovered the parents of one of the museum registrars were from Scottsbluff. Later, she met a professor from the University of Nebraska-Omaha who was at the Hall of Fame for a conference; turns out he once worked with a college friend of my mom's.

2. Husker fan Steve Smith notes in his book, *Forever Red*, "This happens all the time when Nebraskans get together. It's like our version of the Six Degrees to Kevin Bacon game. Everyone either knows you or knows someone who does" (125). Smith offers this observation after explaining that he ran into someone at a Northern Nevadans for Nebraska watch party who knew someone who lived down the street from Smith's childhood home in Rosalie, Nebraska.

3. Garry Crawford (*Consuming Sport*) observes that many sports fans describe their experiences as being part of a community. Although Huskervillers share such a community experience, our use of language such as friend, neighbor, and—especially—family, sug-

gests a bond that is more intimate than inhabiting a shared community.

4. Posted on December 3, 2003.

5. Posted on January 15, 2004.

6. The cab driver meant "Runzas," a cabbage-and-burger sandwich in a bun sold throughout Nebraska.

7. Posted on the HuskerPedia Web site on June 5, 2004, by Da Bear (hence the reference to his wife as "Mama Bear" in the story).

8. Posted on the HuskerPedia Web site on June 3, 2004, by Boulder 'sker.

9. Posted on the HuskerPedia Web site on June 6, 2004, by Uncle Buck.

10. Posted on the HuskerPedia Web site on June 3, 2004, by NoVaHusker.

11. This thread was initiated in early June 2004, by a poster named LutheranHusker, who was responding to an idea offered in another message thread by a poster named Boulder 'sker.

12. Posted on June 2, 2004.

13. Posted on missingnebraska.com. Retrieved on August 24, 2005.

14. Posted on the HuskerPedia Web site on June 2, 2004, by red handed.

15. Posted on the HuskerPedia Web site on June 3, 2004, by Husker 4 Ever.

16. Posted on the HuskerPedia Web site on June 2, 2004.

17. As Raymond Boyle and Richard Haynes (*Power Play*) explain within the context of soccer, "For many fans, versions of tradition and history associated with football [soccer] clubs and their cities provide a tangible link between the past and present. Football teams are always changing (players, managers and the like all come and go), yet the club exists in a space that is in part untouched by these changes" (202).

18. Rituals, write Sally Moore and Barbara Myeroff ("Introduction"), "can be seen as an especially dramatic attempt to bring some particular part of life firmly and definitely into orderly control" (3).

19. Ibid., 17.

20. Posted on the HuskerPedia Web site on January 15, 2004.

21. Relph, *Place*, 38.

22. Giddens, *Modernity*, 35–69.

23. Ibid., 54.

24. Ibid. Later in his book, Giddens notes that the idea of tradition, or what I would call the "kept going narrative," contributes to ontological security because "it sustains trust in the continuity of past, present, and future, and connects such trust to routinised social practices" (105).

25. Stein ("Cult") observes that sports, in particular, help to provide such continuity: "sport, as a 'little world,' offers its followers an island of continuity amidst a sea of chaos" (33).

26. Eric Eisenberg ("Building") observes, for example, that "coping with the uncertainties of one's positionality in the world is key to ontological security" (535).

27. Erdrich, "Writer's," 36.

Chapter 13

1. Roughly 90 percent of those who responded to my questionnaires, e-mail inquiries, or requests for interviews did not want to remain anonymous despite an offer to do so.

2. Among the eight states more desolate than Nebraska, only Wyoming and Alaska do not have two major state universities which field intercollegiate football teams.

3. Schieffelin ("Problematizing"), while writing about performances other than sports, observes that "amongst the various people involved (who often have different agendas) there is always something aesthetically and/or practically at stake, and something can always go wrong" (198). Certainly, the different teams and their fans have different agendas, and—as unscripted performances—the action on the field holds much potential for things to go wrong. In his book *The Joy of Sports*, Michael Novak writes, "The mode of observation proper to a sports event is *to participate*—that is, to extend one's own identification to one side... By an exercise of imagination one places oneself under the fate of a particular group [team], becomes other than oneself, and risks thereby one's security" (144).

4. Basso, *Wisdom*, 148.

5. I would also recommend Tony Hiss's *The Experience of Place*.

6. Basso, *Wisdom*, 145-146.

7. Harold's story about returning for a football game can be found in Appendix A. It was originally posted on www.huskerpowerhour.com. Thanks to John Strope for sharing the story with me, and to Chris Sobczyk for help in finding its author.

8. Basso, *Wisdom*, 148.

9. Quoted from Darren's Internet blog, which can be found at: http://friedmeatandsugarwater.blogspot.com/

10. de Tocqueville, *Democracy*, 95.

11. Ibid.

12. Ibid., 96.

13. Ibid.

14. See *Economist* ("The Glue").

15. Reported in McPherson, Smith-Lovin, and Brashears, "Social Isolation."

16. See Ritzer's *McDonaldization* for a discussion of how the concepts of efficiency, predictability, quantification, and control are

being treated as values in many areas of our lives.

17. Sheldrake, *Spaces*, 2.

18. Egan, "Amid."

19. Basso, *Wisdom*, 148.

20. Eisenberg ("Ambiguity") points out that, used strategically, ambiguous ideas and notions may be more appealing *because* of their lack of concreteness.

21. Walter, *Placeways*, 204.

22. In an essay entitled, "Building Dwelling Thinking," Heidegger explains how humans build in order to dwell, to turn space into lived spaces. This process, he claims, is perpetual: humans "must ever learn to dwell" (Heidegger, *Poetry*, 161).

23. Geertz, "Afterword," 262.

24. This work was published by Dollar and Zimmers ("Social Identity") in the journal *Communication Research*.

25. Hyde, "Introduction," xiii.

26. Ibid., xxi. Hyde's quotation without the bracketed insertions: "rhetorical architects whose symbolic constructions both create and invite others into a place where they can dwell and feel at home while thinking about and discussing the truth of some matter that the rhetor/architect has already attempted to disclose and show-forth in a specific way with his or her work of art."

27. Recall Abrahams' ("Introductory") words in Chapter 11, "each item of expressive culture is an implement of argument, a tool of persuasion" (146).

28. Miller, "A Felt," 72.

29. Feld and Basso, "Introduction," 11; emphasis added.

30. This survey was taken in 1997 as part of the Nebraska Annual Social Indicators survey. People were asked to respond to the statement, "Please tell me three positive characteristics you think Nebraska has." Sixteen people used the phrase "good place to live," three said "good state to live in," three said "great place to live," six said "nice place to live," and two said "nice state to live in." Individual responses included, "it's a good state to live in," "it's a wonderful state to live in," and "it's just a good place to live."

31. Basso, *Wisdom*, 148. Edward Relph (*Place*) adds that "sense of place" might also be called "spirit of place" (48).

32. Welch, *Stories*, 10.

33. Hogan, "Conclusion," 292.

34. Cameron, "When Strangers," 411.

35. Rosowski, "Sense," 2.

Appendix A

1. A former star running back for the Huskers, Phillips was arrested and eventually pleaded no contest to domestic violence when a member of the team (see Kaipust, "Callahan").

2. This note was originally sent to the Capital of Texas Nebraskans alumni chapter, whose e-mails I have received as part of this project. Lt. Col. Caudle gave me permission to reprint his letter in this book.

3. Erik wrote his story prior to the 2003 Kansas State victory in Lincoln.

Bibliography

Abercrombie, Nicholas, and Brian Longhurst. *Audiences: A Sociological Theory of Performance and Imagination.* London: Sage, 1998.

Abrahams, Roger D. "Introductory Remarks to a Rhetorical Theory of Folklore." *Journal of American Folklore* 81 (1968): 143–58.

Alexander, Deborah. "A Big Red Recession?" *Omaha World-Herald*, October 25, 2002, http://www.lexis-nexis.com/.

Allen, John C., Rebecca Vogt, and Sam Cordes. *Quality of Life in Rural Nebraska: Trends and Changes. 2002 Nebraska Rural Poll Results.* Lincoln, NE: University of Nebraska Institute of Agriculture and Natural Resources, 2002.

Allen, John C., Rebecca Vogt, Sam Cordes, and Randolph L. Cantrell. *Attributes of a Successful Community: Responses From Rural Nebraskans. 2002 Nebraska Rural Poll Results.* Lincoln, NE: University of Nebraska Institute of Agriculture and Natural Resources, 2002.

Alswager, Sandi S. "Researchers Get to Root of Sugarbeet Problems." *Research Nebraska*, September 2002, http://ard.unl.edu/rn/0902/sugarbeet.html.

Anderson, Benedict. *Imagined Communities: Reflections on the Origin and Spread of Nationalism.* London: Verso, 1983.

Anderson, Lars. "Road Trip: Lincoln, Nebraska." *CNN/Sports Illustrated*, September 11, 2003, http://si.cnn.com/.

Augé, Marc. *Non-places: Introduction to an Anthropology of Supermodernity.* Translated by John Howe. London: Verso, 1995.

Babcock, Mike. *Go Big Red: The Ultimate Fan's Guide to Nebraska Cornhusker Football.* New York: St. Martin's Press, 1998.

Baggarly, Andrew. "Sweet Home Nebraska." Vallejo, CA, *Times Herald*, July 22, 2005, http://www.lexis-nexis.com/.

Bakhtin, Mikhail. *The Dialogic Imagination: Four Essays.* Edited by Michael Holquist. Translated by Caryl Emerson and Michael Holquist. Austin, TX: University of Texas Press, 1981.

Ballard, Chris. "Finding the Perfect Sports Bar." *Sports Illustrated*, February 7, 2005, 67–77.

Basso, Keith H. *Wisdom Sits in Places.* Albuquerque, NM: University of New Mexico Press, 1996.

Belsie, Laurent. "The New Frontier." *Christian Science Monitor*, February 11, 2003, 10.

_____. "Little Farms on the Prairie Bow to a Wal-Mart Era." *Christian Science Monitor*, February 12, 2003, 1, 12–13.

Berens, Charlyne. *Power to the People: Social Choice and the Populist/Progressive Ideal.* Dallas, TX: University Press of America, 2004.

Berry, Wendell. *The Unsettling of America: Culture and Agriculture.* San Francisco: Sierra Club Books, 1977.

Bizman, Aharon, and Yoel Yinon. "Engaging in Distancing Tactics Among Sport Fans: Effects on Self-esteem and Emotional Responses." *Journal of Social Psychology* 142 (2002): 381–92.

Bly, Laura. "Saga of the Sandhill Crane." *USA Today*, March 31, 2006, 1D-2D.

Blythe, Will. "Blue Blood." *Sports Illustrated*, March 8, 2004, 67–74.

Bodnar, John. *Remaking America: Public Memory, Commemoration, and Patriotism in the Twentieth Century.* Princeton, NJ: Princeton University Press, 1992.

Bohlke, Brent L. *Willa Cather In Person.* Lincoln, NE: University of Nebraska Press, 1986.

Borchers, Tim. "Netsurfers for Nebraska: A Worldwide Virtual Community of Husker

Fans." Paper presented at the annual meeting of the National Communication Association, Seattle, WA, November, 11, 2000.

Bourland, Patrick. "Huskers for Ohio: 'Braska Fans Join Bobcats on Web." *The [Ohio University] Post*, January 20, 2005, 8.

Boyle, Raymond, and Richard Haynes. *Power Play: Sport, the Media and Popular Culture.* Harlow, England: Longman, 2000.

Brennan, Christine. "Solich Turns Ohio U. Red With Excitement." *USA Today*, August 30, 2005, 1C-2C.

Brown, Barbara B., and Douglas D. Perkins. "Disruptions in Place Attachment." In *Place Attachment*, edited by Setha M. Low and Irwin Altman, 279–304. New York: Plenum Press, 1992.

Bryson, Bill. *The Lost Continent: Travels in Small-town America.* New York: Harper and Row, 1989.

Burke, Kenneth. *The Philosophy of Literary Form: Studies in Symbolic Action.* Berkeley, CA: University of California Press, 1974. First published 1941 by Louisiana State University Press.

Buttimer, Anne. "Home, Reach, and the Sense of Place." In *The Human Experience of Space and Place*, edited by Anne Buttimer and David Seamon, 166–87. New York: St. Martin's Press, 1980.

Cameron, Ardis. "When Strangers Bring Cameras: The Poetics and Politics of Othered Places." *American Quarterly* 54 (2002): 411–35.

Campbell, John M. *The Prairie Schoolhouse.* Albuquerque, NM: University of New Mexico Press, 1996.

Caple, Jim. "Red Alert Takes Over Entire State." September 11, 2003, http://espn.go.com/.

Carbaugh, Donal. *Situating Selves: The Communication of Social Identities in American Scenes.* Albany, NY: State University of New York Press, 1996.

Carlson, Allan. *The New Agrarian Mind: The Movement Toward Decentralist Thought in Twentieth-century America.* New Brunswick, NJ: Transaction, 2000.

Casey, Edward. *Getting Back into Place: Toward a Renewed Understanding of the Place-world.* Bloomington, IN: Indiana University Press, 1993.

____. "How to Get From Space to Place in a Fairly Short Stretch of Time: Phenomenological Prolegomena." In *Senses of Place*, edited by Steven Feld and Keith H. Basso, 13–52. Santa Fe, NM: School of American Research Press, 1996.

Cather, Willa. *O Pioneers!* Boston: Houghton Mifflin, 1913. Reprinted in 1995.

____. *My Ántonia.* Boston: Houghton Mifflin, 1918. Reprinted in 1995.

____. *The Kingdom of Art: Willa Cather's First Principles and Critical Statements, 1893–1896.* Edited by Bernice Slote. Lincoln, NE: University of Nebraska Press, 1967.

Cavicchi, Daniel. *Tramps Like Us: Music and Meaning Among Springsteen Fans.* New York: Oxford University Press, 1998.

Chapple, Eliot Dismore, and Carleton Stevens Coon. *Principles of Anthropology.* New York: Henry Holt, 1942.

Chatelain, Dirk. "Ickes is the Talk of the Town." *Omaha World-Herald*, October 21, 2005, http://www.omaha.com/.

Chen, Albert. "Extreme Makeover: Will Bill Callahan's West Coast Offense Fly in Huskerland?" August 11, 2004, http://sportsillustrated.cnn.com/.

Chidester, David, and Edward T. Linenthal. "Introduction." In *American Sacred Space*, edited by David Chidester and Edward T. Linenthal, 1–42. Bloomington, IN: Indiana University Press, 1995.

Cialdini, Robert B., Richard J. Borden, Avril Thorne, Marcus Walker, Stephen Freeman, and Lloyd R. Sloan. "Basking in Reflected Glory: Three (Football) Field Studies." *Journal of Personality and Social Psychology* 34 (1976): 366–75.

Clarke, Varro Jack. "The Year I Became a Cornhusker." *Nebraska Magazine* 96, no. 4 (2000): 28–29.

Claussen, Nick. "Coach Hiring Makes For Strange Bedfellows." *The Athens [OH] News*, January 20, 2005, 1, 10.

Cohen, Anthony. *The Symbolic Construction of Community.* Chichester, Sussex, England: Ellis Horwood, 1985.

Coleman, Bill. Letter to the Editor. *Athens [OH] News*, January 10, 2005, 5.

Conquergood, Dwight. "Ethnography, Rhetoric, and Performance." *Quarterly Journal of Speech* 78 (1992): 80–97.

____. "Homeboys and Hoods: Gang Communication and Cultural Space." In *Group Communication in Context: Studies of Natural Groups*, edited by Lawrence R. Frey, 23–55. Hillsdale, NJ: Lawrence Erlbaum Associates, 1994.

Corcoran, Michael. *The Game of the Century:*

Nebraska vs. Oklahoma in College Football's Ultimate Battle, November 25, 1971. New York: Simon and Schuster, 2004.

Cotten, Stan. "100% Cotten: Red Carpet Treatment." September 11, 2005, http://wakeforestsports.collegesports.com/genrel/091105.aaa.html.

Crawford, Garry. *Consuming Sport: Fans, Sport and Culture.* London: Routledge, 2004.

Daily Nebraskan, "Tradition Gone After Callahan's First Year," November 30, 2004, http://www.dailynebraskan.com/.

Daniels, Bruce C. *Puritans at Play: Leisure and Recreation in Colonial New England.* New York: St. Martin's Press, 1995.

Daniels, George L., and C. Ann Hollifield. "Time of Turmoil: Short- and Long-Term Effects of Organizational Change on Newsroom Employees." *Journalism and Mass Communication Quarterly* 79 (2002): 661–80.

Davis, Fred. *Yearning For Yesterday: A Sociology of Nostalgia.* New York: The Free Press, 1979.

Debnam, Betty. "Nebraska From A to Z." *The* [Athens, OH] *Messenger*, May 21, 2001, 8.

De Cillia, Rudolf, Martin Reisigl, and Ruth Wodak. "The Discursive Construction of National Identities." *Discourse and Society* 10 (1999): 149–73.

de Coppet, Daniel. "Introduction." In *Understanding Rituals*, edited by Daniel de Coppet, 1–10. London: Routledge, 1992.

Deegan, Mary Jo, and Michael Stein. "American Drama and Ritual: Nebraska Football." *International Review of Sport Sociology* 13, no. 3 (1978): 31–44.

Deleuze, Gilles, and Felix Guattari. *A Thousand Plateaus.* Translated by Brian Massumi. Minneapolis: University of Minnesota Press, 1987.

Denney, James, Hollis Limprecht, and Howard Silber. *Go Big Red: The All-time Story of the Cornhuskers.* Omaha: Kratville, 1967.

Denzin, Norman K. *Interpretive Ethnography: Ethnographic Practices For the 21st Century.* Thousand Oaks, CA: Sage, 1997.

de Tocqueville, Alexis. *Democracy in America.* Edited and abridged by Richard D. Heffner. New York: Signet, 2001.

Dick, Everett. *The Sod-House Frontier: 1854–1890. A Social History of the Northern Plains From the Creation of Kansas & Nebraska to the Admission of the Dakotas.* Lincoln, NE: Johnsen, 1954. First published 1937 by D. Appleton-Century.

Dollar, Natalie J., and Brooke G. Zimmers. "Social Identity and Communicative Boundaries: An Analysis of Youth and Young Adult Street Speakers in a U.S. American Community." *Communication Research* 25 (1998): 596–617.

Downs, Roger M., and David Stea. *Maps in Mind: Reflections on Cognitive Mapping.* New York: Harper and Row, 1977.

Driver, Tom F. *Liberating Rites: Understanding the Transformative Power of Ritual.* Boulder, CO: Westview Press, 1998.

Eastman, Susan Tyler, and Arthur M. Land. "The Best of Both Worlds: Sports Fans Find Good Seats at the Bar." *Journal of Sport and Social Issues* 21 (1997): 156–78.

Economist. "The Glue of Society." July 16, 2005, 13–17.

Egan, Timothy. "Amid Dying Towns of Rural Plains, One Makes a Stand." *New York Times*, www.http://nytimes.com/.

Eisenberg, Eric M. "Ambiguity as Strategy in Organizational Communication." *Communication Monographs* 51 (1984): 227–42.

_____. "Building a Mystery: Toward a New Theory of Communication and Identity." *Journal of Communication* 51 (2001): 534–52.

Elliott, Josh. "Field of Dreams." *Sports Illustrated*, October 6, 2003, 32–34.

Erdrich, Louise. "A Writer's Sense of Place." In *A Place of Sense: Essays in Search of the Midwest*, edited by Michael Martone, 34–44. Iowa City: University of Iowa Press, 1988.

Fallik, Dawn. "There's No Place Like Nebraska For Fans, Unless It's Florida or Ohio." Associated Press, September 7, 1999, http://www.lexis-nexis.com/.

Federal Writers Project. *Nebraska: A Guide to the Cornhusker State.* New York: Viking Press, 1939.

Feld, Steven. "Dialogic Editing: Interpreting How Kululi Read Sound and Sentiment." *Cultural Anthropology* 2 (1987): 190–210.

_____, and Keith H. Basso. "Introduction." In *Senses of Place*, edited by Steven Feld and Keith H. Basso, 3–11. Santa Fe, NM: School of American Research Press, 1996.

Fine, Elizabeth C., and Jean Haskell Speer. "Introduction." In *Performance, Culture, and Identity*, edited by Elizabeth C. Fine and Jean Haskell Speer, 1–22. Westport, CT: Praeger, 1992.

Finebaum, Paul. *I Hate Nebraska: 303 Reasons Why You Should, Too.* Birmingham, AL: Crane Hill Publishers, 1996.

Fink, Janet S., Galen T. Trail, and Dean F. Anderson. "An Examination of Team Identification: Which Motives are Most Salient to its Existence?" *International Sports Journal* 6 (2002): 195–207.

Fiske, John. *Power Plays, Power Works.* London: Verso, 1993.

Frei, Terri. "A Place Like No Other." *The Sporting News,* October 31, 1994, http://www.lexis-nexis.com/.

Fujioka, Toru. "Sustaining the World's Water." In *Platte River Odyssey* 23. Lincoln, NE: College of Journalism and Mass Communications, University of Nebraska-Lincoln, 2006.

Furay, Conal. (1983). "The Small Town Mind." In *The Popular Culture Reader.* 3rd ed. Edited by Christopher D. Geist and Jack Nachbar, 41–54. Bowling Green, OH: Bowling Green University Popular Press, 1983.

Garreau, Joel. *The Nine Nations of North America.* New York: Avon, 1981.

Gates, Paul W. *Free Homesteads for All Americans: The Homestead Act of 1862.* Washington, DC: Civil War Centennial Commission, 1962.

Geertz, Clifford. "Afterword." In *Senses of Place,* edited by Steven Feld and Keith H. Basso, 259–62. Santa Fe, NM: School of American Research Press, 1996.

George-Bloomfield, Susanne. "The Happiness and the Curse: Literary Views of the Nebraska Prairie." In *A Prairie Mosaic,* edited by Steven J. Rothenberger and Susanne George-Bloomfield, 138–43. Kearney, NE: University of Nebraska-Kearney, 2000.

Geyer, Joel, producer. *Husker Century, Part I: Pioneer Spirit.* Lincoln, NE: Nebraska Educational Television, 2000.

_____, producer. *Husker Century, Part III: Spirit of Champions.* Lincoln, NE: Nebraska Educational Television, 2000.

Gibson, Heather, Cynthia Willming, and Andrew Holdnak. "'We're Gators ... Not Just Gator Fans': Serious Leisure and University of Florida Football." *Journal of Leisure Research* 34 (2002): 397–425.

Giddens, Anthony. *Modernity and Self-Identity: Self and Society in the Late Modern Age.* Stanford, CA: Stanford University Press, 1991.

Glasser, Marvin. "Weather and Climate: Arbiter of Life on the Prairie." In *A Prairie Mosaic,* edited by Steven J. Rothenberger and Susanne George-Bloomfield, 26–43.

Kearney, NE: University of Nebraska-Kearney, 2000.

Glennon, Sean. *This Pats Year.* Boulder, CO: Taylor Trade Publishing, 2004.

Gongaware, Timothy B. "Collective Memories and Collective Identities: Maintaining Unity in Native American Educational Social Movements." *Journal of Contemporary Ethnography* 32 (2003): 483–520.

Goodall, H. L. Jr. *Divine Signs: Connecting Spirit to Community.* Carbondale, IL: Southern Illinois University Press, 1996.

Greene, Bob. *Once Upon a Town: The Miracle of the North Platte Canteen.* New York: William Morrow, 2002.

Gruchow, Paul. *The Necessity of Empty Places.* New York: St. Martin's Press, 1988.

_____. "Thinking of Home." In *Sacred Ground: Writings About Home,* edited by Barbara Bonner, 334–47. Minneapolis: Milkweed Editions, 1996.

Grumbach, Doris. "Foreword." In *O Pioneers!* by Willa Cather, vii–xxiv. Boston: Houghton Mifflin, 1995.

Guffey, Kim. "Nebraska Going Green and White." *The* [Athens, OH] *Messenger,* January 1, 2005, 1, 7.

Gusfield, Joseph R. *Community: A Critical Response.* New York: Harper and Row, 1975.

Guttmann, Allen. *From Ritual to Record: The Nature of Modern Sports.* New York: Columbia University Press, 1978.

_____. *Sports Spectators.* New York: Columbia University Press, 1986.

Hamar, Bob. "Huskerville an Interesting Place to Be." *Grand Island* [NE] *Independent,* August 31, 1998, http://www.theindependent.com.

Hanson, Victor Davis. *Fields Without Dreams: Defending the Agrarian Idea.* New York: Free Press Paperbacks, 1996.

Harris, E. Lynn. "Black + White = Red." *Sports Illustrated,* December 1, 2003, 36.

Hassebrook, Chuck. "The State of Rural America." *Center for Rural Affairs Newsletter,* March 2004. http://www.cfra.org/newsletter/2004_03.htm

Heidegger, Martin. *Poetry, Language, Thought.* Translated by Albert Hofstadter. New York: Harper & Row, 1971.

Hendee, David. "Osborne: 'All You Can Do is Do All You Can.'" *Omaha World-Herald,* May 10, 2006, http://www.omaha.com/.

Hickey, Donald R. *Nebraska Moments: Glimpses of Nebraska's Past.* Lincoln: University of Nebraska Press, 1992.

Hilliker, Roger. "See the State First." *Lincoln Journal Star*, October 10, 1999, 3E.

Hiss, Tony. *The Experience of Place*. New York: Knopf, 1990.

Hogan, J. Michael. "Conclusion: Rhetoric and the Restoration of Community." In *Rhetoric and Community: Studies in Unity and Fragmentation*, edited by J. Michael Hogan, 292–302. Columbia, SC: University of South Carolina Press, 1998.

Holbrook, Morris B. "On the New Nostalgia: 'These Foolish Things' and Echoes of the Dear Departed Past." In *Continuities in Popular Culture: The Present in the Past and the Past in the Present and Future*, edited by Ray B. Browne & Ronald J. Ambrosetti, 74–120. Bowling Green, OH: Bowling Green State University Press, 1993.

Holloway, Marguerite. "A Great Echelon of Birds." *Scientific American* 290, no. 1 (2004): 102–103.

Hord, Bill. "Bad Season + Bad Business." *Omaha World-Herald*, November 22, 2004, http://www.lexis-nexis.com/.

Howells, William. "William Howells Remembers Neighborliness in Ohio." In *Witness to America: An Illustrated Documentary History of the United States From the Revolution to Today*, edited by Stephen Ambrose and Douglas Brinkley, 60–62. New York: HarperCollins, 1999.

Hufford, Mary. "Thresholds to an Alternate Realm: Mapping the Chaseworld in New Jersey's Pine Barrens." In *Place Attachment*, edited by Irwin Altman and Setha M. Low, 231–52. New York: Plenum Press, 1992.

Huizinga, Johan. *Homo Ludens: A Study of the Play Element in Culture*. New York: Harper & Row, 1970. First published 1938.

Hyde, Michael J. "Introduction." In *The Ethos of Rhetoric*, edited by Michael J. Hyde, xiii–xviii. Columbia, SC: University of South Carolina Press, 2004.

Israel, David. *The Cornhuskers: Nebraska Football*. Chicago: Regnery, 1975.

Johnsgard, Paul A. *Crane Music: A Natural History of American Cranes*. Washington, DC: Smithsonian Institution Press, 1991.

Kaipust, Rich. "Callahan to Evaluate Walkons." *Omaha World-Herald*, January 24, 2004, http://www.omaha.com/.

_____. "Turning the Corner? Carrying the Baggage of His Past, Lawrence Phillips Recently Returned to Omaha; Friends Say He's Made a Change For the Better." *Omaha World-Herald*, December 24, 2004, http://www.omaha.com/.

_____. "NU to Look at Reliance On Juco Players." *Omaha World-Herald*, February 2, 2006, http://www.omaha.com/.

_____. "Spring Game a Recruiting Tool." *Omaha World-Herald*, April 14, 2006, http://www.omaha.com/.

Kawar, Mark. "Rural Poll Finds Concern About Future." *Omaha World-Herald*, July 31, 2002, http://www.lexis-nexis.com/.

Kelsey, Timothy W. "The Agrarian Myth and Policy Responses to Farm Safety." *American Journal of Public Health* 84 (1994): 1171–77.

Kentuckiana Huskers. "Husker Game Watch Parties a Huge Success," November 1999, 1.

Klein, Gary. "USC Football; Optimism, Concern at Scrimmage." *Los Angeles Times*, April 10, 2006, http://www.lexis-nexis.com/.

Knopp, Lisa. *The Nature of Home*. Lincoln, NE: University of Nebraska Press, 2002.

Kobayashi, R. H. "Responding to Katrina." *Nebraska Magazine* 101, no. 4 (2005): 3.

Krantz, Les. *Jobs Rated Almanac*. 6th ed. Fort Lee, NJ: Barricade Books, 2002.

Lane, Belden C. *Landscapes of the Sacred: Geography and Narrative in American Spirituality*. Expanded edition. Baltimore: Johns Hopkins University Press, 2002.

Larkey, Linda, and Calvin Morrill. "Organizational Commitment as Symbolic Process." *Western Journal of Communication* 59 (1995): 193–213.

Lasch, Christopher. *The True and Only Heaven: Progress and Its Critics*. New York: Norton, 1991.

Lawrence, Denise L. "Transcendence of Place: The Role of *La Placeta* in Valencia's *Las Fallas*." In *Place Attachment*, edited by Irwin Altman and Setha M. Low, 211–30. New York: Plenum Press, 1992.

Lippard, Lucy. *The Lure of the Local: Senses of Place in a Multicentered Society*. New York: The New Press, 1997.

Low, Setha M., and Irwin Altman. "Place Attachment: A Conceptual Inquiry." In *Place Attachment*, edited by Irwin Altman and Setha M. Low, 1–12. New York: Plenum Press, 1992.

Lowe, David, Jr., director. *Johnny Goes Home*. Carson Productions Group, 1982.

Lowenthal, David. "Fabricating Heritage." *History & Memory* 10 (1998): 5–24.

_____. "Nostalgia Tells It Like It Wasn't." In *The Imagined Past: History and Nostalgia*, edited by Christopher Shaw and Malcolm Chase, 18–32. Manchester, UK: Manchester University Press, 1989.

Lowery, Courtney. "Dropping Enrollment in Small Towns Brings Back an Age-old Game." Associated Press, November 18, 2004, http://www.lexis-nexis.com/.

Luebke, Frederick C. "Ethnic Group Settlement on the Great Plains." *The Western Historical Quarterly* 8 (1977): 405–30.

Maisel, Ivan. "The Coaching Carousel Begins." *Sports Illustrated*, November 12, 2001, 74–76.

Malpas, J. E. *Place and Experience: A Philosophical Topography*. Cambridge, UK: Cambridge University Press, 1999.

Massey, Doreen. *Space, Place, and Gender*. Minneapolis: University of Minnesota Press, 1994.

McFeatters, Dale. "There Can Be Life in Dead-End Jobs." [Torrance, CA] *Daily Breeze*, September 24, 2005, http://www.dailybreeze.com/.

McHoul, Alec. "On Doing 'We's.'" *Journal of Sport and Social Issues* 21 (1997): 315–20.

McPherson, Miller, Lynn Smith-Lovin, and Matthew E. Brashears. "Social Isolation in America: Changes in Core Discussion Networks Over Two Decades." *American Sociological Review* 71 (2006): 353–75.

Meredith, Mamie J. "Cornhusking and Other Terms." *American Speech* 13, no. 1, (1938): 19–24.

Merrill, Elizabeth. "Osborne Vents Over NU Changes." *Omaha World-Herald*, February 6, 2004, http://www.omaha.com/.

_____. "Walk-on Schroeder No Stranger to Work." *Omaha World-Herald*, August 29, 2004, http://www.lexis-nexis.com/.

_____. "Some Former Huskers Plan to Complain." *Omaha World-Herald*, December 3, 2004, http://www.lexis-nexis.com/.

Middleton, Catherine A. "Roots and Rootlessness: An Exploration of the Concept in the Life and Novels of George Eliot." In *Humanistic Geography and Literature: Essays on the Experience of Place*, edited by Douglas C. D. Pocock, 101–20. London: Croom Helm, 1981.

Miller, Jackson. "'Legal or Illegal? Documented or Undocumented?' The Struggle Over Brookhaven's *Neighborhood Preservation Act*." *Communication Quarterly* 51 (2003): 73–89.

Miller, Jim Wayne. "A Felt Linkage." In *Sacred Ground: Writings About Home*, edited by Barbara Bonner, 68–75. Minneapolis: Milkweed Editions, 1996.

Miller, Richard L., and Joseph J. Benz. "Conceptions of Human Nature: The Value Orientations of Students From Central Nebraska." In *A Prairie Mosaic*, edited by Steven J. Rothenberger and Susanne George-Bloomfield, 226–31. Kearney, NE: University of Nebraska-Kearney, 2000.

Mitchell, Innes. "Seeing Big Red Through Tartan Eyes In Texas." Paper presented at the annual meeting of the National Communication Association, Seattle, WA, November 11, 2000.

Momaday, N. Scott. "Native American Attitudes to the Environment." In *Seeing With a Native Eye: Essays on Native American Religion*, edited by Walter Holden Capps, 79–85. New York: Harper and Row, 1976.

Moore, Sally F., and Barbara G. Myeroff. "Introduction: Secular Ritual: Forms and Meanings." In *Secular Ritual*, edited by Sally F. Moore and Barbara G. Myeroff, 3–24. Assen, The Netherlands: Van Gorcum, 1977.

Moran, Malcolm. "In Nebraska, Hardships Ease on Each Fall Saturday." *New York Times*, August 21, 1988, sec. 8, 1, http://www.lexis-nexis.com/.

_____. "Where Football is Way of Life." *USA Today*, October 27–29, 2000, 1A, 17A–18A.

Morrison, Frank B. "Where the West Begins." *Omaha World-Herald*, May 5, 1963, 21.

Morrison, Kara G. "From Farm to Forbes; Nebraska Roots Keep Exec Grounded." *Lincoln Journal Star*, October 10, 1999, 1B, 11B.

Moseman, Andrew. "Nature's Underground Storage." In *Platte River Odyssey* 13. Lincoln, NE: College of Journalism and Mass Communications, University of Nebraska-Lincoln, 2006.

Murphy, John M. "Presence, Analogy, and Earth in the Balance." *Argumentation & Advocacy* 31 (1994): 1–16.

Myeroff, Barbara G. "We Don't Wrap Herring in a Printed Page: Fusion, Fictions and Continuity in Secular Ritual." In *Secular Ritual*, edited by Sally F. Moore and Barbara G. Myeroff, 199–224. Assen, The Netherlands: Van Gorcum, 1977.

Nack, William. "Bang for the Bucs." *Sports Illustrated*, October 23, 2000, 66–81.

Nagel, Harold G., and Marvin C. Williams, "The Prairie Below Ground." In *A Prairie Mosaic*, edited by Steven J. Rothenberger and Susanne George-Bloomfield, 44–53. Kearney, NE: University of Nebraska-Kearney, 2000.

National Geographic, "Live From Nebraska," 205, no. 3 (2004): 1.

Nebraska Magazine, "Continued Population Decline Expected in Smallest Counties," 98, no. 2 (2002): 9.

Nolan, Mike. "The Huskers Just Aren't Important to Nebraska, They ARE Nebraska." *Lincoln Journal Star*, December 8, 2002, 8A.

Nora, Pierre. *Realms of Memory: Rethinking the French Past*. Vol. 1. Edited by Lawrence D. Kritzman. Translated by Arthur Goldhammer. New York: Columbia University Press, 1996.

Norman, Geoffrey. "Bear Necessity." *Sports Illustrated*, November 24, 2003, 40.

Novak, Michael. *The Joy of Sports: End Zones, Bases, Baskets, Balls, and the Consecration of the American Spirit*. New York: Basic Books, 1976.

O'Donnell, Hugh. "Mapping the Mythical: A Geopolitics of National Sporting Stereotypes." *Discourse & Society* 5 (1994): 345–80.

Olson, Eric. "I. M. Hipp Says Walk-On Cuts Will Take Away Dreams." Associated Press, January 29, 2004, http://www.lexis-nexis.com/.

———. "Small Colleges Open Door to Would-Be Husker Walk-Ons." Associated Press, January 29, 2004, http://www.lexis-nexis.com/.

———. "Big Red Isn't Dead, It's Just Different." Associated Press, December 9, 2005, http://www.lexis-nexis.com/.

———. "Retired Two Years, Tenopir Can't Get Big Red Out of Blood." Associated Press, March 27, 2005, http://www.lexis-nexis.com/.

Olson, James C., and Ronald C. Naugle. *History of Nebraska*. 3rd ed. Lincoln, NE: University of Nebraska Press, 1997.

Omaha World-Herald, "Two NU Football Walk-ons Get Scholarships." May 22, 2005, http://www.omaha.com/.

O'Neil, Danny. "Home Away From Home." *The Seattle Times*, August 20, 2000, F2.

Oriard, Michael. *Sporting With the Gods: The Rhetoric of Play and Game in American Culture*. Cambridge, UK: Cambridge University Press, 1991.

Osborne, Tom. *More Than Winning*. Nashville, TN: Nelson, 1985.

———. "Big Red Planet." *Sports Illustrated*, June 14, 2004, 37.

Pearlman, Jeff. "Worth Clucking Over." *Sports Illustrated*, September 15, 2003, 34–36.

Perelman, Chaim. *The Realm of Rhetoric*. Translated by William Kluback. Notre Dame, IN: University of Notre Dame Press, 1982.

Plante, Charles, and Ray H. Mattison. "The 'First' Homestead." *Agricultural History* 36, no. 4 (1962): 183–93.

Plaschke, Bill. "Corn on the Mob." *Los Angeles Times*, December 11, 2001, http://www.latimes.com/.

Pluto, Terry. "The Red Menace: Nebraska Football Has to be Experienced to be Believed." Akron [OH] *Beacon Journal*, November 10, 1996, D1.

———. "Small Town Big Dream." Akron [OH] *Beacon Journal*, November 12, 1996, C1.

Popper, Frank J., and Deborah E. Popper. "The Buffalo Commons: Metaphor as Method." *Geographical Review* 89 (1999): 491–510.

Posnanski, Joe. "Nebraska Fans Deserve a Hand." *The Kansas City Star*, October 5, 1997, C1.

Pride of Place. "Poetry of the Plains: Land Offers Powerful Metaphors for Poet Charles Fort." Winter 2001, 14.

Putnam, Robert D. *Bowling Alone: The Collapse and Revival of American Community*. New York: Simon and Schuster, 2000.

Quantic, Diane. *The Nature of the Place: A Study of Great Plains Fiction*. Lincoln, NE: University of Nebraska Press, 1995.

Queenan, Joe. *True Believers: The Tragic Inner Life of Sports Fans*. New York: Holt, 2003.

Ramsey, Ramsey Eric. *The Long Path to Nearness: A Contribution to a Corporeal Philosophy of Communication and the Groundwork for an Ethics of Relief*. Atlantic Highlands, NJ: Humanities Press, 1998.

Rathe, Tracy R. "Lots of Attractions." *Lincoln Journal Star*, October 10, 1999, 3E.

Relph, Edward. *Place and Placelessness*. London: Pion Limited, 1976.

Ritzer, George. *The McDonaldization of Society*. Thousand Oaks, CA: Pine Forge Press, 1996.

Roeder, Vivian. *Memories are For Sharing*. Sun City, AZ: Self-published, 1980.

Rooney, Phil. "Nebraska Faces Identity Crisis at Start of 21st Century." *Grand Island Independent*, January 2, 2000, http://www.theindependent.com/.

Rosenblatt, Richard. "HuskerNation Heads West to Pasadena." Associated Press, December 31, 2001, http://www.lexis-nexis.com/.

Rosenthal, Brian. "What Anxiety?" *Lincoln Journal Star*, December 16, 2004, http://www.lexis-nexis.com/.

Rosowski, Susan J. *The Place of Literature and the Cultural Phenomenon of Willa Cather*. Lincoln: University of Nebraska Press, 1998.

Rosowski, Susan. "A Sense of Place." *Nebraska Magazine* 94, no. 4 (1998): 2.

Rothenbuhler, Eric W. *Ritual Communication: From Everyday Conversation to Mediated Ceremony*. Thousand Oaks, CA: Sage, 1998.

Rushin, Steve. "Hockey's Miss Havishams." *Sports Illustrated*, June 19, 2006, 17.

Sampier, Larry. Letter to the Editor. *Omaha World-Herald*, December 3, 2004, http://www.omaha.com/.

Sandoz, Mari. *Sandhill Sundays and Other Recollections*. Lincoln, NE: University of Nebraska Press, 1970. First published 1930 by North American Review.

____. *Old Jules*. 20th anniversary ed. New York: Hastings House, 1955. First published 1935.

____. *Love Song to the Plains*. Lincoln, NE: University of Nebraska Press, 1961. Reprinted 1966 by Bison Books.

Sano, Patrick. "The Sower Sees All." *Nebraska Magazine* 97, no. 4 (2001): 2.

Sartore, Joel. *Under a Big Red Sky: Nebraska*. Lincoln, NE: Nebraska Book Publishing Company, 1999.

Schaller, Bob. *I Played for Coach Osborne*. Lincoln, NE: Nebraska Book Publishing, 1998.

Schechner, Richard. *Performance Theory*. Revised and expanded ed. New York: Routledge, 1988.

Schieffelin, Edward L. "Problematizing Performance." In *Ritual, Performance, Media*, edited by Felecia Hughes-Freeland, 194–207. London: Routledge, 1998.

Shapiro, Gerald. "Why I Like Nebraska: A Selection From an Alphabetical Index of Reasons." *Nebraska Alumnus* 85, no. 1 (1989): 13–14.

____. "Some More Reasons Why I Like Nebraska." *Nebraska Alumnus* 86, no. 3 (1990): 4–7.

Shatel, Tom. "Wild Finish Is Wonderful for Walk-on." *Omaha World-Herald*, September 18, 2005, http://www.omaha.com.

____. "In Defeat, Osborne Still Rules." *Omaha World-Herald*, May 11, 2006, http://www.omaha.com/.

____. "Tom Shatel: He is 'a Hick,' But He is Happy." *Omaha World-Herald*, September 21, 2006, http://www.omaha.com/.

Sheldrake, Philip. *Spaces for the Sacred: Place, Memory, and Identity*. Baltimore: Johns Hopkins University Press, 2001.

Sherman, Mitch. "Group of Recruits Pleases Osborne." *Daily Nebraskan*, February 6, 1997, http://www.dailynebraskan.com/.

Simers, T. J. "Putting Out Red Carpet for Cornhusker Folks." *Los Angeles Times*, December 11, 2001, http:www/latimes.com/.

Smith, Jonathan Z. *To Take Place: Toward Theory in Ritual*. Chicago: University of Chicago Press, 1987.

Smith, Rachel A., and Norbert Schwarz. "Language, Social Comparison, and College Football: Is Your School Less Similar to the Rival School Than the Rival School is to Your School?" *Communication Monographs* 70 (2003): 351–60.

Smith, Robert Lee. "The Plainsman." *Nebraska Magazine* 99, no. 3 (2003): 21.

Smith, Steve. *Forever Red: Confessions of a Cornhusker Football Fan*. Lincoln, NE: University of Nebraska Press, 2005.

Snook, Jeff, ed. *What It Means to Be a Husker*. Chicago: Triumph Books, 2004.

Snyder, C. R., MaryAnne Lassegard, and Carol E. Ford. "Distancing After Group Success and Failure: Basking in Reflected Glory and Cutting Off Reflected failure." *Journal of Personality and Social Psychology* 51 (1986): 382–88.

Speer, Jean Haskell. "Communication, Culture, and the Invention of Tradition." In *Culture and Communication*, edited by Edith Slembeck, 83–94. Frankfort, Germany: Verlag fur Interculturelle Kommunikation, 1991.

Sports Illustrated, "Lincoln Logs On." September 4, 2000, 24.

Starita, Joe, and Tom Tidball. *A Day in the Life: The Fans of Memorial Stadium*. Lincoln, NE: Nebraska Book Publishing Company, 1996.

Stein, Michael. "Cult and Sport: The Case of Big Red." *Mid-American Review of Sociology* 2, no. 2 (1977): 29–42.

St. John, Warren. *Rammer Jammer Yellow Hammer*. New York: Three Rivers Press, 2004.

Tambiah, Stanley Jeyaraja. *Culture, Thought, and Social Action: An Anthropological Perspective*. Cambridge, MA: Harvard University Press, 1985.

Taylor, Gordon A. "No. 1 Fans." *Nebraska Magazine* 100, no. 4 (2004): 3.

Thomas, Bob. "Defense Dominant at FSU." *Florida Times-Union*, April 9, 2006, http://www.lexis-nexis.com/.

Thompson, Paul B. *The Spirit of the Soil: Agriculture and Environmental Ethics*. London: Routledge, 1995.

Tuan, Yi-Fu. *Passing Strange and Wonderful: Aesthetics, Nature, and Culture*. Washington, DC: Island Press, 1993.

Turner, Victor. *Dramas, Fields, and Metaphors: Symbolic Action in Human Society*. Ithaca, NY: Cornell University Press, 1974.

Tyson, Rae. "In Rural Nebraska Town, Playing Field Has Changed." *USA Today*, October 25, 1995, 9A.

Tysver, Robynn. "Heineman Benches Osborne." *Omaha World-Herald*, May 10, 2006, http://www.omaha.com/.

Volpe, Vernon L. "Prairie Views." In *A Prairie Mosaic*, edited by Steven J. Rothenberger and Susanne George-Bloomfield, 92–99. Kearney, NE: University of Nebraska-Kearney, 2000.

Wahl, Grant. "Wilt's World." *Sports Illustrated*, November 10, 2003, 40.

Walter, Eugene Victor. *Placeways: A Theory of the Human Environment*. Chapel Hill, NC: University of North Carolina Press, 1988.

Wann, Daniel L., and Frederick G. Grieve. "Biased Evaluations of In-Group and Out-Group Spectator Behavior at Sporting Events: The Importance of Team Identification and Threats to Social Identity." *Journal of Social Psychology* 145 (2005): 531–45.

Wann, Daniel L., Merrill J. Melnick, Gordon W. Russell, and Dale G. Pease. *Sport Fans: The Psychology and Social Impact of Spectators*. New York: Routledge, 2001.

Warsaw [IN] *Times-Union*, "Nebraska: Lincoln Means Football, Steaks and Football," July 8, 1999, 16C.

Weil, Simone. *The Need for Roots*. London and New York: Routledge, 1997.

Welch, Bob. *Stories From the Game of Life*. Eugene, Oregon: Harvest House, 2000.

Welch, Don. *The Platte River*. Kearney, NE: Self-published, 1992.

Welsch, Roger L. "Germans From Russia: A Place to Call Home." In *Broken Hoops and Plains People*, 193–235. Lincoln, NE: Nebraska Curriculum Development Center, 1976.

_____. *Sod Walls: The Story of the Nebraska Sod House*. Broken Bow, NE: Purcells, 1968.

Williams, Hattie Plum. *The Czar's Germans*. Lincoln, NE: American Historical Society of Germans From Russia, 1975.

Winkler, Charlie. *My Big Red Obsession*. Grand Island, NE: Winkler, 1982. First printing 1981.

Wright, Richard. "NU Grad Oversees Restoration of State's Tallest Citizen." *Nebraska Magazine* 97, no. 3 (2001): 28.

Wunder, John. "Change Causes Culture Clash." *Jnews* [a publication of the University of Nebraska College of Journalism and Mass Communication] 13, no. 2 (2003–2004): 7–11.

Zerubavel, Eviatar. *Time Maps: Collective Memory and the Social Shape of the Past*. Chicago: University of Chicago Press, 2003.

Index